The Woman Behind the Letters

Laura Lee McKellips

Laura Lee McKellips

This book is dedicated to everyone who read, and loved Cursed Soldier. Thank you for taking a chance on a first book.

Cover Art ShutterStock Image: 149258657
Cover Art ShutterStock Image: 129298562
Cover Design by Christina Malone
Editing by Catherine DePasquale

TABLE OF CONTENTS

Prologue

"You know, if you keep looking at the ring long enough, it might disappear." Ben teased, as he moved them across the dance floor.

Kathryn's brown curls bounced, as they danced to the music. "I just can't believe we are engaged," she remarked, smiling into his eyes. Anyone could see the love reflected in her blue eyes, especially when she looked at Benjamin.

"I've wanted to ask you for weeks but I couldn't think of the perfect place. It finally came to me, and I'm happy you accepted." Benjamin spun them around in time to the music.

"Was there any doubt?" Kathryn asked, glancing around the room before looking back at him.

"A little," he admitted.

Kathryn laughed and eased closer to him.

"You know, you are not supposed to be dancing this close to me."

"Who cares? We are engaged now." Kathryn intended to dance as close to Benjamin as she could. She looked around them. "Anyway, we are at the back of the room so no one can really see us."

"Kathryn, what would Ms. Maybelle think of your behavior?" Benjamin asked.

Kathryn smiled, as he pulled her closer. She knew he didn't care how close they were dancing; he just didn't want to ruin her reputation. "If my mother weren't talking to your mother at this very moment, she would likely come and separate us to the required inches apart." She gave a knowing smile. "As long as those two talk about our upcoming wedding, we are fine dancing this close."

"As long as you don't get me in trouble with my momma, we're fine." Benjamin laughed, spinning them once more around the crowded ballroom. This was the first party of the season, and people had ventured out to show off their new dresses and to shake off the winter blues.

This year had been hard due to the recent election. Months and months of arguing had finally resulted in Abraham Lincoln becoming President last November. Lincoln hadn't yet taken office, but the Union was already broken up. In January, their beloved Georgia left the Union as another seceding state. Things happened fast as more and more states left the Union. Their representatives were also leaving Congress. Three days ago, shots were fired on Fort Sumter. The people waited anxiously for a response from their new President.

Reflecting on this, Kathryn asked, "Are you worried about President Lincoln declaring war?" It was something the couple had discussed at length over the past few weeks. Tensions across the nation were running high, and there seemed to be a common expectation - war. Kathryn didn't like this, and although she prayed it wouldn't come to that conclusion, she feared that it would.

Benjamin, noticing their mothers looking at them, sighed and stepped back. "I am worried, yes, but if war is declared, I will fight."

This statement broke Kathryn's heart. Benjamin was a good man, and she knew he would fight for Georgia. Still... "Why?" Kathryn pressed, "You don't believe in war."

"I know, but I will support my state and my rights," Benjamin answered. "Kathryn, this war could mean the end of the United States, or it could make us stronger."

"It's already the end of the United States," she muttered. She continued, a little louder. "They are already calling themselves the Confederate States of America. We left the Union in January, and more states have left since then."

"I know, and I hope things can be resolved, but with Lincoln becoming President only five months ago, I fear the worst."

The couple continued to dance as if in their own private world.

"Why can't he just let us leave in peace?"

Benjamin shook his head. "Would you willingly give up land?" he asked.

"No, of course not."

"Exactly. He does not want to fight, but he does want to preserve the Union. If that means war, then war it is."

"You talk like a politician," Kathryn remarked slowly.

"No, it's the truth. Every nation has been tested at one time or another," Benjamin explained sadly. "A nation is only strong when tested."

"Yeah and most of those nations have fallen," Kathryn muttered. "I just want our way of life to stand."

"Nothing stands forever." Benjamin whispered.
Just then, several men entered the ballroom shouting. Benjamin and Kathryn stopped dancing and lowered their arms as they tried to figure out what was happening.

Guests rushed into the ballroom and waited with bated breath to hear what these men would say.

"LINCOLN HAS DECLARED WAR!"

Kathryn closed her eyes and felt the shift in Ben with those four words. Their world was forever shattered. Breathing slowly, she opened her eyes and looked up at him and saw his resolution. Benjamin had always known it would come down to this, and in the back of her mind, Kathryn had known it, too.

"Ben?" she asked, as he looked down at her. Her heart broke again in those moments.

"Marry me tonight," he whispered. "We can get married before I leave."

"What?" she asked, not understanding what he wanted.

"I will leave in a few days now that Lincoln has called for war. We can get married before I leave. I know it will not be the wedding you have dreamed of, but at least we will be together."

Kathryn shook her head. She tried to think of the right words to say, but nothing came to her. "I'm sorry," she whispered, "I want us to get married but not like this." Tears pooled in her eyes, blurring her vision.

"I understand," Benjamin said, cupping her face. "Believe me, I understand." He brushed his lips across hers before pulling back to look down at her. "I love you, Kathryn."

"I love you," she said, wrapping her arms around his waist. She had held him like this before, but it was different this time. It was as if someone had placed something between them, and she feared it would never be removed. Their easy, loving relationship was forever changed in those moments, and she knew she would never get it back. Benjamin didn't even have to leave. He was already gone.

Chapter One

Opening her eyes, she realized last night wasn't a dream. War had been declared, and it took away the love of her life. She understood why Ben joined the cause. He felt it was his duty to stand up for the rights of the states. She just wished all the tensions would not have bubbled over and resulted in war. The men who fired on Fort Sumter were praised for an act that resembled dumping the tea in Boston Harbor all those years ago.

It wasn't the same for her, though. Dumping the tea didn't take Ben away from her. This war did. She didn't know when or if she would see him again. All she had was her memories and his ring on her finger. It wasn't a wedding band because she chose not to marry him before he left. It was a decision she hadn't made lightly, but she still wondered if she should have made the other choice. Should she have married him? He was going to war, and he could die. Last night might have been the *last time* she would see him.

Getting out of bed, she walked over to the window and saw nothing different. It was as it was yesterday morning, when she went to the park with Ben. How could she go from being the happiest girl in the world to this? She never would have thought her life would change over the course of a few hours, but it did. When President Lincoln declared war on the Confederate Southern States, life as she knew it was over. Four words, and everything she knew faded to black. Four words destroyed everything she had ever known. Everything came down to one word, war.

"Kathryn, you need to eat," her mother said behind her. She had been so lost in her thoughts she didn't even hear her mother come into her room.

"I know, Mother." She mumbled. "Do you think I should have married him before he left?" she asked, turning to face the woman who gave her life.

"Benjamin is a good man and I want him as my son-in-law, but it was your decision, and I support you," her mother replied walking into the room. "You know what's best for you in your heart, and no one can fault you. I know you love him."

"I feel I broke his heart," she shared, as she sat on the edge of her bed.

"You might have, but he understands. He loves you for you."

"Does he understand?" she asked. "I'm not sure anymore," she whispered, as her mother sat down beside her and wrapped her arms around her.

"Baby, you know your heart, so trust in your decision. This war won't last long, which means he will be back before you know it," her mother said, as she rubbed her back and shoulders. "In the mean-time, you can start planning your wedding."

Kathryn nodded, as she eased out of her mother's embrace and stood up. "I'll get dress and be down to eat," she said, as her mother nodded before leaving the room.

Standing up, she began to get dressed for the day. She was tempted to dye her clothes black to signal she was in mourning. She wouldn't, though, because Ben wasn't dead. It would send out a bad omen, if she started wearing black, and she didn't want his death on her conscience.

~ ~ ~ ~

"Well how is she?" Gregory Alexander asked, as Maybelle walked back into the morning room.

"She's not good, Gregory." Maybelle sighed as she sat down next to her husband. "I am worried about her."

"Our daughter just said goodbye to the only man she has ever loved, give her time," he said, placing his hand on her back. "She will settle down and be her old self in time."

"I do not like seeing our daughter like this." She whispered leaning into his side. "Promise me he will come back."

"You know I can't, my dear. He is traveling to join the Army of Northern Virginia," Greg supplied slowly. His heart was heavy for his daughter, as Benjamin journeyed north.

"What does it mean?" she asked, pulling back to look up at him.

"It means he might not come back," he stated gravely as tears formed in her eyes. She was worried about their daughter and how she would take it if Benjamin died. She feared her daughter would shut herself off completely. Benjamin must survive the war if only to put the smile back on her daughter's face.

~ ~ ~ ~

Kathryn leaned against the wall, as she listened to her parents. She knew Ben was traveling north, but she never thought it would be that far. Closing her eyes, she held back the tears that threatened to spill. Why hadn't she just agreed to marry him? He could have stayed here a few more days. She still would have said goodbye to him.

Breathing deep, she straightened away from the wall and walked into the morning room. She saw her parents when they noticed her. They quieted down and watched her closely.

"Since we are all here, let's move to the dining room," her mother said jumping up. She watched her father stand up slowly. "Come on," her mother said, as she looped her arm through Kathryn's and led her out of the room, down the hall, and into the dining room.

They did not have a big house but there were still several rooms.

It was nothing like Twin Willows, though. Benjamin's house was huge and had been in the family for years. His grandmother loved the land so much she built a home there with her husband. The name even came from her. She birthed twin stillborn sons and in her grief she planted two willow trees side by side. The willows protected those graves to this day. The estate was renamed in the following weeks as she healed.

Kathryn didn't know if she would be able to live through the death of a child. She knew she wouldn't be able to live through Ben's death. Closing her eyes, she quietly said a quick prayer for him to come back to her once the war was over.

"Since we have time on our hands, where do you want to get married?" Maybelle asked her daughter.

"I don't know," Kathryn replied as she thanked the servant who set her plate in front of her.

"What about Twin Willows?" her mother asked. "You love the house, and there is enough room to get married there."

"I know but can we not talk about it right now?" she asked. "I'm sorry; I just don't want to discuss a wedding that might not happen."

"Oh dear, Ben will come back home," Maybelle said, jumping up and rushing to her daughter's side. "You have to believe."

"You don't know that!" Kathryn yelled as her emotions burst forth. "You cannot guarantee me he will come home. You cannot tell me he will not die!" she shouted as pain clogged her throat.

"No I can't, but you have to be hopeful." Her mother said softly.

"Mother, please." She whispered as Gregory cleared his throat.

"Dear, Kathryn has a point. You have plenty of time to discuss the wedding," he stated. "She needs time to settle down. There have been many changes in her life," he said, as Maybelle nodded.

"May I be excused?" Kathryn asked as Maybelle sighed and walked back to her chair.

"You need to eat."

"I know, but I'm not hungry," she said.

"Fine, you're excused," her mother said as she nodded and left the room. She grabbed her bonnet before leaving the house. She couldn't stay in the house a moment longer. Walking swiftly, she found herself in the park. It was busier than yesterday, but she still felt all alone. She walked to their spot and closed her eyes. She pictured him as he was yesterday and heard his words echoed.

"Kathryn..." he started as she looked up at him.

"Benjamin," she said as he took a deep breath. She never saw him this nervous except when he asked if he could court her. Something was up with him; she just didn't know what it was.

"I love you," he said slowly. She loved hearing him say those words. They always made her feel special.

"I love you, too," she said with a smile.

Ben squeezed her hands before coming down on one knee in front of her. "Will you marry me?" He asked simply as she squeezed his hands. It was such a simple proposal, but it was perfect for her.

"Yes," she said simply as he smiled, released her hands, grabbed the ring from his pocket, before slipping it on the ring finger of her left hand. He stood up and pulled her close to brush his lips against hers to seal their engagement.

"I've wanted to kiss you for a week now," he stated pulling back from her.

"Oh Benjamin!" she whispered. "The ring is beautiful," she said holding her hand up to look at it closely.

"I've been carrying it around for a while," he admitted. "Thankfully, your father can keep a secret from you," he said as she smiled.

"You asked my father before me?" she asked still somewhat dazed he asked her to marry him.

"Yes," he replied. "When I asked to court you, he made me promise I would ask him for your hand in marriage first," he explained.

"He just wanted to know before my mother," she remarked, as she picked up her parasol.

"I think he might have mentioned that," he muttered still smiling. "Since I'm sure your parents are waiting for us, we better make our way back," he said as she looped her arm through his. They made their way back to the carriage, both walking on clouds and lost in their own thoughts.

"Our mothers will want to start discussing a date for our marriage," she informed him.

"You can count on it," he said as he helped her up into the carriage and tucked in the step, before grabbing the reins from the boy and climbing in.

She was in bliss during the ride back. The world was beautiful and full of color. It stayed that way until four words, shouted in the ballroom, drained the color from her world. It was a dull gray now.

Why hadn't she told him she would marry him last night? It would have been wrong to marry him under those circumstances. These things couldn't be rushed. She didn't want to be rushed. She deserved to have a husband with a wedding. With the war, he would have left only a few days later. Several of her friends were rushing to the altar so they could be married before the men left for war. It was their choice, not hers. The moment the war was over, though, she would be the one dragging Ben up the aisle.

Sighing, she cleared her head and made her way out of the park. The streets were busy with families sending their boys away. The fathers were smiling and slapping the boys on their backs, while the mothers were crying and waving their handkerchiefs around. The boys were about to become men. They were already men, she guessed, but they were very young men. If they survived, they would come back changed.

She knew several men rushed to sign up last night and again this morning. Everything was happening fast. She hoped they were right and the war wouldn't last long. President Lincoln even believed the war would be over quickly.

"Kathryn, how is Benjamin?" Robert Jackson, one of her childhood friends, asked. He was in a light gray uniform that looked like Ben's.

"He left this morning," she replied. "When do you leave?" she asked.

"Two days; Henrietta is marrying me tomorrow."

"Congratulations," she said keeping her emotions under control.

"It's not going to be anything big, but she's okay with it. She says we'll do it up right when the war is over."

"I'm sure it will be lovely. Give her my blessings," she said, as he nodded. "I better let you go so you can get everything in order before you leave."

"Take care, and don't worry; we'll lick those Yankees in a month," he stated with a smile as she nodded before walking away.

She glanced once more at Robert and prayed he was right. She wanted them to lick the Yankees in a month so Ben would be back. The one lingering thought was what war only lasted a month?

~ ~ ~ ~

"Kathryn, you are looking well," Lydia Sawyer commented the next day. Lydia was Ben's mother but she loved her too. She got their invitation to dine this morning and knew she couldn't say no even if she wanted too, which she didn't. They were to be her future in-laws.

"Thank you, I am finally accepting the fact he had to fight in this war," she stated, as she sat down in the parlor. "Thank you for inviting me over today."

"Oh, Joshua and I wanted to see you. I feel it has been way too long since I've seen your pretty face," she said, smiling as Kathryn smiled back.

"It hasn't been long, Mrs. Sawyer." She commented.

It had only been a few days since she had seen them in the ballroom.

"How are you, Kathryn? I still think my son should not have left you," Joshua stated as he walked into the room. Kathryn knew Joshua didn't support his son's decision to join the war. He was mad Benjamin decided to do this on his own.

"I am good today, but it is a constant battle," she replied. "He asked me to marry him before he left, and I'm the one who said no," she informed them because she didn't want them to think he hadn't done right by her.

"You had every right, my dear. My son should not have expected you to say yes under those terms," Joshua commented.

She knew he was still angry, but she didn't like it. Father and son shouldn't fight especially when the son was fighting in a war.

"Mr. Sawyer, I love your son and I understand why he chose to fight," she said, placing her hands in her lap.

"Oh please not this subject again," Lydia stated. "I cannot hear you talk about Benjamin again," she said, as Joshua nodded.

Apparently, there had been fights about Ben. Lydia would always support her son even if she didn't agree with his decision either.

"Where is Hannah?" Kathryn asked changing the subject.

"She is on her way; in fact I suspect she will be walking through the door in a matter of moments," Lydia remarked, as she nodded.

Hannah was Ben's little sister. She was only a year younger than herself, so they got along great. Hannah was the reason she met Benjamin in the first place. They were at a ball, and his sister pointed her out to him. Apparently, he saw her earlier in the park and wanted to talk to her. She was pulled out of her thoughts by the sound of the front door slamming.

"Ah, there is my daughter now," Joshua stated, as he stood up. "Hannah," he called out, before she appeared in the doorway.

"Oh Kathryn, I didn't know you were coming tonight," Hannah said rushing into the room.

"It was a last minute invite," Lydia supplied. "You were already gone so I couldn't tell you."

"Let me change, and I'll be back down in time for dinner," she said as Lydia nodded to her daughter.

Kathryn smiled as Joshua sat back down. "How are your parents?" he asked her.

"They are well," she answered. "Mrs. Sawyer, my mother is ready to start planning the wedding. She wanted you to let her know when you are ready."

"Is now too soon?" she asked as everyone laughed.

"For her, no it's not too soon," she remarked. "I am sure she would love for you to call on her tomorrow to discuss some details."

"Then I will be over bright and early," Lydia stated. "A wedding," she sighed. "Thank you for allowing us to help you plan."

"There are so many details for a wedding, and I know I can't do it by myself," Kathryn voiced. "You will probably want to bow out after meeting with my mother."

"Oh no, I love planning parties. Your wedding will be amazing," she stated.

"Well, if the groom comes back," Joshua muttered.

Kathryn still heard him, and she was sure Lydia did too. Lydia didn't say anything though; she continued to talk about what she thought Ben and Kathryn should do for the wedding. She already had lots of ideas, so it would be interesting to see her and her mother discuss everything.

Hannah finally came down. She changed out of her green morning dress to a pale blue dress.

"Since everyone is here, let's take this to the dining room," Joshua stated as he stood up. Lydia and Kathryn stood up as well. He led them into the dining room and signaled for their food. Ben's family owned slaves as hers did. He had more, though, but she knew it always made him uncomfortable. He hated the thought of owning people, but this was his father's estate. It was one of their fights before Ben left.

Once dinner was served, they talked more about the wedding. They finished up, and Joshua drove Kathryn home in his carriage. It wasn't Ben's, but it was okay with her. She didn't know if she could ride in it with anyone else especially since he gave up his horses for the war effort.

"You know Ben still loves you," she said, breaking the silence.

"I know, dear. I love him, but I'm worried," he stated. "Fathers are not supposed to bury their sons."

"I'm sorry," she whispered as he pulled up in front of her house. "Thank you."

"You are welcome, and Kathryn, I hope for your sake he does come home," he said, as she nodded before walking into her house.

She thought about what Mr. Sawyer shared with her. He was hurting and in pain just like the rest of them. He was just hiding it under anger which wasn't a good thing. His anger could eat him alive. He needed to make peace with Ben's decision, and she was going to help him.

~ ~ ~ ~

The next day Mrs. Sawyer showed up at her house bright and early. Her mother was excited to see Lydia. Hannah came along as well, which put her at ease. She didn't have two mothers to wrangle alone.

"I think they should get married at Twin Willows," Maybelle stated as they sat down to eat breakfast.

"Oh I agree, it would be perfect," Lydia said. "It should be under the willow trees."

"Are you ladies going to talk about the wedding all morning?" Her father asked.

"Of course, dear," Her mother said, as he nodded and stood.

"Then I will bid you good day. Lydia, it is always a pleasure to see you," he said, before leaving the room.

Lydia and Maybelle watched him leave before laughing. "Men," they said at the same time.

"Now what about those willow trees?" Lydia asked as Hannah rolled her eyes for only Kathryn to see. The two of them sat back and ate while their mothers discussed everything including what Kathryn would wear.

"I thought about a white wedding dress," she said breaking into their conversation. It was her wedding day after all.

"White?" her mother gasped. "No, it is just not done. You will wear blue for your purity."

"Queen Victoria wore white to her wedding to Prince Albert," Kathryn pointed out.

"Good for her but you are not the Queen of England," Maybelle stated. "You will wear blue just like I did, just like your grandmother did, and just like Lydia did," she said, as Lydia nodded.

"Mother, it is fashionable to wear white," she said, trying again.

"I do not know what you have been reading but you are not wearing white," Maybelle stated.

"We will have to order the dress, but I'm afraid it will be almost impossible to get it from Paris," Lydia stated.

"What do you mean?" Anna asked.

"Well, the Yankees are trying to bottle up our harbors. Jefferson Davis is working on a plan to combat the problem," Lydia explained. "There are some men who did not sign up to fight who are sailing through the blockades."

"This just adds to the fact the postal service has been suspended," Lydia commented.

"What?" she asked.

This was news to her. She hadn't heard the service was suspended. It wasn't the best news for her right now.

"I heard from the Millers that Lincoln suspended the postal service to the rebellious states."

"No, the post offices split," Hannah explained. "We still have service, just limited at the moment. The blockade runners will be helping with getting letters to the troops as well."

"How do you know?" Kathryn asked.

"I talked to the post master. He confirmed it," she replied. "They wanted to make sure the soldiers got their letters from home."

"Makes sense," Lydia said. "Has Ben written to you?" she asked, looking at Kathryn.

"No, not yet," she answered. "Hopefully soon though."

"Don't worry; he will write you," Lydia promised. "He loves you."

"Now back to your wedding; I think we need to order some lace," Maybelle said, as Kathryn sighed and listened to what they were saying without processing it.

She was thinking about why she hadn't received a letter from Ben yet. He promised to mail her when he reached camp. He left in mid-April; he should have been there by now. Had something happened to him? She prayed not.

~ ~ ~ ~

Tension was high as rumors started flying around. She along with everyone else wondered when the first battle would happen. Everyone waited for those first gunshots throughout all of May and June. It was near the end of July on the 21st that the first battle was fought. She waited with everyone else at the telegraph office the next day for the lists of the wounded and dead. They won the battle, but there was still loss of life. The idea this war would be over in 90 days was long gone. This battle proved neither side was really ready for battle, never mind a war. It was going to be a long hard fight before a victor could be named.

Closing her eyes, she sent up a quick prayer hoping Ben was still alive. She hadn't heard from him since he left early that April morning. She wasn't sure if it was good or bad news. He had to travel a distance, so she wasn't really sure if he made it to the camp or not.

"I need everyone to stand back; I have the lists of the wounded. The dead are still being identified. Please stay calm and pass around the lists. We do not have enough paper to print everyone a page," Mr. Smithville called out.

He was one of the older men who wanted to go to war but felt his duty was here.

He started passing out the pages. Screams pierced the air as everyone began to read the lists. After 10 minutes she finally got one and quickly read down the list. She held back tears for those she knew. She couldn't hold back her relief, when she didn't see Ben's name, but then she remembered this was only the wounded list. The death list still needed to be read.

Twenty minutes later, Mr. Smithville passed out the death lists. She toned out the screams and crying from the people around her. He could not be dead. He could not be dead. As soon as she got a list, she scrolled down the names. Tears rolled down her cheeks as she read the names of her friends and people she knew all her life. There was one name she did not see, thankfully. Ben was alive at least as far as this battle was concerned. How could she handle this after every battle? She would be out here, though, because she would need to know if he survived. She wouldn't be alone, thankfully. There would always be someone out here trying to find out about their loved ones.

~ ~ ~ ~

Over the next several days, more and more men signed up for the war. So many men signed up and left that there were more women in town than men now. The only men left were either too old, too young, or ran a major business. Thaddeus Morgan was one of the men who stayed in town. He was unmarried but helped out with his mother Grace, who was still grieving over her husband. His father died suddenly last year making him the head of the bank. He ran the Bluff City Bank where her family did business. Grace was one of the tellers. They were family friends and people she held dear, which is why she stopped beside the town church to talk to Grace.

"Kathryn, your mother said you were not well," Grace said, as she placed her hand on Kathryn's shoulder.

"Oh I'm fine. Don't worry about me," She voiced, hoping she didn't look as lost as she felt.

She still hadn't gotten a letter from Ben, and she was starting to worry. He promised to write as much as he could.

"Dear, you have been walking around in a daze," Grace mentioned, and she could hear the concern in Grace's voice. "Is this about Benjamin leaving?"

Kathryn sighed and nodded. "It is about him leaving. I question whether I should have married him before he left," she shared. It was a question she asked herself at least ten times a day.

"Do you really believe it or are you worried you may never see him again?" she asked knowingly.

"I don't know, but I am worried. This is a war not some game."

"I know, but you have to trust in your own decision. Sweetie, you know your own mind better than anyone else. He will come back. He is a strong one," Grace said stepping closer to Kathryn.

"Thank you," she whispered.

"No problem, I know it's hard saying goodbye to the only man you've loved, but it will get better," she stated, and Kathryn knew it was advice from her experience. "Now if you need to talk, just come by the bank."

"What about your son? Won't he get mad if I visit you at work?" she asked.

She didn't know much about banking, but she did know Grace had a job to do.

"Thaddeus won't care," she stated with a smile. "Believe me, I have him under control."

"Okay, I'll remember that little fact," Kathryn said. "I better get back home before my father comes looking for me."

"Have a nice day," Grace said, before walking in the opposite direction from her.

Kathryn finally made it to her house. She looked at the mail stacked on the side table in the entryway. Lying on top was a letter, she never expected. She screamed out, smiled, and started spinning around.

"What's wrong?" Her father asked rushing into the entryway.

"Ben sent me a letter!" she shouted, holding the letter close to her chest, while still bouncing up and down.

"Calm down, it's only a letter. The man isn't back yet," he said with a smile, before leaving the room again.

She shook her head and raced upstairs to her bedroom. Jumping on her bed, she carefully opened the letter and began to read it. She couldn't believe she finally got a letter from him.

Dear Kathryn,   *May 1861*

I pray that this letter finds you well. I know you are reading this with bated breath wondering if this letter finds you too late. We have finally reached the camp. I know you have been worried about me and the other guys, as we journey north to join Robert E. Lee's Army. The journey was rough, since I knew that it carried me miles and miles away from you and our sleepy little town.

I wish that Lincoln would have just let the South leave the Union peacefully, but after Fort Sumter I knew that he would not. April 15, will forever be etched in my mind as the date that our lives ended. I knew when Lincoln called forth for troops that everything we knew was about to change.

You know I do not support the war, but I do support the reason for the war. I heard more states have joined the Confederate States. The guys say Tennessee finally left the Union, so we all wonder when the first official battle will be.

There are rumors that Lincoln wants to attack some of our boys at Manassas Junction, which the Yankees are calling Bull Run for some strange reason. I fear, if the Yankees do attack there, that General Jackson will stand his ground. He and his men are ready to die for the cause. The Yankees are not as prepared as those men, though. Even though I am in the mist of the camp, I feel like the war is still just a dream. We all wait in anticipation of where the Yankees will strike first, still hoping that the war will be over in 90 days and we come out the victors.

Please know that I love you, and if I could, I would have married you before I left. If you change your mind, when I come home on my furlough, I will have you in front of the preacher that day. I cannot wait until the day that you become my wife.

Please give my love to my mother. I know she worries as much as you do.

Pray for a short war,
Your soldier preparing for battle

She noticed the date at the top and saw it was already two months old. The mail was always slow but with the suspended service, she was shocked the letter even made it to her. Those blockade runners deserved a medal or something. They brought her hope from the Army of Northern Virginia. She re-read the letter three more times before getting off the bed and sitting down at her writing desk. The way he signed his letter made her sad but she understood. He explained before he left that he couldn't sign his name to any letter due to others possibly getting ahold of it. Smiling she penned her letter to him.

My love,　　　　　　　　　　　　　　　　　　*July 1861*

It was great to receive your letter. We heard about the battle at Manassas Junction, but the papers are calling it Bull Run. I am not sure why there are two different names for the same battle. Apparently, the Yankees name places differently than we do. Were you there in the battle? I did not see your name among the list of dead or wounded, so I still have hope that you are alive and well. Please stay that way throughout this war. I could not bear it if you were to die that far away from me.

Your mother wanted to let you know that she loves you and that she was happy to see you had time to write. She also wants you to be careful, and come home to give her grandbabies to spoil. Your father is still not saying much, but I know that he is proud of you for joining the cause, even if you do not support the war.

I will not change my mind on marriage until the war is over. I do not want to be a widow because of this war. Many of my best friends are already widows with only this one battle. Please do not pressure me to change my mind because I will not. I love you and will marry you the minute that the war is over and you come home to me. Not a moment sooner.

I wait for your next letter to know that you are alive and well. Please do not be heroic during battle like I know you want to be. I do want you to come home to me. Remember I love you, and know that I am praying for a short war as well.

All my love,
Kathryn

Once she was finished, she rushed to the post office so she could get it in today's mail. With the split of the post offices, the mail only went out on certain days. Today was one of those days and she wanted to hurry up and get some of home back to Ben.

Chapter Two

Kathryn was in a better mood after receiving Ben's letter. She reread his letter every morning and again before she went to bed. After the first battle, she realized Bluff City would never be the same. Several of her friends were dead, leaving widows and children. More and more of the women wore black. They were in grieving for their husbands, sons, and grandsons.

She saw a notice in one of the store windows, calling for more nurses. Men poured in town to get extensive medical attention they could not receive on the battlefield. She tried to volunteer as a nurse, but since she was unmarried, they would not let her. They were worried about her virtue, but she didn't care. She wanted to do something for the war effort, but there was nothing for her to do.

The town held fundraisers to send money to the men fighting. She just wanted to do her part. Nothing seemed to be enough for those men, or for Benjamin.

Walking down the street, she saw Grace leaning against the side of the church. Grace didn't look well. She knew something was wrong with the older lady.

"Mrs. Morgan, are you okay?" she asked rushing to her side.

"No, I'm not," she gasped, as Kathryn tried to see if anyone was close by to find Thaddeus, but no one was around.

Grace needed help, now.

"Are you okay here alone?" she asked as Grace nodded. "Okay let me get your son, stay right here."

"Please hurry," she whispered as Kathryn nodded.

She hurried to the bank. He had to be there; Ms. Grace could not afford for him to be anywhere else. She rushed into the bank, and saw him sitting behind his desk. "Thaddeus," she huffed out trying to take some deep breaths.

"Kathryn, what's wrong?" he asked, rushing to her side.

He was almost as tall as Benjamin. She never realized how tall he was. He looked nothing like Benjamin with his blond hair and gray eyes.

"It's your mother," she breathed out as she pushed aside the thoughts of how Thaddeus looked.

Grace needed her to focus.

"Take me to her," he demanded, as she nodded and grabbed his hand.

She took him to his mother who, thankfully, was still in the same place.

"Mother, what's wrong?" he asked, when he reached his mother's side.

"I got dizzy and couldn't breathe," she gasped.

Thaddeus nodded and scooped his mother up into his arms. "Do you know where the doctor is?" he asked looking at Kathryn.

"He's at the hospital," she replied, as he nodded again.

"Will you please bring him to the house? I want to get her home as soon as possible," he said, as she nodded before rushing to the hospital.

It took her a few minutes to get inside the hospital and a few more minutes before she could locate the doctor. He was bandaging a little boy's arm, when she finally did find him.

"Kathryn, what's wrong?" the doctor asked, when he saw her rush in. He knew something was wrong because Kathryn never rushed anywhere. Proper ladies did not rush.

"It's Thaddeus' mother," she said as the doctor motioned to one of the nurses to finish what he was doing.

"What's wrong?" he asked.

"She was dizzy and is having trouble breathing," she replied. "He took her back to the house, and wants you to meet him there."

"My rounds are finished, I can go now," he said reaching for his medical bag. "Lead the way, Kathryn." They left the hospital and arrived at the Morgan house a few minutes later. Thaddeus let them in as soon as the doctor knocked.

"Glad you could make it, doctor," he said looking relieved.

"No problem. Where is Grace?" the doctor asked as he walked inside.

"She is in the parlor," he said, as the doctor nodded and moved past them. They followed close behind him.

"So what happened?" he asked, sitting on one of the chairs close to Grace. She looked better than she did, but Kathryn could tell she still couldn't breathe well.

"I don't know; Kathryn found her like this," Thaddeus stated, while rubbing the back of his neck.

He looked helpless at his mother's state. She wanted to comfort him, but she didn't know if it was proper.

"Grace, were you rushing around again?" the doctor asked, as he moved his stethoscope under her blouse between her shoulder blades. He unbuttoned the top buttons to have easier access.

"No, doctor," she gasped slowly.

"Oh I don't like that sound," the doctor said, listening to her lungs again.

"What's wrong?" Thaddeus asked.

"I think your mother has a touch of the grippe," the doctor said, looking up at him. "Have you had any pain or cramps in your extremities?" he asked looking back at Grace, as he placed a thermometer under her arm, inside her blouse.

"My what?" She asked.

"Your arms, legs, or joints?" he asked, holding the thermometer still.

"Yes I've had pain in all my joints; I thought it was because I was getting older," she answered.

"Mother, why didn't you tell me?" Thaddeus asked concerned about his mother's condition. It was barely a year since he lost his father; he was not ready to lose his mother, too.

"I didn't want to worry you," she replied, as the doctor finally removed the thermometer.

"Well, I think we've caught it early enough," he said reading the thermometer. "You have a slight fever. You will need to rest and take a pinch of quinine in hot water, every hour," he said standing up to get the medicine from his bag.

"Is this serious?" Grace asked, concern written clearly on her face.

"It can be, and if left untreated it could develop into pneumonia," he explained as she nodded.

"Don't worry doctor; she will not leave the house until she is better," Thaddeus promised looking from his mother to the doctor.

"Have either of you been exposed to the grippe?" The doctor asked looking at Thaddeus and Kathryn.

"Since my mother lives with me; I have been exposed through her," Thaddeus remarked. "But no one else."

"What about you, Kathryn?" he asked placing the stethoscope and thermometer inside his bag.

"I have through Ben's sister, Hannah," she said remembering how sick Hannah had been.

The house was quarantined due to the highly contagious nature of the disease. Since she was there on a visit, she was quarantined as well. They hadn't been sure Hannah would make it, but finally her fever broke in the early morning, and the quarantine was lifted three days later.

"Well the good news is, you two have a low chance of catching it. The bad news is, I have to place the house under quarantine. She will not be allowed to leave the house, and neither will the two of you until she is better."

"What?" Thaddeus asked in shock.

Kathryn stayed silent because she knew it would happen when the doctor diagnosed Ms. Grace.

"You cannot leave; I'm sorry. This town does not need an outbreak while most of its boys are fighting," he explained. "It is standard practice in this situation."

"I have a business to run," Thaddeus pointed out. "How can I afford to be locked in the house?" he asked in frustration.

"I am sorry, but I have to do this," the doctor commented.

Kathryn stayed back as she listened to the doctor instruct Grace and Thaddeus on her care. She would need sponge baths when her fever peaked, as well as constant monitoring. Twenty minutes later, the doctor left them with his promise to send a nurse over to monitor Grace's progress. Since he was the only doctor, he wouldn't be quarantined with them, even though he was exposed as Kathryn was. The town trusted him to take precautions and not get sick.

"Thank you again for finding my mother," Thaddeus said as Kathryn nodded.

"Yes thank you, dear," Grace said placing her hand on Kathryn's sleeve. "I am sorry you are trapped in the house with us."

"It's okay; I pray you get better," Kathryn stated, as she placed her hand on top of Grace's. She remembered when Ben's sister, Hannah, was diagnosed. There were some tense moments throughout the quarantine before Hannah's fever broke. No one wanted an outbreak in town; she couldn't blame them. People died of the grippe or influenza as some doctors were now calling it. "I will need to let my parents know what's going on," she said, as Grace nodded.

"I have pen and paper in my office," Thaddeus said. "You can write a letter, and I will have someone get it to them," he stated moving toward the door.

"Thank you."

"It is the least I can do, since you found my mother," he said leaving them alone to grab the pen and paper for her.

"My son is a good man," Grace mentioned as Kathryn nodded.

"Yes ma'am he is," Kathryn voiced with a smile.

"Oh, none of that ma'am stuff while we are under quarantine. You may call me Grace," she said looking at Kathryn.

"Ms. Grace," Kathryn said.

"I am okay with Ms. Grace; your mother raised you right," she commented.

Kathryn laughed. "She would love to hear you say it," she said, as Thaddeus walked back with the paper and pen.

"Do you require anything else?" he asked.

"No, thank you. I'll get this done quickly so my mother doesn't worry. I should have been home by now," she stated, as he nodded.

"You may use the desk in my office, if you would like."

"Thank you, I won't be too long," she said, as he nodded. "If you will excuse me?"

"Go right ahead; it is the second door to the left down the hall," he said, as she stood and left the room.

"I do hope her mother doesn't blame me for being quarantined. It's not at all proper for her to be here without a chaperone."

Thaddeus sat beside his mother. "I don't think Ms. Maybelle will blame you, Mother. She likes you," he said, taking his mother's hand in his. "I want you to focus on getting better. The doctor warned us. You will get worse before getting better."

"Don't worry about me; I have a strong constitution," she stated.

"I know, but I can't lose you," he said squeezing her hand.

"I promise you, it is not my time to die," she said, as Kathryn came back into the room with her letter.

"That was quick," Thaddeus noted, as he stood up.

"Well I didn't want to worry her, so I kept it short and simple," she remarked. "Thank you for getting this to her," she said handing him her letter already folded and ready to go.

"It's not a problem," he said, leaving the room.

"I am sorry for the trouble I have caused you," Grace said, leaning back against the cushions.

"It was no trouble; please get some rest so you can get better," she said, as Grace nodded.

~ ~ ~ ~

"I wonder where Kathryn is," Maybelle stated, as she paced the room.

"She might have gotten held up," Gregory commented, as one of the servants walked into the room and handed Maybelle a letter.

"Thank you," she mumbled, as she opened the letter. "What? This can't be right," she exclaimed, as she walked over to her husband, and thrust the letter in his face.

"She is under quarantine with Grace and Thaddeus," Gregory read before looking at his wife.

"Grace has the grippe!" she exclaimed.

"I know, I read the letter but, Kathryn has been exposed before through Hannah," he stated calmly trying not to worry his wife.

"What does it mean?" she asked, sitting beside him.

"If you have been exposed, it is less likely you come down with it," he explained. "Don't worry our daughter has a strong constitution. She will be okay."

"I don't like this. She will be alone with Thaddeus," she remarked.

"And Grace, as well as a nurse, there is nothing improper about it. The people in town will see," he reminded her gently. "She will need clothes, though."

"Yes she will; I will pack a few for her," she said, standing up.

He stood and walked over to the side table. "Make sure you pack this letter," he said, handing it to her.

"It's from Ben," she noted, looking at it.

"Yes, and I know our daughter will want to read it," he stated, as she nodded before leaving the room.

It took her several minutes to pack Kathryn's things. She wasn't sure what she would need or how long the quarantine would last. If Kathryn needed more clothes, she would send them later. Hopefully, the quarantine wouldn't last long. She wouldn't be able to bear it if Kathryn got the grippe.

~ ~ ~ ~

"Kathryn, your mother sent your things," Thaddeus said, while knocking on the bedroom door.

She opened the door of the room she was given for her time here. "How did she get it over here?" she asked stepping to the side to allow him into the room.

"She stopped the nurse, and handed your case to her," he said, placing the Lindy trunk on the bed.

"I didn't think about asking her to pack anything," she commented. "It must have been my father's idea."

"I will leave you to unpack. If you need anything, I will be either in my office or with mother," he stated, as she nodded.

"Thank you again," she said.

"Well, I would have loved to repay you for helping my mother in some other way, but this is the best I can do," he said as she laughed. "You have a wonderful laugh."

"Thank you, and don't worry about repaying me. I want your mother to get better," she said, as he nodded before leaving her alone.

Kathryn opened her case, and noticed a letter sitting on top. "Ben," she whispered, as she pushed the case aside, and sat on the bed to read his latest letter.

Dear Kathryn,   *September 1861*

I never realized how slow the mail was until the war. It seems like it was months ago that I sent you that letter. I will try not to pressure you for marriage, but why are you asking me not to be heroic? You know I would not let anyone die if I had the chance to save them. It would be wrong of me to sit back and watch them die because I just stood by. This war is a test to those ideas.

I am sorry about your friends. I know most of the guys from Bluff City are dead. The war has not been easy on us, but with each battle we win, we believe victory is within our hands. After our defeat at Cheat Mountain, Lee was sent down to Georgia to secure the port at Savannah. The Yankees are trying to bottle up the harbor and attack from that way. I'm not sure why they had to send Lee, since he is needed on the front lines.

We are now under the command of General Johnson. I do not like him as well, but he is a fair man, and we have won a few battles already. We march most of the time until we are near the enemy. It is times like these that I do miss my horses.

I do pray this letter finds you well. Please tell momma I love her and that I will be home soon. This war can't last too much longer. We are gaining more ground every day and soon we will take Washington.

Love from the battlefield,
Your Soldier

Once she finished, she noticed her mother included paper and a pen for her. She knew she would want to write Ben back quickly. It had been months since she got a letter from him. Before she could write him back, a knock sounded on her door. She got up and opened it to find out dinner was ready. She would have to wait until after dinner to write to Ben. A few hours wouldn't matter. The mail wouldn't go out until tomorrow. Sighing, she made her way into the dining room where Thaddeus was waiting for her.

"If you would prefer to eat in your room, I would be okay with it," he stated.

"No, I'm not sick, and this will be less work for the servants," she stated, as he nodded. "Also I do not like eating alone."

"I don't either," he said walking to her side. "Allow me." He pulled out her chair.

"Thank you," she said, as she sat, before he pushed her closer to the table. Once she settled, he walked back to his chair and sat. "How is your mother?" she asked.

"The nurse got her settled in her room. She was sleeping when I checked on her, a few minutes ago," he informed her.

"I pray she doesn't get worse," she voiced.

"Me too, but this has made me realize she needs help," he said.

"Why?" she asked, as their food was set before them.

Everything looked and smelled great.

"She is still grieving over my father, and I know she needs time away from the bank. She needs to spend time with her friends instead of working as much as she does," he explained.

"Who will you hire in her place?" she asked between bites.

"Do you need a job?" he asked.

His question was a little shocking to her. "Well, I tried to sign up as a nurse, but I was unable too," she informed him.

He swallowed before speaking. "You would make a perfect nurse, why won't they take you?" he asked.

"I am unmarried," she explained. "They are worried about my virtue, even though they are short on help. Men are dying, but my virtue is more important."

"A young woman's virtue is a prize," he teased, as she shook her head.

"I'm sure it is, but I want to help the cause in any way I can," she stated.

"So work for me," he suggested. "It would help me out, and keep you busy while waiting for news."

"Okay, but Grace will have to teach me," she warned, as he nodded.

"I knew she would, and it would make her feel involved without pushing her to the side," he said before taking a drink. "Tell me about your fiancé; its Benjamin, right?" he asked.

"Yes, his name is Benjamin; he is good man. He is quiet, but able to carry the weight of the world," she said, and wondered if Thaddeus had met Benjamin.

"Where is he stationed?" he asked wanting to know more about the man she loved. He knew of Benjamin but nothing more.

"He is serving in the Army of Northern Virginia. He was under Robert E. Lee's command, but Lee was reassigned," she mentioned.

"I heard Lee was sent to the Port of Savannah to reinforce the city against the Yankee ships, circling the harbor," he mentioned, as she nodded.

"Yes he was, but I would rather Lee stay with the Army."

"In your position, I would too," he remarked. "Was Benjamin ready for the war?"

Kathryn sighed. Everyone asked her this question, and she was tired of lying. "No, in fact, he didn't want the war," she replied.

"Then why did he leave?" he asked, as she took a sip from her water.

"Because he is fighting for our state's rights; he knew the moment we left the Union, he would fight," she stated, as their plates were cleared.

"How do you feel about his choice?" he asked, as the next course was set in front of them.

She took a moment to compose herself before answering him. "I'm mad at him," she stated. "Wow, I am mad at him," she remarked, finally voicing her feelings.

"I can understand," he muttered. He could see the anger at her fiancée. She was more than hurt at Benjamin actions. He wondered if anyone else saw this side of her. He would bet they hadn't.

"He hates war, but he still chose to fight. He chose to leave me, so yes, I am mad at him," she exclaimed.

"Did he not want to marry you before he left?" he asked softly, wondering why any man who would ask this woman to marry him, would not want to marry her before he left.

She smiled sadly. "He did, but I said no," she said shocking him.

Why would she turn him down?

"Why? You said yes to his proposal, so why didn't you want to marry him before he left?" he asked. "You don't have to answer. I know it is your business on why you said no."

"It's okay. I love him, and I do want to marry him when he comes home, but I didn't want to be rushed into it. I want a husband as well as a wedding," she explained. "I know I could have had him for a day or two as my husband, but then he still would've left."

"True, but you would have been a married woman and could have worked as a nurse," he commented.

"I know, but what if he dies? He is at war, and many men have already died," she voiced.

"You can't think the worse. God willing, Benjamin will come home, and you will be married."

"I pray for him daily," she whispered glancing at her plate.

"We all pray for an end to this war," he stated, as she looked back at him. He paused before continuing. "I am sorry about the sour topic tonight."

"It's fine, I am happy not to hide behind a smile," she revealed. "I'm also happy to have finally nailed what I'm feeling about Ben and his decision to fight."

"I'm happy to help," he said, as she laughed.

"If your offer is still good, I would love to work in the bank."

"Oh, it's good, I'm sure you will do wonderful work," he stated before pausing. "Will Benjamin be upset you are working?"

"No, I don't think so, but I will have to speak with momma. She might have something to say about it."

"She doesn't want you to work?" he asked, as they finished their dinner.

"I don't know, but I will write to her, and ask since we do not know how long the quarantine will last," she stated, as their plates were cleared.

"If you write it now, I can send it out with my letters to the tellers at the bank," he stated, as they stood.

"I will write it now. Thank you, and thank you for a lovely meal," she said, as he nodded. Turning, she made her way back to her temporary room to write the letter.

~ ~ ~ ~

The next morning, she got a response from her mother. She didn't like the idea of her daughter working, but if it helped the cause, then it was okay. After reading her mother's letter, she realized she never answered Ben's letter from yesterday. Grabbing the paper and pen, she sat at the desk and wrote back to him. She didn't tell him about the quarantine because it would worry him. He did not need to worry about her while he was fighting. He wouldn't be able to help her from the battlefield.

My Love,   *October 1861*

I do wish that the mail was faster. I hate having to wait for your letters. I fear one day I will get one after I have read your death in the paper. I am asking you to not go rushing into the midst of the battle just to save someone. I know you, and I know you will rush into a situation without thinking about it. This war has lost its focus. Those ideals that we held so dear seem gone with the wind now.

I was sorry to hear about your defeat at Cheat Mountain, but I know that your troop will bounce back and start winning, so this war will be over sooner rather than later. I was happy to hear Lee was sent to protect the Port of Savannah. It is one of the ports the block aid runners are able to get through at the moment. The block aid runners are our only hope at the moment for supplies. Hopefully, Lee will take care of those Yankees and get them out of our waters.

Will I even recognize you after all this walking and fighting? I'm sure I will because I would know you anywhere. The only thing I ask is you do not cut your hair. I love your long hair because it reminds me of pirates. It will also keep you warm in those cold winter months up North.

Your letters always find me well. I love hearing from you as does your momma. She wanted me to tell you that she loves you and to be careful. Remember, I love you and want you to come home to me so that we can start our life together.

Oh, I do have some good news. Thaddeus Morgan the one that owns the bank, asked me to work for him. He needs help, and since I cannot help in the hospitals because I am an unmarried woman, I told him yes. I start my new job on Monday. Momma's not happy that I am working, but she said that if it would help the cause, then it was okay to work there.

All my love,
Kathryn

Finishing his letter, she read over it quickly, then sealed it. Hopefully, it would go out today. She wished she had another letter from him. His letters were a sign he was alive and still fighting.

~ ~ ~ ~

A full week passed before the quarantine was lifted. Grace got worse, but the nurse handled it wonderfully. The doctor told them yesterday they could leave the house this morning. She spent the morning packing what little she had. She didn't want to forget anything or leave the room in a mess.

As she made her way to the entryway, she saw Thaddeus and Grace waiting for her. Thaddeus took her case so he could carry it. She wasn't surprised because he was a gentleman.

"Oh my dear, I will miss you and our conversations," Grace said as she hugged Kathryn. "My son is not the conversationalist you are," she whispered, as Kathryn smiled.

Grace hadn't heard them during their dinners. Thaddeus liked to talk, and he liked to ask her questions.

"I will miss being a guest in your house," Kathryn commented, as she stepped back from Grace. "I am thankful you are better. I was worried about you when the fever took hold."

"I am thankful you were here to keep my son company," she said. "I know if it had just been the two of us, he would have tried to sneak out and go to work."

"I think you're right," Kathryn remarked glancing at Thaddeus, who was trying to hid his smile.

"Mother, we have detained Kathryn long enough. I am sure her family would love to see her and make sure we have treated her properly," Thaddeus interjected.

Grace sighed and nodded. "You're right," she said. "Thank you again," she said before hugging Kathryn once more. "I do expect to see you dining with us soon."

"All you have to do is send the invitation," Kathryn said stepping away from Grace.

"Let's get you home before mother traps you in the house again," Thaddeus said, as he ushered her outside and into his buggy.

"Thank you for everything."

"It was no trouble, and I hope your time with us was pleasurable for you. I know it was not the way you would have spent your week," he said, as he drove the horses toward her house.

"I enjoyed my time, no worries," she said, as he pulled up outside her house.

He jumped down before helping her step down and grabbing her case. They walked up to her door as it opened to reveal her mother.

"Oh Kathryn, are you alright? You didn't get sick or anything did you?" she asked, rushing out to hug her daughter.

"I am perfectly fine, Mother. They took great care of me," she stated, pulling back from her mother to look at Thaddeus.

"Good, and how is Grace?" Maybelle asked Thaddeus.

"Mother is well, and I think healthier than she was before she got sick," he replied. "Kathryn was a great blessing to us during my mother's illness," he informed her.

"I'm happy your mother is better. I have been so worried about her."

"I will let her know," he said, as he handed Kathryn's case to one of the servants. "I will see you tomorrow for your first day," he stated, looking at Kathryn.

"Yes, I will be there," she said as he nodded and left them.

Maybelle ushered her daughter inside. "Are you sure you are alright? You are not sick or feverish?" she asked, as they entered the parlor.

"I am fine, mother," she assured her mother. "The doctor checked us to make sure we were not sick."

"We were so worried about you," she stated, as her father came into the room.

"Yes we were," he said. "I trust they treated you well."

"Yes, Father, they did. The doctor sent a nurse to make sure Grace was okay, and to check on Thaddeus and me," she explained, as they nodded.

"Breakfast is ready for you whenever you want it," her mother said.

"Thank you, Mother, I will eat it now before I call on Ben's parents."

"They will be happy to see you," her father stated. "They have been worried about you almost as much as we have."

"They are good people, and I will assure them I am fine," she said, before leaving the room.

~ ~ ~ ~

After breakfast, she went out to Twin Willows. She was embraced as soon as she stepped inside.

"We were so worried about you," Lydia stated. "I am happy Grace is feeling better. I would hate for Thaddeus to lose both his mother and father so close together."

"Ms. Grace is stronger than anyone knows," Kathryn commented, as she was ushered into the parlor.

"Yes she is. Now your mother tells us you are going to be working in the bank," Lydia stated.

"Yes, ma'am, Thaddeus doesn't want Ms. Grace working too hard," she explained. "I will start tomorrow."

"Are you nervous?" she asked, as Hannah came into the parlor.

"A little, but Ms. Grace will be teaching me what I need to know," she stated.

Hannah sat down, before turning to Kathryn. "Why do you need to work?"

"I want to do my part for the war," Kathryn answered. "Also, I cannot just sit around and wait to hear from your brother."

"Oh, I wish this war was over already," Hannah mumbled. "All the boys my age have gone to fight, and some of them will never come home again."

"Hannah, this is not a proper conversation," Lydia mentioned, while glancing at Kathryn.

"It's fine; I do understand the wages of war. There is a price to be paid for one's rights," Kathryn voiced. "I wish the price didn't include a man's life, but unfortunately, it does."

"Yes it does," Lydia commented.

Kathryn stayed through the afternoon, before heading home. She didn't want her parents to worry about her after being quarantined for a week. She also wanted to get plenty of sleep tonight. Tomorrow was her first day of work.

Chapter Three

After a few weeks, Kathryn was in a routine at the bank. Grace was patient with her while she learned. It seemed as if she asked hundreds of questions, but Grace answered each one with a smile and plenty of explanation. Grace never made her feel she asked stupid questions either, which helped ease her mind. She learned Grace did not deal with money directly. Instead, Grace balanced everyone's work throughout the day, which was something she knew she could handle.

Everyone at the bank was nice and made sure she was okay throughout the day. It appeared as if they wanted to make sure she enjoyed her job. They always asked her about Ben and helped cheered her up on the days she was sad. She tried to smile, and not show how worried she was, but she knew it didn't work all the time.

She waited every day for another letter. Some days were almost unbearable for her. It had been weeks since she sent her letter. When would another letter arrive? It would at least let her know he was still alive on the day he wrote it.

"You know you can cry if you want too," a calming voice said from behind her. She knew who it was before even turning to face him. He always seemed to stop by her desk at least once a day, since she started work.

"Thaddeus," she whispered, as she looked at him. "I'm sorry I was thinking about something," she muttered, hoping he wouldn't be mad at her for drifting off at work. She didn't lose herself during work hours, but she was missing Ben too much today.

"More like thinking about someone," he stated quietly, his voice full of sympathy. It almost made her cry. "Come on, let's go outside," he said cupping her elbow.

"I just got here," she protested, as he helped her to stand.

She didn't put up too much of a fight, because deep down she knew she needed to get out of the office.

"I need some fresh air, and I think you do too," he stated, as he grabbed her wrap from the back of the chair. "Tell mother, I will be back before the noon meal," he said to one of the older woman standing nearby.

She nodded, as he ushered Kathryn out of the building, and into the cool morning air.

"I am fine; you do not have to treat me any different than one of your other employees," she stated looking at him. It would be weird if people noticed he treated her differently. She didn't want the people at the bank to be mad they didn't get special treatment from the boss.

"I'm not treating you any different than any of my other workers," he stated evenly. "You needed to get out of the office," he commented, as he placed her arm on his while walking down the street.

Kathryn sighed before looking around. Women and older men were milling about getting their business finished before heading back home. They were buying goods from the general store along with the feed store. They acted as if the war wasn't even going on in another part of the country.

"Have you heard anything about the troops?" she asked, as they made their way through the park entrance. Her father was hiding the paper from her, so she couldn't read the battle updates. His plan was to keep her from worrying, but his plan wasn't working. It made her worry more. She wanted to know the troop movements to see how close Ben was to the action.

"No but that's a good thing," he replied. "Benjamin is fine," he tacked on, and she knew it was for her benefit.

"I wish I could believe you, but my heart tells me he is not fine," she voiced, as she pulled her wrap tighter around her shoulders. The temperatures were cooling down as winter got closer. She could imagine how cold Benjamin was. She hoped his wool uniform kept him warm. She visited Boston a few years ago during the winter, and it was not just cold, but bitter cold. It was as if the cold seeped through her clothes and settled in her bones. Benjamin didn't need to be cold while he fought.

The other concern was where he was sleeping. She hoped they would have somewhere other than a tent, but she knew they wouldn't. It was a soldier's lot in life, and it hurt her knowing he was sleeping outdoors.

"You have to stay positive until there isn't a reason too," he stated sadly pulling her from thoughts of Benjamin and the cold. She wondered at his tone, but she wouldn't ask him because it wasn't any of her business. People were entitled to their heartache. He was a private man, and reminded her of Benjamin.

"Oh, I know, and I pray he is safe," she mentioned. "I wish I could talk to him. It is hard to go from talking almost every day to nothing but a letter every few months."

"I know, and I know not hearing anything from the war is worrying you," he commented, as she nodded. He was the only person who guessed not hearing any news was worrying her. "You know I feel guilty about not signing up."

"Why didn't you?" she asked because she was curious why he didn't join the Army.

"I couldn't leave my mother," he replied. "She just lost my father; she needs me more than the cause."

"You made the right decision. Your mother does need you here," she agreed, as they strolled through the park. This morning reminded her of all the times she and Ben walked in the park. "You know Benjamin proposed to me here," she shared glancing up at him.

"In the park?" he asked looking at her with an odd expression. It probably sounded weird that Ben proposed to her in a park, but it was perfect. If she could have planned it, she wouldn't change anything. Ben did everything perfectly.

She smiled, as she remembered the morning so clearly. "This is one our favorite places in Bluff City," she explained, as he nodded. "He came by the house early in the morning, and drove us out here. No one was around so we had the entire park to ourselves. We walked to our spot, and he asked me to marry him. I was surprised when he asked."

"He put a lot of thought into asking you," he remarked, as she laughed.

"Yes he did."

They looped the park before finally exiting. "Are you ready to go back to work?" he asked.

"I never wanted to leave," she stated, even though it wasn't true. It was his idea, though. "You are the one who claimed I needed fresh air," she pointed out, as he nodded.

"I guess so, but are you okay?" he asked, as she sighed.

Somehow he saw the sadness and sorrow she tried to hide from everyone.

"I'm better than I was," she answered truthfully. "Remembering the best day of my life helped."

"I'm happy to help you in any way I can," he said. "If you ever need to talk, let me know. If you're not comfortable sharing with me, talk to my mother. She loves cheering people up, and she would love to repay you for taking care of her."

"Thank you, Thaddeus," she stated, as they walked into the bank. He walked her to her desk, before leaving her alone.

"Are you okay, dear?" Grace asked as soon as Kathryn sat. She didn't even wonder how Grace knew she was back. The woman had a mystic side to her.

"Yes ma'am, I am," she replied with a smile. "Your son wanted to help take my mind off of worrying about Benjamin."

"He doesn't want anyone to worry," Grace said pulling a chair next to her. "Have you heard from Benjamin lately?" she asked placing her hand on Kathryn's arm.

"No, but the mail is really slow."

Grace nodded. "I heard they are trying to speed it up for the soldiers and family members," she informed her.

"I hope so; I would love to hear from him more," she commented.

Grace smiled, and patted her arm. "I'm sure you will hear from him soon, dear. He loves you, and I know he wants nothing more than to be with you," she said as Kathryn nodded. "I will leave you to your work, but if you need to talk, please come find me."

"I will," Kathryn said, as Grace nodded, and left her alone with her work.

The rest of the day was a blur for her, but she was actually happy. Thaddeus and Grace helped ease her mind about the war and Benjamin. They didn't do anything except talk, but she needed to talk. It wasn't as if she couldn't talk to her parents or Ben's family, but they accepted when she told them she didn't want to talk. They never pushed her to discuss Ben. But maybe they needed to. Talking really helped her.

The end of the work day came quickly. She left work on time and walked to her house in a much better mood than when she left. Once she got home, she discovered another letter from Benjamin sitting on the entry table. It was wrinkled and creased, but it was perfect. It was his words from the battlefield. Today turned out better than it started. Grabbing the letter, she rushed to her room to read it in privacy. She didn't want anyone to interrupt her while she read it.

Dear Kathryn,   *November 1861*

I will try to make sure I don't die so you will not get my letter after reading of my death. We are on the move again trying to secure more ground farther North. Every step I take makes me feel like I'm losing you a little more. The thought keeps me up most nights.

I am happy to see you have a job. I know sitting around waiting for news was never to your delight. Thaddeus is a good man, and I trust he will not overwork you even if you ask for it. The one good thing is you will be working in a bank with set hours.

Talk around camps is of the Yankee soldier named Grant moving south. I pray our troops will stop his path and keep our land safe. We cannot afford to lose Tennessee at this stage, especially with the access to the Cumberland and Tennessee Rivers. Steamboats, on those rivers, provide our supplies at this stage. I fear if they ever gain control of that area, they will win the war because we will be cut off from our main supply route.

Please continue to be safe and give momma my love. I know she worries about me as much as you do.

Love,
Your Soldier from the front lines

The Yankees were planning to take Tennessee. This was not great news. It was driving home the fact; this would not be a short war. The North was moving the fight farther south than anyone could have anticipated, especially this early in the war. She knew the Tennessee and Cumberland Rivers were essential to getting supplies to the troops farther north. They could not lose access to them this early. It would spell the end of the Confederacy, if they were to lose them to the Union forces.

Standing, she walked over to her desk, and placed his letter with the others he sent her. She grabbed a pen to write him a letter because she wanted him to get it as soon as possible. She wanted to send her love and a piece of home to him.

My Love, *December 1861*

I was so happy to get your letter. I feel like the mail is getting slower and slower. It seems like it has taken months to get this letter instead of weeks. I do at least know that you are safe or was from the last death report from the latest battle. I still pray you make it through this war and back home to me.

Every step you take is not taking you farther from me. I love you more than the day you asked me to be your wife. I fall more in love with you every day because I envision our life together once this war is over.

My job is great. Thaddeus doesn't let me work overtime at all. He makes me leave in time for dinner and doesn't want me to come in until after I've had breakfast. He is a good man and speaks highly of you. I think he wishes he could have joined the fight, but with the bank and his mother's health, there was no way he could have. I think it makes him feel guilty; others are fighting while he is stuck here in Bluff City.

Grant is moving south? This is not good news about Tennessee, since it is a Confederate State now. I pray he is defeated shortly and run back up into Kentucky where he belongs.

Your momma said hi, and she loves you. She also wants you to be safe.

I love you,
Kathryn

Once she finished her letter, she read over it before sealing it. It would go out in tomorrow's mail. It was a mail day. In addition, if she got it out, it would mean she would get one back from him. She hoped it would be sooner rather than later, but she knew not to get her hopes up. She promised herself she would not be disappointed when she didn't get a letter as soon as possible. Ben was fighting in a war, and she had to remember he couldn't always sit down to write.

~ ~ ~ ~

The following weeks flew by, and before she knew it, it was Christmas. This year was her first Christmas as an engaged woman. It should have been a happy time for her, but with Benjamin gone, it wasn't. The annual Christmas party hosted by Ben's parents at Twin Willows was tonight. She was looking forward to it, even though Ben was gone. Many people from town would be there, including Thaddeus and his mother.

They missed the last Christmas party because his father recently died. They stayed at home not wanting to bring the Christmas mood down; besides the fact, they were in mourning.

She couldn't imagine losing a loved one, let alone losing one around Christmas. It emphasized the loss more than any other time of the year. Ben wasn't dead, but she felt his loss more so now than when he first left in April. Christmas was a time when family gathered together and celebrated the year. She didn't have anything to celebrate with Ben gone.

"Are you ready?" her mother asked knocking on her door. She knew her mother would be the one to check on her. It was a good bet her father was pacing downstairs, waiting on them.

Sighing, she smoothed her hands over her skirt before walking over to her door to open it. "I'm ready," she informed her mother.

"Oh, you look beautiful," her mother said as she looked over Kathryn. Her mother convinced her to be measured for a new dress even though she wasn't in the mood. The dressmaker finished the dress last week and sent it over. She wore her largest hoop, and it really made the dress shine. It was the traditional red, but with white lace around the top and sleeves. Her hair was pinned to get it off her shoulders. It was exactly what she would have picked, if she were in the mood for a new dress.

"Thank you, Mother, you look beautiful too," she said looking at her mother's red and green dress. The dressmaker made her mother's gown as well.

"Are you okay?" her mother asked really looking at her.

She knew she wouldn't be able to hide her feelings from her mother if she tried.

"I'm sad. This is my first Christmas as an engaged woman, but I'm still alone," she explained. "I don't know if Ben is alive or if he's fighting for his life."

"Honey, I know he is alive. He loves you and doesn't want to leave you," Maybelle said, reaching out to tuck a wayward strand of hair behind Kathryn's ear.

"I know," Kathryn whispered. "Shouldn't we be going?" she asked wanting to change the subject. She knew her mother would continue on Ben's welfare all night, if she let her.

"As long as you're ready," Maybelle said, as Kathryn nodded. "Okay, I know your father has the carriage ready and waiting for us."

"Then let's head out, I'm sure daddy is pacing in front of the door," she remarked, as she grabbed her gloves. She would need them once she got outside.

"I'm sure he is," Maybelle mused, as she ushered her daughter out of her room and to the front door. "We are ready," she announced, as her husband smiled.

"My two beautiful women," he stated looking them over. "I must give my regards to the dressmaker."

"She did amazing work this year," Maybelle said looking down at her dress, as Gregory nodded and opened the front door. Maybelle and Kathryn walked outside as Gregory shut the door and led them to the carriage.

Kathryn saw they were traveling in the enclosed one today. It would keep them warm on the ride back tonight. Winter had hit full force; the only thing they were missing was snow. Normally, it didn't snow here until late winter. She wondered if Ben encountered any snow yet.

"Kathryn, do you know if Thaddeus and Grace will be there tonight?" her mother asked, looking at her as they settled inside the carriage.

"They will be there. Grace told me yesterday she was excited to attend this year," she explained. "She told me it was the perfect way to remember her husband."

"How is a party the perfect way to remember her husband?" Maybelle asked in wonder.

Kathryn smiled before answering. "She told me her husband loved the Christmas party at Twin Willows. He never missed a year."

"You know Ben's grandparents hosted their first Christmas party to cheer up after the death of their twins," Gregory informed them.

"Really?" Kathryn asked, thinking about Ben's grandparents.

She didn't know how she would have got out of bed after losing a baby, never mind hosting a Christmas party for the neighbors.

"They continued the tradition every year until his parents moved into Twin Willows. His parents then continued the tradition, since they met at one of the Christmas parties."

"I never knew the party started so long ago or that his parents met at one of the parties," she mentioned, thinking about his grandmother the first year.

She was a strong woman to have gone through what she did and still hosted a party. It was something she would strive to do. It would help her until Ben came home.

They finally made it to Twin Willows and greeted everyone when they got inside. The house was decorated from the floor up with greenery and candles. There was a huge Christmas tree across from the front door. It was the first thing you saw as soon as you walked in. She couldn't believe the transformation of the house. She was here a few weeks ago and nothing was decorated then.

"The house looks amazing," her mother whispered, as she nodded. "Lydia has outdone herself this year," she said, as Hannah rushed over to her. She wasn't running, because she would have tripped over her new green dress.

"Kathryn, come with me," Hannah whispered, as she reached for Kathryn's hand.

"Okay," she whispered, as Hannah pulled her along and up the stairs. "Hannah, where are we going?" she asked, as Hannah continued down the hall. Normally guests did not come upstairs during a party. There was plenty of room downstairs so there wasn't a reason for people to be up here.

"My room," she replied, as they reached her door. They slipped inside before Hannah shut the door. The noise of the party could barely be heard once they were inside.

"You're not going to try to kill me, are you?" she teased, as Hannah laughed.

"No, but I do have a question to ask you," Hannah said as she sat down on her bed. "Have you ordered your wedding dress yet?" she asked.

"No, because I want a white dress, and mother is determined I wear a blue one," Kathryn remarked, thinking back to one of their fights this week. "We are at a stalemate. I decided it would be better not to fight over the holidays."

"I think you should order it." Hannah commented.

"Where would I put it until Ben comes home?" she asked. "I can't hide it away from my mother in my room," she pointed out.

"You could leave it here," Hannah said, motioning around her room. "I know Ben told me you probably would before he left," she mentioned, as Kathryn smiled.

"Your brother really thinks of everything," she noted.

Benjamin was still looking out for her, from an unknown battlefield in Virginia. It warmed her heart.

"Yes he does," Hannah voiced. "Did you tell him you are working at the bank?" she asked, changing the subject.

Kathryn smiled and nodded. "Of course I told him. He thought it was a great idea and would keep me from sitting around worrying about him."

"Maybe I should go work at the bank," Hannah muttered glancing around the room. "All I do is worry about Ben and the other men fighting," she explained, as Kathryn nodded. It was hard sitting at home worrying about the people you love; Hannah was young, so the war was harder on her.

"You know, your brother doesn't want you worrying about him," she remarked, as Hannah nodded.

"I know, but I can't help it," Hannah said. "When he left, he tore our family apart. Our father barely talks about him, while mother sits and stares out the window most days."

"I'm sorry Hannah," she said, placing her hand on Hannah's shoulder. "He had his reasons, even if you don't agree with them."

"It's not that I don't agree; it's just hard knowing he could die."

"I know it's hard for me, too," she shared. "I spend most of my nights trying to picture him alive and well."

"How is it going for you?" Hannah asked.

"Not too well, since I'm losing sleep," she replied sadly. "His letters help. He tells me about his time in camp. It's almost as if I'm there with him."

"He's been sending me and Momma letters, too. Daddy doesn't read them, but he listens when Momma reads them," Hannah informed her. "His letters make me sad and happy at the same time."

"Yeah, they do the same for me," Kathryn shared. "Hannah, if you need to talk about your brother please come to me."

Hannah sighed. "Okay," she muttered. "We better get back to the party; I'm sure my mother will be looking for us."

"If she doesn't, then my mother will be," Kathryn stated, as they made their way out of Hannah's room and back down to the party.

Kathryn spotted Thaddeus and Grace, as they entered the house and greeted Joshua and Lydia. "You know I wonder what Thaddeus thinks about this time of the year," Hannah whispered beside her.

"Why?" Kathryn asked, as she watched Grace embrace Lydia. They were old friends, so it wasn't unusual.

"Well, he lost his father last Christmas and his fiancée two Christmases ago," Hannah explained. "It has to be a hard time of year for him," she muttered.

"Thaddeus was engaged?" she asked in shock, as she turned to look at Hannah. This was news to her, and she wondered why she hadn't heard about a fiancée. She couldn't believe Thaddeus was engaged two years ago.

"Yes, he was engaged," Hannah replied. "How is this news to you?" she asked, cocking her head to the side.

"Who was he engaged to?" Kathryn asked instead of answering Hannah. She just couldn't seem to move past the fact Thaddeus was engaged.

"Her name was Sarah," Hannah replied. "Did you really not know?" she asked.

"No, how long were they engaged?" Kathryn asked, looking back over at Thaddeus and Grace.

They were talking to her parents now. She wondered if it had been a secret engagement, or did everyone know, but her? It seemed impossible she would miss something as big as an engagement, but it looked as if she did.

"I'm not sure, but I don't think long," Hannah answered. "She died of cholera a few days before Christmas. It was a bad time for him."

"Oh, that's so sad," Kathryn remarked. "I wonder if it's the reason he stays pretty much to himself now."

"I would say so," Hannah commented. "I know he really loved her."

"I can't believe I didn't know about his engagement."

"Come on, let's go say hi," Hannah said, as Kathryn nodded and followed her over to Thaddeus and Grace.

"Hannah, you are beautiful as always," Grace said, as she pulled Hannah into a hug. "Your parents will be beating the boys off when this war is over."

"Oh, thank you Ms. Grace," Hannah said with a smile. "Thank you for coming tonight."

"I couldn't miss this year," she stated, as Hannah nodded and moved to greet Thaddeus. "Kathryn, you look beautiful, as well."

"Thank you, Ms. Grace," she said hugging Grace. "You look beautiful, too."

"Mother always looks beautiful." Thaddeus stated behind her. He was smiling at the three of them.

"Now, I know you both are lying," Grace stated with a smile. "I think I will join the other parents, but you three need to be in the ballroom dancing. Young people are meant to be dancing at parties," she said, before leaving them alone.

"You know I think my mother just ordered all of us to dance," Thaddeus muttered.

Kathryn smiled. "She didn't phrase it as an order, but it was," she said, as Hannah nodded.

"Don't worry momma already told me I wasn't doing my duty, so I'm on my way there now," Hannah said. "Are you two joining me?" she asked.

"I am," Kathryn replied.

"I will, if I can persuade both of you ladies to honor me with a dance," Thaddeus stated, sweeping his arm in front of him.

Kathryn glanced at Hannah before looking back at Thaddeus. "As long as you don't step on my toes, I will dance with you," she said.

"If you're stepping on toes now, I can't dance with you," Hannah teased.

"Your toes will be fine, ladies," Thaddeus said, as he ushered them into the ballroom. "You know this ballroom is amazing."

"Thank you, I thought momma could've done without the tree in here," Hannah commented. "It takes up a corner of the dance floor."

"No, I think the tree in here is the best one," Kathryn said looking at the Christmas tree in the corner. "I know Ben would love it."

"True, my brother is all about Christmas," Hannah said, as the band started playing.

"Kathryn, would you honor me with the first dance?" Thaddeus asked holding out his hand to her.

"I will," she said placing her hand in his.

Hannah watched as Thaddeus led Kathryn out to the floor. "Would you like to dance?" William asked. He was a friend of the family and one of the last boys her age still in town.

"I would," Hannah replied, as she let William lead her out to the dance floor. Thankfully, the band wasn't playing a reel. William didn't know the steps for a reel and she hated dancing it with him.

"I see Hannah found a dance partner already," Thaddeus mentioned, looking over at the couple. "I thought William would have joined the Army already."

"He probably will in about another week," she commented, looking at William and Hannah. Everyone assumed they would get married but she couldn't see Hannah marrying him.

"Why in a week?" he asked, spinning her around the dance floor.

"He will turn 16 next week, and his mother told him he could join once he turned 16," she explained. "He is hoping to join his older brother, Robert. I don't know where Robert is, but Henrietta told me he is not stationed with Benjamin."

"He is stationed in Tennessee," he informed her. It amazed her he knew where the men in town were stationed. He must be keeping up with the troop movements through the papers. It was the only way to explain his knowledge.

"What?" she asked, remembering Benjamin's letter about the Yankee Grant planning to move the fighting into Tennessee. If Robert was stationed in Tennessee, he could be fighting at this moment.

"He is in the Army of the Central Kentucky under General Albert Sydney Johnston," he said. "I spoke with his father about it yesterday."

"Benjamin wrote about a Yankee by the name of Grant moving south to fight in Tennessee," she stated, trying not to worry. It was hard, because she had so many friends fighting there.

Thaddeus looked at her and sighed. "Benjamin's right. Grant is planning on fighting for control of the Cumberland and Tennessee Rivers. He knows it is the main supply route to our troops up north," he said. "Grant is in Kentucky according to reports."

"Where is the fighting right now?" she asked, hoping it was far away from all of her friends and Benjamin.

"Do you really want to know?" he asked, turning her once again weaving through the other couples dancing.

It was a good thing he was leading her, because she would have stopped and stood in the middle of the dance floor, especially after he delivered his news about Grant.

She closed her eyes and took a calming breath. "Please tell me the fighting is nowhere near Benjamin," she begged.

"I would if I could but most of the fighting is in Virginia. Kentucky and Missouri are seeing a lot of action as well," he informed her. "I'm sorry; I shouldn't have told you any of this, everyone wants you to not worry about the war."

"No, I want to know," she said. "I need to know what's going on."

"It will only make you worry more," he pointed out as she nodded. "Kathryn, this isn't good for your health."

"I'm not sick," she said quickly. She was tired of people thinking they know what's best for her. "You do not have to worry about my health."

"I'm sorry," he apologized, as the music changed. "I do believe our dance is over." He said as he led her off the dance floor. "Thank you," he said, before bowing to her.

"Thank you for being honest with me," she said, as he nodded and stepped away from her. She watched him lead Hannah out on the dance floor, as she tried to process everything he told her.

Ben was in the middle of battle which was the reason he couldn't write to her. She would speak to her father about not hiding the paper from her anymore. She needed to know what was going on. The war was affecting her and the country; she deserved to read about it along with everyone else.

~ ~ ~ ~

The rest of the night was a blur to Kathryn. She danced almost every dance and even enjoyed them. Once she made up her mind about talking to her father, she let herself enjoy the party. She and Thaddeus danced two more times. Normally it would have been unheard of for her to dance that many times with someone who wasn't her fiancée, but since most of the younger men were at war, it was fine. Her mother did give her an odd look after the third dance, which she took to mean, don't dance with him again. It was okay with her since the night was winding down.

They left the party before the last guests left. Once they made it home, she went to her room. Thankfully, her maid was there to help her out of her dress. She thought about what Hannah said about ordering her dress. She should order her wedding dress. It was her wedding, not her mother's. If she wanted to get married in a white dress, she would get married in a white dress.

Climbing into bed, she thought about what her ideal dress would be. She closed her eyes and dreamed about what her wedding day would be like. The main thing, her dress would be white. Her dreams quickly took a turn for the worse as the night wore on. She was standing in her white wedding dress, but when she looked down at it, there was blood staining it. The blood covered her dress as she screamed out.

Chapter Four

Christmas and New Year's passed quickly for Kathryn. She didn't receive a new letter from Ben. The holidays kept her busy enough not to dwell on it. She started keeping up with the war more and more against her father's wishes. It was important to her, because she needed to know if he was killed or injured. His name hadn't appeared on any list yet, which kept her spirits high.

It was hard to have high spirits when she read the papers. Every page contained grim reports from the various battlefields. There were wins and losses for both sides. The Union would lose some ground, but the next day on another battlefield, the Confederacy would lose some ground. There wasn't a clear victor, which meant the war would continue.

The war was getting closer and closer to them as more and more men died. The people in town already suffered losses, and if the war continued, those losses would only rise. Many women in town were dyeing their dresses black. It was easy to see who lost a loved one. Several families lost more than one loved one already. It was a growing list, and she wondered if anyone would survive the war.

Sighing, she looked out her bedroom window and watched the rainfall. The weather was mimicking her mood. The sun shined when she didn't read Ben's name on the dead lists, but it rained when she heard about another battle close to him. This morning she felt Ben was a lifetime away from her. Their shared days of joy and love were nothing but a dream. Closing her eyes, she steeled her mind against those thoughts. Ben would come home to her. They would get married at Twin Willows and start their life together.

Their mothers were pressuring her to marry him when he came home on furlough, whenever it would be. She refused to marry him at least until the war was over. She didn't want to have him for only a few days only to lose him again. It was the same reason she didn't marry him before the war started. They were relentless in wanting her and Ben married, but she would not move on this issue.

They would marry once the war was over and there was peace once again.

She did visit the dressmaker, without either mother, who promised to order the material and lace for her dress. The dressmaker cautioned it would take longer to get the items in because of the blockade. It wasn't a problem for her, since the war wasn't over.

The North was trying to bottle up the harbors, but the blockade-runners were staying one step ahead of them. It was crazy the things the war effected, such as linens and lace. No one traveled to see family if they were located in the North or if their family sided with the Union. No one spoke of the Northern states unless in a slur. Lincoln was not President here; instead, their President was Jefferson Davis.

Planning the wedding was taking her mind off of Benjamin fighting on some Northern field. She just wished he was here planning it with her. It would seem real if he was here. He would provide support for her against their mothers.

"Kathryn, I have something for you," her mother said tapping on her door, which in turn interrupted her thoughts. It was okay, because she needed to get ready for work.

She spun around, walked to the door, and opened it for her mother. "Why do you sound odd?" she asked looking at her mother.

Nothing seemed off, but there was something different about her mother.

"Your father did not want me to give this to you," she said instead. "I told him he could not continue to shield you from the war," she stated, as Kathryn nodded. "You need to get ready for work," she said, handing Kathryn a letter before walking away.

Looking at the letter, she smiled for the first time today. It was from Ben. She wondered if she had time to read it before work. If she didn't, she would make time. She called for her maid, as she opened the letter.

Dear Kathryn,   *January 1862*

The mail is getting slower. The postal service has been suspended to the Confederate States, since we are not a part of the

Union. Thankfully though, there are a brave few that take the letters to the block aid runners so they can sail them into one of the Southern ports and get them to everyone. Don't worry, I am still alive, and I plan to stay that way. Also, please stop reading the death reports. I do not want you to learn about my death that way.

I am in love with you as well. I cannot wait for this war to end so I can make you my wife.

You can tell Thaddeus not to feel guilty over not joining the cause. He is doing his part by watching over you and keeping you entertained while I'm gone.

The Yankees are closing in on Fort Henry and Fort Donelson, which is not good news at all. Apparently, Grant is preparing to attack the middle of Tennessee first, before spreading down. Hopefully our boys will take care of them before they move lower.

Tell momma I love her, and I'm being safe.

I love you,
Your Soldier

Once she finished reading, she knew she didn't have time to write him back. She would have to wait. Her maid arrived, as she tucked his letter away, and she got dressed before leaving.

~ ~ ~ ~

As soon as she got to the bank, she learned Grant attacked Fort Donelson and Fort Henry. He now controlled the Tennessee and Cumberland Rivers around the Nashville area. This wasn't good news, but it didn't ruin her mood. Ben's letter made everything seem better than it was. The news of Grant's capture of the rivers would upset her another day once she thought about it, but not today.

"I haven't seen a smile on your face in a while," Thaddeus commented walking toward her. "You must have gotten a letter from Benjamin," he stated.

Turning slightly, she glanced at him. "My mother gave it to me this morning," she informed him.

"How is he?" he asked.

"In love with me," she joked not losing her smile.

"And why wouldn't he be?" he asked, smiling back at her. "He has you waiting on him to return. What man wouldn't want a beautiful woman waiting on him?" he teased.

"Yes he does," she admitted. "He asked me not to read the death lists anymore," she shared.

Thaddeus nodded. "I agree with him," he said, as she lost her smile.

"What? How will I know if he's wounded or …"

"Dead?" he asked, as she nodded. "Kathryn, reading his name on a death list is not the way to find out about his death."

"How will I find out then?" she asked. "He is hundreds of miles away in a different state."

She thought Thaddeus understood why she needed to read the lists.

"You don't understand how reading his name will affect you," he said sadly. "It is a feeling you cannot describe, and it would be better if you didn't feel it at all."

"How would you know?" she asked.

His comments made her think he'd read someone's name on a death list but whom? He knew when his father died, because He was there. What name did he read on a death list? It was really bugging her. There were secrets behind those eyes of his, but it wasn't her place to ask him.

"Kathryn," he paused, while rubbing the back of his neck. "Now is not the place or time to get into this."

She nodded in understanding. He was right this was not the time or the place for this discussion.

"I'm sorry, I shouldn't have asked," she voiced, looking away from him.

"No you can ask because you share your secrets with me," he sighed heavily before continuing. "I was engaged to a woman from the next county. I met Sarah at one of the house parties I attended with my parents. We corresponded for a year before I asked her to marry me. We were only engaged for two short weeks when there was a cholera outbreak. The town was quarantined as a result. Nothing could come or go, including the mail. I didn't learn of her death, until the paper published a death list after the outbreak was over," he explained.

"Oh, Thaddeus," she breathed, as she placed her hand on his sleeve. "I'm sorry."

"It's been two years, since I read her name, but the wound is still there," he shared, as she bit her lip. "Trust me, reading a death list, and finding the name of your loved one on it doesn't leave you. The feeling stays and torments you in your weakest moments," he said before backing away from her. "I will leave you to your work."

She watched him walk away with a heavy heart. Two weeks. He had two weeks of bliss with Sarah, before she was taken away from him. It was worse than her few hours with Benjamin. She never really got to celebrate as he did. Two short weeks, before disease and death took the love of his life away. She wondered if they planned anything, or if they were floating on love. It was something she wouldn't ask him. She didn't want to remind him of the heartache again.

The rest of the day passed as she completed her work. She pushed her conversation with Thaddeus to the back of her mind.

"It's time for you to go home," Thaddeus said, walking to her desk.

"Sorry, I didn't realize it was already time," she said, cleaning her desk.

She didn't like leaving a mess when she left.

"You've been busy," he muttered, as she nodded.

"Oh, I forgot to tell you, Ben said for you not to feel guilty over not joining the cause," she stated, standing up.

"You told him I felt guilty?" he asked.

"Yes, I also told him about you giving me this job. He said you should not feel guilty. You are here entertaining me and keeping me from worrying about him," she stated with a smile.

Thaddeus stood there a moment thinking about what she told him. She wasn't sure what he would say.

"You know he is the first man to tell me not to feel guilty," he stated. "Everyone else looks at me and tells me I'm not a true Southern gentleman for not joining the cause."

"I'm sorry, I didn't know," she whispered.

"It's fine because I knew I would not leave my mother, but it was not a popular choice," he shared. "Thank him for me."

"I will," she said.

"You can also tell him I try to entertain you, but you are stubborn and want to bask in your sadness some days," he said with a smile.

"I'll be sure to share it with him. It will make him laugh and ease some of his worry over me," she commented.

"You two are quite a pair, worrying about each other," he said as she nodded.

"Thank you for sharing earlier."

He nodded, as Grace walked over to them. "Are you keeping Kathryn late?" she asked.

"No, in fact, I was the one to remind her it was time to leave," he answered, looking at his mother.

"Yes he did," Kathryn voiced.

"You look happy today, did you get a letter from Ben?" she asked, as Kathryn wondered how sad she looked.

Everyone commented on how happy she looked today. She would have to work harder on being happy, while Ben was away from home or at least keep her sadness to herself.

"I did, ma'am," she confirmed. "He seems to be in good spirits, which is better than I could have hoped."

"He has a beautiful woman waiting on him to return, I'm sure it keeps him from going crazy," she commented.

"I hope so," Kathryn said in agreement. "I guess I better leave. My parents will be worried if I am not home soon."

"See you tomorrow, dear," Grace said as Kathryn nodded and left the bank.

She quickly made her way home so she could write Benjamin a letter.

~ ~ ~ ~

Maybelle smiled when she saw her daughter come home. "I told you it was better not to hide his letters from her," she said looking over at her husband.

"I wasn't against Benjamin's letter," Gregory stated. "I was against her reading the battlefield reports."

"It helps her focus," she said, once their daughter was out of earshot. "She needs to know where the fighting is."

"I still don't like it, but I will agree she seems better," he voiced, picking up his paper.

The editor remarked about the recent loss of the Tennessee and Cumberland Rivers. The South would need another route to get supplies to the troops. No one knew which way Grant would head, but he would bet further down the Tennessee River. It made sense for Grant to head in that direction. Only the coming months would reveal his plan. He just hoped the Confederate troops were ready for his attack.

~ ~ ~ ~

Kathryn entered her room, sat at her desk, and read Ben's letter again before writing hers to him.

My Love,   *February 1862*

I cannot help but read those death reports. It is just a sick obsession that I have to do. In a small way, if I do not see your name, I can rest easy because I know you are alive for at least another battle.

Our mothers are pressuring me to marry you when you come home on your furlough. I have told them we are not getting married until after the war is over, but they just do not listen to me. They want us married with a baby on the way. Apparently, there is talk about me getting too old to have a child if we wait any longer. It is just utter nonsense. I pray every day for Lincoln to call an end to the war. It just seems never ending, even though it has not yet been a year since it started and Fort Sumter seems so long ago now. I guess it is because our lives have changed from what we had envisioned.

Well, Grant has finally attacked Fort Henry and Donelson, reports confirm. I cannot believe that the Yankees are in Tennessee at all. It is only February, and I can only imagine what the rest of the year will bring for us and Tennessee if they have already lost that much ground.

Thaddeus wants to say thank you for telling him not to be guilty about not being able to join the cause. He said you are the only one that has not made him feel less than worthy of being a man. He also wanted me to tell you he is doing his best to keep me entertained, even though it is a difficult job. Apparently, I worry too much about you, or at least that is what he told me the other day.

Your momma says hi, and she loves you too. Your father is still silent on the issue of you joining. I know he is proud of you; it is just hard for him to think about you fighting. Remember, I love you, too, and expect you to return to me in one piece so we can get married and provide our mothers with grandchildren and great grandchildren.

All my love,
Kathryn

~ ~ ~ ~

February and March passed quickly with no letter from Ben. She knew he was alive since she still read the death lists and kept up with troop movements. The weather was getting warmer as April rolled around. She made an effort to be happy, even if she wasn't. She didn't want other people pitying her. Some days she actually found herself really happy, even though she hadn't heard from Benjamin. It was weird, but she was finding her feet with Ben gone.

As she made her way through town, she saw a crowd gathering around the telegraph office. The size of the crowd could only mean one thing, a battle. It must be a big battle, since most of the town was gathered there. When she made it to work, she ran into Thaddeus as soon as she stepped inside.

"What battle is being fought?" she asked.

"Somewhere in the lower part of Tennessee, along the banks of the Tennessee River," he replied. "It's near a church called Shiloh along Pittsburg Landing," he informed her.

"Shiloh?" she asked, as he nodded.

"General Johnston and the Army of the Mississippi were stationed close to there in Corinth," she voiced, as he nodded. "So he moved his army up to stop Grant?"

"Yes, the fighting started two days ago and finished in a Confederate defeat yesterday," he explained.

"Several of the men from town are in the Army of the Mississippi, including Robert," she commented, as he nodded.

She didn't notice his nod, because she closed her eyes to gain control of her thoughts. "Henrietta is probably worrying herself sick over this news."

"Take today off and go to her," he stated.

"What?" she asked, opening her eyes to look at him.

"She needs you more than you need to be at work," he stated. "I don't think you will get any work done today anyway. Most people in town will be waiting on any news from the battlefield."

"Are you sure?" she asked.

"I am; go to her. She will need a friend when she receives the news."

"If you need me, come find me," she stated, as he nodded.

Turning around, she left the bank and went in search of Henrietta. She sent up several prayers before she found her. Henrietta was standing between her parents, while Robert's parents were standing behind her. They were waiting on news for Robert and William. She knew it was hard enough waiting on news for one man, she couldn't imagine waiting for two.

She took a deep breath and walked over to Henrietta. Robert got to come home for a few days between Christmas and New Year's, which she knew made Henrietta happy. The married soldiers got leave before the single ones. It made her wonder when Ben would be home.

"Kathryn, why are you not at work?" Henrietta asked.

"Thaddeus explained what was going on and thought you needed a friend while you wait," she replied.

Henrietta nodded before throwing her arms around Kathryn. "I can't lose him," she cried, as Kathryn wrapped her arms around her friend.

"I know," Kathryn whispered as she let Henrietta cry.

"I haven't told him yet, but he's going to be a father," she whispered, as tears pooled in Kathryn's eyes. "The doctor confirmed it yesterday," she shared.

"Oh, Henrietta, I'm sorry," she whispered, as she rubbed Henrietta's back.

There was a big chance Robert would never find out he would be a father. This is what she was afraid of, if she married Benjamin before the war was over.

"I just want him to live through this battle," Henrietta cried, as Kathryn nodded.

"Do you know any news?" she asked, looking around at the people.

Henrietta shook her head before pulling back. "They just told us it could take all day while they identify the bodies," she explained.

"You need to eat and rest for the baby's sake," Kathryn commented. "Let me take you home."

"No, I need to be here when the list is released," she protested.

Kathryn sighed and nodded. She wrapped her arm around Henrietta's shoulders.

Throughout the day, the families who were not waiting for news bought food and water to them. Kathryn convinced Henrietta to sit in the carriage to get her off her feet. It was late afternoon before the telegraph operator rushed out with the lists. People rushed forward to grab one. Robert's parents got one and came back to them to read it. They read through the names starting at the J's.

"Ashley Jacks, Robert Jackson, William Jackson..."

"No!" Henrietta screamed, as Kathryn gathered her close and let her cry.

"Both my boys," Robert's mom cried, as his dad pulled her close.

Kathryn closed her eyes to the screams, wails, and crying. So many families lost loved ones in one battle. Two days of battling resulted in all this heartache. Life would never be the same again for those families.

She wondered how she would react if Ben died. It wouldn't be pretty, and she didn't know how she would muddle through each day. Holding Henrietta and listening to her complete breakdown, she steeled her resolve. She would not marry Ben until this war was over. She would not have him one day then have him taken away the next.

~ ~ ~ ~

Over the next few days, the businesses in town were closed due to so many in mourning. In fact, it was a week later before Thaddeus opened the bank. She was glad to be back at work, because while she was off, she ran errands for her mother and spent a good deal of time with Henrietta. Maybelle sent food over daily for Henrietta and her parents, since she lived with her parents. She and Robert were going to buy a place when the war ended.

Kathryn was worried about the baby. Henrietta barely ate and slept even less. It was as if she couldn't function with Robert dead. He had been gone for months, and she functioned fine. The doctor ordered her to eat and warned her if she didn't; she would lose the baby. The warning seemed to get through to Henrietta, because she ate before going to sleep.

Two months passed, and Henrietta was still barely living. She walked around in a fog most of the time, but she was at least eating and sleeping more. Kathryn visited with her for several hours yesterday. Henrietta spoke maybe ten words while Kathryn did most of the talking. She tried to cheer her up, but nothing appeared to get through to Henrietta.

The next morning she found a surprise waiting for her downstairs on the entry table.

"Mother, when did Ben's letter come?" she asked, waving the letter around.

"Late yesterday, but you were tired and needed your rest after visiting Henrietta. One day wouldn't make any difference," Maybelle replied, looking at her daughter. "You can read it now."

"I'll be late for work, but I will read it sometime today," she stated, as Maybelle nodded.

Kathryn quickly ate breakfast before making her way to work. The letter was safely tucked in her clutch. She was tempted to read it on the way to work, but she decided it was better not too. A few minutes later, she walked into the bank and saw Grace waiting for her.

"How is Henrietta?" Grace asked, as soon as Kathryn drew near.

She sighed before answering, "She's not good. The doctor warned her again if she didn't eat and sleep she would lose the baby."

"Oh my, she is pregnant?" Grace asked, as Kathryn closed her eyes.

Henrietta wasn't telling anyone about the baby yet. She would when she started showing, she promised.

"She is, but you cannot tell anyone," she stated. "She isn't sharing her news yet."

"I will not tell anyone, not even Thaddeus. You have my word," she promised, as Kathryn nodded. "How are the Jackson's?" she asked.

Kathryn tried to visit them several times over the past two months, but they always turned her away. They weren't receiving callers at all. It didn't matter who knocked on their door.

"They are not receiving visitors, so I'm not sure," she revealed. "My father did get to talk to them after the funeral. They said they may take a trip to get away from everything."

"I cannot imagine losing two sons at once and so far away," Grace mumbled. "Losing a husband is one thing, but a son is a part of you. You carry him for nine months before sharing him with the world. It is hard to let him go and be a man, but it's even harder to have him die so soon. His life cut short in battle," Grace said, as Kathryn nodded. "Give them time, they will learn to live again. They will need to find comfort in each other."

"I hope so," Kathryn whispered thinking about how hollow Mrs. Jackson's eyes looked the last time she tried to visit.

"Oh, my dear, you haven't read Benjamin's name, have you?" she asked, placing her hand on Kathryn's arm.

The past two months saw an increase in battles between the Union and Confederacy.

"No, I haven't read his name," Kathryn stated and sent up another quick prayer hoping she wouldn't read his name on those dreaded lists. "In fact, I just received a letter from him. I haven't had a chance to read it yet."

"I hope it contains good news."

"Thank you, I hope so," she said, sitting down. "Will Thaddeus be here today?" she asked.

He'd been coming in later and later as he dealt with the families of dead soldiers. They didn't want to leave their houses so he made house calls.

"He will be here later this morning," Grace replied. "He said he had some business to attend to, and then he would be here."

Kathryn nodded before getting to work. It was an easy day for her, which was good since she was thinking about Ben's letter most of the day. She found a few minutes, so she quickly pulled his letter out and opened it.

Dear Kathryn,   *April 1862*

It is getting tough here at camp. Winter just seems to drag on which is not good for us. I don't think any of us were really prepared for this cold. Some of the guys do not even have shoes to wear. I am not sure how much longer we will be able to hold out with this cold.

If you must read the death reports, please do not get mad if you do read my death. If they do let you rest better, I cannot tell you not to read them even though I would like to. I will say, please remember I am not fighting in every battle, and I hope that small fact gives you comfort.

You can tell my mother I said to leave you alone. You can also tell your mother that too, but I am sure that would not go over very well. I am sorry they are pressuring you and I am not there to protect you, but I am with you in spirit. I pray this war is over soon, as well, so we can get married and start our family.

We heard about Henry and Donelson. Grant is on a mission, but no one seems to know his next target. For the moment, we are in wait-and-see mode, but hopefully, that will change as soon as possible. General Johnston is ready and waiting for anything to suggest where Grant will be next.

Of course, you are not making Thaddeus' job easy. You were always a difficult woman to entertain, but it is just one of the reasons that I love you. Please be a little nicer to him since he did give you a job.

Wishing I was back home in the warmth,
Your Soldier

Rubbing her face, she read the date. He wrote the letter before Shiloh. It was evident in his words. She wondered if he heard the news, but then thought better about it. He knew about the battle, but he couldn't possibly know the losses the town suffered. She debated about telling him who died, but decided it wouldn't be a good idea. He didn't need to worry about her or anyone but himself. He needed to stay strong and focused, so he could come home to her. He had to come home to her.

"Bad news?" Thaddeus asked, breaking through her thoughts.

She looked up at him and shook her head. "No, it's a letter from Benjamin. He wrote it before Shiloh, and I debated telling him who died there."

"I wouldn't think it would be a good idea," he stated, as she nodded.

"Yea, I know, I decided against it almost as soon as I thought it," she stated, as she stood up. "Can I get you anything?"

"No, I'm fine. I just needed a moment before getting to work."

"Well, if you need anything, let me know," she said, as he nodded and left her alone.

She sat back down, and read Ben's letter again. Once she finished she grabbed some paper and wrote back to him.

My love,   *June 1862*

I was so happy to receive your letter today. We heard about the battle at Shiloh. Grant has gained access to the lower part of the Tennessee River, which is not good news for your troop. We all thought Spring would bring better news but not anymore. The reports of the battle are horrific, and it is being called the bloodiest battle to date.

I am thankful you are still in Virginia now instead of closer to me. Tennessee is taking a beating, and I fear it will only get worse in the coming months. With the war a year old now, I fear everyone has been wrong. This will not be a quick war. I fear it will take years to resolve, and even after it is over, will there even be peace.

I did talk to our mothers and finally made them see my side. They are backing off, but I am not sure if it is because I am barely holding it together, or if they have accepted that I am firm in my decision not to marry you until the war is over.

I love you, and I await your furlough so I can hold you in my arms and know you are really alive and well, as your letters made me think you are.

Your wife to be,
Kathryn

Once she finished her letter, she read over it before sealing it. She wasn't sure when he would get the letter or how long it would be until he got to write back. It still gave her hope. He was alive and fighting for a war that was only a year old. She thought about how much a year made a difference. What would the next year bring and could she handle it?

~ ~ ~ ~

Dear Kathryn,   *August 1862*

We received the news of Shiloh after I had sent your last letter. I cannot believe we lost that battle. I know if General Johnston would have survived, we would have won. The fighting is getting more intense, much more than we ever thought it would that far south.

Tennessee is all but fallen into Yankee hands. I fear its loss will spell trouble for us and the entire Confederate Army. I still wish I was closer to you, but I know I am needed here more. I agree this will be a long-fought war, and I can only hope there will be peace once the fighting is finished.

I am thankful that our mothers are backing off. I do not like reading you are barely holding it together. The only reason I am strong in battle is because I know you are staying strong at home. Please continue to be my strength.

I am afraid my furlough has been delayed due to General Lee rumored to be taking control once again. I have been promoted to sniper, so I should not be on the front lines. I hope this news brightens your spirit and brings a smile to your face. In the last battle, the generals were impressed I could shoot as far as I can. I did explain that I practiced long range shooting at home.

Give momma my love.

Your soldier awaiting the end of the war,
Your Soldier

Chapter Five

May 1863

Months passed as the war continued on different battlefields spread across the nations. The two nations questioned when or if the war would end. Everyday more and more names were added to the death lists. The battles seemed to grow deadlier daily. Men littered the battlefield in places such as Shiloh, Antietam, Stones River, and recently Fort McAllister, which was located here in Georgia.

There were rumors the Confederate dead were thrown into trenches, or left lying on the ground where they fell. It was disheartening to hear, and she hoped it wasn't true. The men who fought and died in those battles deserved a burial for their service to Confederacy just as the Union soldier who fought. They deserved to be sent home and buried by their loved ones, or at least an honorable grave.

Sighing, she got out of the carriage and looked up at the house in front of her. A black bow indicting mourning still hung on the door. It was faded from the passage of a year. A smaller blue bow now hung beside it. The blue one should be the only one on the door for the family, but the battle of Shiloh destroyed this family. It would be broken forever because Robert would never leave. His spirit probably still fought the battle, his body lost.

She made her way to the door and knocked. This wasn't the first time she visited the house, but this was the first after the baby was born. Henrietta was confined to her parent's house for most of her pregnancy due to complications. Kathryn knew it didn't bother Henrietta being confined, because she was still in mourning.

As she raised her hand to knock again, Henrietta's mother opened the door. "Oh Kathryn, it's great to see you, I wondered when you would be by," she said ushering Kathryn inside. "Henrietta is in the parlor with the baby," she informed her.

"Thank you, is it okay if I see her?" she asked because she wasn't sure of Henrietta's frame of mind. This was a delicate time for her. "Is she up for visitors?"

"I know she will love to see you, honey," she said with a smile. "You have been a dear friend to my daughter during this black time in her life. I cannot thank you enough."

"There is no need to thank me; she kept my mind off of Benjamin fighting on some unknown battlefield."

"Have you heard anything from him recently?" she asked, shutting the door.

"Actually I just received a letter from him this week. He is feeling old even though he just turned 25," she said with a smile. "They are on their way to Chancellorsville."

Henrietta's mother smiled. "I'm so happy he writes to you. I know you worry less when you hear from him."

"I love hearing from him, even if it is months between letters," Kathryn commented, as they walked into the parlor.

"Henrietta, Kathryn is here," she said, as Kathryn stepped into the room. "I will leave you two ladies alone; if you need anything, ring the bell."

"Thanks, Mother," Henrietta said, as she smiled at Kathryn. "How are you, Kathryn?"

"I'm great, just wanting to see your precious baby," she said, as she walked over to Henrietta, who was seated near the fireplace.

"Do you want to hold him?" she asked, as Kathryn nodded. "Here," she said, as she handed the baby to Kathryn. "I'm sure he will be happy you're not my mother."

"Why?" Kathryn asked, as she sat on the chaise with the baby.

Henrietta stood and stretched before sitting back down. "My mother tends to squeeze him too tight," she explained. "He's not too fond of the squeezing."

"Henrietta, he is handsome," Kathryn stated, as she looked down at Robert Jr. He had a light dusting of brown hair. She didn't know the color of his eyes, since he was sleeping, but he was amazing.

"Thank you," Henrietta said softly. "He reminds me so much of his father," she voiced, and Kathryn heard the pain in her voice.

Robert died a year ago last month, and she was impressed at how far Henrietta had come. Henrietta used to dissolve into sobs whenever anyone mentioned Robert. She was happy to see her healing.

"How are you feeling?" she asked, looking over at Henrietta.

It had been a hard year on Henrietta. She didn't have an easy pregnancy or an easy birth. Her parents told Kathryn the doctor was worried about losing Henrietta and the baby, throughout the long birthing process. Losing Robert started a bad series of events for her life.

"I'm actually feeling better this week," she replied smiling. "It's been a year since I lost Robert, but looking at our baby keeps me from slipping away. I can't imagine my life without him, even if I can't have his father," she explained, as Kathryn nodded. "I wasn't sure if I would ever get to hold him after everything I've been through."

"Has Robert's parents been by to see him?" she asked tucking the blanket tighter around the baby. She didn't want him getting cold.

"No, they haven't," she answered. "I can't blame them. It's harder for them since they lost their family in one day."

Kathryn sighed as she cuddled the baby closer. "I'm sorry," she voiced, as she wondered who wouldn't want to see this baby. They might have lost their sons, but a baby couldn't be punished for it. This would be their only grandchild, and they needed to be here to watch him grow. It would help heal some of their pain.

"It's fine," Henrietta said. "Thank you for visiting. I feel like I've lost everyone around me but my parents and you."

"I will always be here for you and baby Robert," she stated. "I'm not sure I can stay away from this precious baby," she admitted, smiling down at Robert Jr. who was finally opening his eyes. "Oh, he has blue eyes," she noted quietly.

"Most babies have blue eyes when they are born; at least that's what the doctor told me," Henrietta informed her. "I hope they stay blue, since his father had blue eyes."

"I'm sure they will," she commented, still staring down at the baby. He was a miracle, and she hoped Robert's parents would see it.

Kathryn stayed a little longer before taking her leave. She wanted to get home before it got too late, and little Robert needed his afternoon nap with his momma. Once she reached town, she saw a crowd gathering. A huge crowd meant a battle was being fought somewhere. The carriage stopped, and she got out to see where the fighting was and if it was close to Benjamin.

"Kathryn, I'm so glad I found you," Joshua stated, as he reached for her.

He was starting to respect his son's decision for joining the cause and fighting. Each letter helped him understand Ben a little more. She hoped his relationship with Ben was healed by the time Ben came home.

"Mr. Sawyer, what's wrong?" she asked, seeing the panic in his eyes. Normally, he was calm, but it wasn't the case today.

"Did Ben mention where he was heading in his last letter?" he asked in a rush.

"Yes, he told me Chancellorsville, why?" she asked starting to worry.

"He's there then," he muttered, as he released her and started to turn away.

"Wait, what's going on?" she demanded, reaching for his hand.

"A battle, reports are coming in of Lee going crazy with his plan," he stated. "I prayed Benjamin wasn't there."

"Mr. Sawyer, please tell me. When do they expect the death lists?" she asked holding back tears.

She couldn't lose him, not now.

"They do not know; the battle is still raging," he informed her. "I'm sorry; I shouldn't have told you any of this."

"No, I need to know. I'm tired of being treated as if I will break," she voiced before storming off.

She made her way into the bank and tried to find Thaddeus. He gave her the day off to visit Henrietta, so he wasn't expecting her when she stormed into his office.

"Kathryn, what are you doing here?" he asked when he saw who it was busting into his office. He stood slowly when he saw the crazed look in her eyes. Had she gone mad?

"Do I look like I will break?" she demanded after shutting his office door. She didn't need the rest of the bank hearing this.

"No, you do not," he answered evenly. "Do you want to sit down?" he asked, motioning to the chairs in front of her.

"I'm sorry; I shouldn't have come in here acting like a crazy woman," she muttered, as she sat down. He then sat back down as he watched her closely. "I'm just tired of everyone trying to keep the war from me. My fiancée is fighting, and I need to know if he's alive or dead or fighting in said battle."

"I understand, but they only want to ease your pain," he said calmly.

"They are not easing my pain," she snapped back. "They are adding to it."

"I thought you were visiting Henrietta today," he stated. "What has bought this on?" he asked, resting his arms on his desk.

"There is a major battle going on in Chancellorsville, which is where Ben was heading in his last letter," she explained. "I just saw his father, and he didn't want to tell me there was a battle," she huffed.

"Kathryn, they do not mean you any harm," he said. "Trust me; your parents, Benjamin's parents want to protect you from any news of Benjamin's death. They know how it will affect you, if you ever read his name on those lists."

Kathryn sighed as she thought about his comments. He was right, they were trying to protect her, but they were doing it all wrong. "I know they are trying to protect me from learning of his death from a piece of paper, or from some random person," she said. "They don't understand; I can take reading it from a piece of paper, more than I can from them."

"Why?"

"Because I will break down in front of them," she whispered. "I don't want them to have to break my heart or to see my heart breaking," she explained.

Thaddeus sat in silence for a moment, while he processed what she said. "Kathryn, I understand what you're saying," he sighed. "I do pray Benjamin lives through the war, so no one will have to tell you of his death."

"I hope so," she whispered, finally calming down. "I better let you get back to work," she said standing. "I'm sorry for unloading all this on you, especially during work hours."

"It's fine," he said standing up. "Don't bottle everything up; you will only suffer for it."

"I'll try not to," she said, before leaving his office.

She was at least in a better mood after talking to him. Worry still plagued her mind about Ben, but she would trust everything would work out.

She made her way home, and avoided the crowd of people still waiting on news. When the battle ended, she would be there with them. There wasn't a point to stand out there now. The death lists would not be released until after the battle ended.

~ ~ ~ ~

My love,   *May 1863*

I just heard the news! Please tell me you are alright. I must know. The death reports are still coming in, and I hope my letter reaches you and finds you safe. How could Lee lead the army in like that? How could he split up his troops who were already outnumbered against two Union armies waiting for you? We heard General Stonewall died as well.

Oh, please be alright. I cannot lose you this close to getting to seeing you.

Waiting in fear,
Kathryn

~ ~ ~ ~

The battle lasted several days until Lee claimed victory. His plan was risky and she worried until the news spread he won. She stood with the other people in town for three days waiting on the death and wounded lists. Once they were finally released, they were incomplete. Since the battle was so long, no one knew if everyone would be identified. She wondered if Benjamin was one of the nameless dead lying on the battlefield waiting for someone to discover his body. She had written him, but still hadn't received an answer back.

A week later she picked up one of the papers to see where the troops were located. It was all about the Battle of Chancellorsville and the death of Lt. General Thomas 'Stonewall' Jackson. The Confederacy was in mourning for one of their beloved soldiers. They might have won the battle, but Jackson's death was a devastating blow. There was even mention of Lee stating he had lost his right arm. Lee always depended on Jackson and considered him his right arm. Lee loved Jackson as did everyone else. The man was brave in battle. He earned his nickname 'Stonewall' in the First Bull Run when he stood firm against the Union Army.

"Any news on Benjamin?" her mother asked, as she walked into the room. The family was on eggshells around her, and knew they would be until she heard from Benjamin.

"No, but hopefully soon," she said, refolding the paper and laying it to the side. "I haven't read his name, and they print a new list every few days."

"It's good news at least," Maybelle stated, watching her daughter closely.

"Maybe, but it could mean they haven't found his body yet," she muttered, as her mother sat.

"I know," she agreed. "I think you need a day not thinking about the war," Maybelle stated, as Gregory walked into the room.

"I will be at work for most of the day, so it will provide some distraction," she said, as their breakfast was set before them.

She ate quickly, before leaving the house. She didn't want to stay around the house too long.

A few minutes later she got to bank and saw Thaddeus. He was talking with his mother.

"Kathryn, you look good this morning," Grace said with a smile. "Have you heard from Benjamin?"

"No Ms. Grace, not yet," she replied. "I hope I get a letter from him soon."

"I'm sure you will; the mail is probably really slow after Chancellorsville. It was a long battle," she stated, patting Kathryn's arm.

"Mother's right, the mail is just backed up, and I'm sure you will get something from him soon," he said with a smile.

"I'm sure that's the reason," she commented, as she sat down, and got to work for the day.

Work was a good thing for her, because it gave her something to focus on besides Benjamin.

~ ~ ~ ~

Dear Kathryn,   *June 1863*

I am perfectly fine. I received both of your letters within days of each other. I am sure the reports of the battle are nothing compared to what I have seen. It was torture watching all those men dying. Lee's plan worked though. We won and pushed the Yankees back. Yes, Lee is saddened by the death of General Stonewall. He said it was like losing his right arm. I do not know what Lee will do now with that troop. General Stonewall was already a legend before his last breath. This is a blow to the Confederacy that I fear will spell trouble for us.

Do not worry; I am just happy I receive your letters at all. We are on the move so much now I fear I will not get them. I will say after that battle, I am more than thankful I feel anything at all. We lost so many good men.

Well, at least Bluff City hasn't changed on that account. They were always protective of their own.

As long as you did not think I was dead then I am happy. I would hate to have my words come back and haunt me. There are enough ghosts of this war already.

Yes, Hooker was raiding the towns, which was why Lee had moved that way. He also needed to start gaining more ground. With our win here, we are closer to securing more Union ground. We now make our way North to Pennsylvania. The countryside is beautiful, and someday I would like to bring you here after we are married. I know that you will like it.

Love,
Your Soldier

She cried the day she got Ben's letter after the Battle of Chancellorsville, and she explained they were happy tears to her parents. They heard her sobs when she read the letter alone. They rushed into her room to see what was wrong. It was the longest wait for this letter, and she prayed she would not have another long wait.

During the same time she waited for his letter, her wedding dress came in. It was just as pretty as she dreamed it would be. She took it out to Twin Willows to show Hannah.

"Oh, Kathryn, this is beautiful. My brother will not know what to say," she breathed, as she circled the dress. They set it up in Ben's room, while he was gone. It would be moved into Hannah's rooms once the war was over, so Ben didn't see it before their wedding.

"I love the lace," Kathryn stated, as she brushed her fingers over the neckline of lace. This dress looked delicate, and she didn't want to touch it too much.

"I'm glad you went with white," Hannah said, looking over at her. "Blue would not be the same."

"I'm glad you like it. I was nervous about ordering it. The dressmaker did an amazing job. I saw the fabric when it came in and panicked. She calmed me down and told me it would be beautiful when she was finished," Kathryn explained.

"And it is," Hannah said. "I love the detail she put into the stitching."

"She told me not having a deadline gave her time to create it," Kathryn told her with a smile. "She outdid herself on this one."

"Yes, she did," Lydia said from the doorway. "I'm not sure your mother will like the white, though."

Kathryn glanced over at Hannah. "I know," she admitted.

"As long as I can't be blamed for you choosing another color, I love it," Lydia stated.

"Don't worry; my mother will know I did this all myself," Kathryn said with a smile. "She will blame no one but me."

"I want this war over now so we can plan your wedding," Hannah said, as Kathryn nodded.

"I just want Benjamin home," Kathryn voiced, as she took one last look at her dress. "I better get home before it gets dark."

"Okay, no problem," Lydia said as they left Ben's room. "Are you coming to the Independence Day barbeque?" she asked, as they walked down the staircase.

"Yes, I will be there along with my parents," Kathryn replied. "I love the barbeque every year," she said, before hugging them. "I'll see you in a few days."

"Bye dear," Lydia said as Kathryn left their house and got in the carriage. It was only four days until she would be back for the barbeque, and she couldn't wait. She would show her mother the dress, and hoped she liked it.

~ ~ ~ ~

The next day Kathryn walked into the bank, the same time she always did. Normally, it was calm and peaceful when she walked in, but not today. It was chaos. She didn't even make it a few feet inside before Thaddeus was ushering her outside.

"Whoa, what's wrong?" she asked, because he wasn't acting normal.

"Kathryn, I need you to remain calm," he stated.

"I am calm," she stated looking at him. "What's going on?" she asked.

She watched as he took a deep breath before speaking. Whatever he had to tell her, she wasn't sure she wanted to know what it was.

"There is a major battle going on," he informed her.

"Where?" she asked feeling the panic set in.

"In a small town in Pennsylvania called Gettysburg," he replied, as her vision blurred and she lost feeling to her hands. "Lee is there with the Army of Northern Virginia," he explained.

"No," she whispered, as she closed her eyes.

Panic settled inside her heart as the numbness spread.

"Kathryn, please breathe," he stated, cupping her shoulders.

She tried to breathe deep, but she couldn't. Everything felt on fire as the news of the battle sunk in. She never felt like this before over any other battle. Something was wrong with Benjamin, she just knew it. The world around her narrowed to one image of Benjamin falling to his knees in pain. Was he shot? Was he dying?

"KATHRYN!" Thaddeus yelled, as she collapsed.

Thankfully, he was quick because he grabbed her before she fell to the ground. Swinging her up into his arm, he made his way to her house. He needed to get her home so a doctor could see her.

"Thaddeus, what's wrong with Kathryn?" Grace asked, when she saw her son walking toward her away from the bank. Kathryn was in his arms, and she looked pale and almost dead.

"She fainted from news of the battle," he replied, trying to remain calm.

"Oh, the poor dear, I'll walk with you to her house," she said, as he nodded. "I want to sit with her until she wakes up."

~ ~ ~ ~

Kathryn opened her eyes and found herself in the parlor of her house. How did she get here? The last thing she remembered was standing outside the bank with Thaddeus. He told her about a battle in some small town called Gettysburg. She saw Benjamin falling to his knees as if in pain before trying to stand up. She saw him stumble again, before everything went black.

"You're awake," Grace mentioned, as she looked over to the woman sitting beside the chaise lounge. "Your mother will be happy," she stated, as she stood up and left the room.

What was Grace doing here? Nothing made sense. Was Ben dead?

"Kathryn, are you alright?" her mother asked, as she rushed into the room.

"I'm not sure," she answered. "I don't know what happened."

"You blacked out," Thaddeus stated, as he walked into the room. She was happy she was in the parlor and not in her bedroom. She didn't want Thaddeus to be in her bedroom, especially when she was in this condition.

"I fainted?" she asked. "I've never fainted," she countered.

"I'm not sure you've heard news like that before either," Grace said, glancing at her son. "Thaddeus should have told you the news somewhere else."

"No, it's fine," Kathryn said, sitting up in her bed. "I'm glad he told me."

"Do you want something to eat or some water?" Maybelle asked her daughter, as she hovered next her.

"Water would be nice," she replied, as her mother nodded and rushed out of the room. "How did I get here?" she asked looking at Thaddeus.

He leaned against the wall before answering her. "I carried you here and on the way mother saw me," he explained.

"I wanted to be here when you woke up," Grace commented.

"How long was I out?" she asked, hoping it wasn't long.

"Only a few minutes, don't worry," Thaddeus replied. "The doctor hasn't even made it here yet," he noted.

"Oh, I don't need to see him," she said. "I'm perfectly fine."

"Perfectly fine young women do not faint," her mother said, as she walked back into the room with a glass of water. "You will see the doctor. Your father has gone to fetch him and should be back shortly."

"Fine," she muttered before looking back at Thaddeus. "Tell me more about this battle."

"I don't think it's a good idea, since you've already fainted once from news of it," her mother noted.

"I'm fine," Kathryn said. "Please, I want to know."

"This is the second day of the battle," he informed her. "The Army of the Potomac is under the command of General Meade. They are trying to hold back Lee from advancing in his Northern campaign. The Union line fell yesterday, but I do not know what has happened today."

"So Benjamin is in another major battle?" she asked, as he nodded. "This is too much. They basically just finished Chancellorsville."

"Lee has an aggressive plan of attack," Grace voiced, as Maybelle nodded.

"He wants this war over," Kathryn whispered, as her father and the doctor came into the room.

"Now Kathryn what happened to you?" The doctor asked, as he knelt down in front of her. "I've known you since you were a child, and I know you do not faint."

"I'm not sure what happened exactly; I couldn't breathe and everything went black," she explained.

"I just told her about the battle," Thaddeus supplied.

"If this wasn't Kathryn, I would say the news caused this, but I know she can handle it," he , as he opened his bag. "Do you feel like you can breathe now?" he asked.

"Yes and my vision is normal," she answered. "I've never felt like this before," she said, as he grabbed his stethoscope.

The doctor listened to her breathing and heartbeat. "I don't hear anything out of the ordinary," he stated. "I guess the news was too much for you, but if it is something more, please get plenty of rest," he said, packing up his bag. "Send for me if you feel faint again," he ordered, as she nodded.

Everyone watched the doctor leave before turning to look at Kathryn.

"I think it's time we took our leave, Mother," Thaddeus said, walking over to Grace.

"Of course, now Kathryn please do as the doctor ordered," Grace stated. "If you are feeling better, you can come into work, but I will be there to make sure you do not over do it."

"Thank you Ms. Grace," Kathryn stated, as she watched Thaddeus and his mother leave the house.

"Are you sure you're alright?" Maybelle asked her daughter once they were alone.

"Mother, I'm fine," she sighed. "I think I let the news overwhelm me. I will rest now. If there is any news, please wake me," she said, as Maybelle and Gregory nodded before Kathryn stood and left the room.

~ ~ ~ ~

My Love,   *July 1863*

I just received your last letter before the most devastating news reached me. You said you were on your way to Pennsylvania, and I pray you were wrong or delayed. I pray you were not in that little town of Gettysburg where thousands of men lost their lives. I could not bear it if you were. The death tolls are not expected for another week due to the heavy rains, so every hour I will be praying you were not harmed or even there.

Please write to me as soon as you can because this waiting is killing me. I need to know you are alive and well.

I love you,
Kathryn

As she sealed her letter, she closed her eyes and prayed. He had to be alright. He had to be.

~ ~ ~ ~

1863, July 4
Bluff City Chronicle
Battle Update

A crushing blow was delivered to the Confederacy yesterday in the quaint little town of Gettysburg, PA. After three days of intense battling, the Union Army claims victory over General Robert E. Lee's troops. This news is sure to cause heartbreak in the South as the possibility of outside help from other countries is only a memory now. Families all over the South are mourning the loss of their fathers and sons, as the death tolls continue to rise. Heavy rains delay most death reports, so we may never know the total number of soldiers lost in this gruesome battle. We will strive to keep everyone informed.

Our prayers are with every soldier who lost their life for the cause and with the ones still fighting.

Three days. The Battle of Gettysburg lasted three long, hot days. She held back tears as she read the paper. The news wasn't good for the Confederacy, but she didn't care. The only thing she cared about was finding out if Benjamin was still alive. Today's barbeque was cancelled as families crowded the telegraph office, once again waiting on the wounded and death lists.

She decided she would not go down there. It would be hard enough reading Ben's name, but she refused to do so in public. She knew something was wrong with him. It was a feeling deep inside, but she wasn't sure if it was because he was dead or something else entirely. The visions of him falling down in pain plagued her sleep now.

"Are you going to the telegraph office?" her father asked her, as she set the paper to the side.

"No, I decided it's best for me to stay here," she replied.

"I agree," he commented. "I will bring you back a list if you want."

"Ben's parents will stop here after the lists are sent out," she informed him. "They stopped by yesterday."

He nodded. "Kathryn, will you be alright if his name is on one of those lists?" he asked gravely, as her control snapped.

"Honestly, I don't know," she cried. "I can't lose him when he is so far away, but I know something is wrong with him," she whispered, as the tears made tracks down her cheeks.

Her father walked over to her side, and put his arms around her. "I know, baby girl," he whispered into her hair. "I know it's hard."

"Daddy, I love him," she moaned, as she wrapped her arms around his shoulders. "Please tell me he's alive," she pleaded through her tears.

"If I could, I would," he said. "You know I don't want to ever see you in pain."

Kathryn nodded against his shoulder, as she tried to dry her tears. She controlled her emotions for the past two days, but she couldn't any longer. In her heart, she knew something had taken Ben from her. It wasn't something she could explain, but it was there. Only the coming days would ease her worry, but she feared her worry would only end in heartache.

~ ~ ~ ~

Kathryn walked around in a fog for the next several weeks. She read the paper and death lists looking for Ben's name, but it never appeared. People in town told her she should be happy, since it wasn't on there, but she wouldn't be happy until she received proof he was still alive. She couldn't let herself believe he was alive, because if she did then read his name, she wasn't sure she would survive.

No one understood her pain, except Thaddeus. He was supportive and made her talk through her feelings and emotions so they weren't bottled up. He knew what she was going through with waiting for any news concerning Ben. It helped because she didn't want to explain why she was acting this way. Thaddeus never pushed but instead sat silently waiting for her to speak.

It was already September and she still didn't have proof Ben was alive. She didn't have proof he was dead either, but it offered little comfort these days. Walking into her house after work, she saw one lone letter on the entry table. She learned not to get excited about the mail. There never seemed to be a letter from Benjamin. She did walk up to the table as she always did and almost fainted. It was a letter from Ben.

Tears pooled in her eyes before spilling out. She silently cried, as she clutched his letter against her chest. She knew it could have been written before Gettysburg, but something told her it wasn't.

She rushed to her room, before opening it and shouting out. Closing her eyes, she counted to ten, and then looked down at his letter to start reading it.

Dear Kathryn,   *August 1863*

I received your letter, and I am fine. The battle was intense, and we lost many good men over the course of those three days. I cannot even begin to explain what I saw on the battlefield, not that I would ever describe it to you. I will tell you that I never want to step foot on that hallowed ground again. I am sure you are wondering why I call it hallowed ground. Well, it is hallowed now because it has been bathed in the blood of Yankee and Confederate alike. I do not know if I can ever get those images out of my head.

I thought when I was chosen as a sniper I would not have to deal with death close up. I was wrong. Death surrounded us for three days, and I am not sure I can even remove it from my skin. It has seeped into my bones and lodged there. Death had always been a part of the war, but nothing like this. This was horror to ever face or even think about.

I experienced something life changing there. I cannot discuss it at this time, and I am not sure I ever could discuss it with you. I do know I am not sure of my future with you any longer. It seems further away than it has ever been. I used to have a clear picture on how our life would be, but now that picture has been covered in blood, my blood. There are some things a man cannot overcome in his life. I do believe Gettysburg will be that one thing for me. I beg that you not worry about me, but pray for those that have died in this war. They are the ones that have been given peace in the time of war.

Please do not ask me about the battle, town, or anything related to those three days. I want to be able to push it to the far reaches of my mind and never have to worry about it again. The course of my life has been forever changed.

Your Battle Changed Soldier

As she read the letter a second time, she started crying again. She was right; something had changed in Benjamin. He was no longer the man who asked her to marry him two years ago or even the soldier he was only a month before Gettysburg.

She wanted to know what he saw different from any other battle he fought. She needed to know if she was to help him move past it. The problem was Ben didn't seem to want to talk about it. The wound would never heal if he didn't air it out. She knew she couldn't press him about it. He would not share if he didn't want to. Pulling out paper and pen, she wrote back to him.

My love,   *September 1863*

I finally received your letter, and I had to shout for joy. I could not believe you are alive. The death tolls from Gettysburg are still being printed each week when a new body is discovered. I would never ask you to describe the battle, even if I wanted to know which I do not. I pray those images leave your mind and give you peace.

I pray you begin to see our future blood-free. I want you to come home to me so we can start out lives together. Please do not turn away from me. I can help heal those demons that haunt you and ease that pain if you will let me.

Loving you through this pain,
Kathryn

Chapter Six

Kathryn made her way to Thaddeus' house the following Sunday afternoon. Wrapping her shawl tighter around her shoulders, she walked faster. She really needed someone to talk to, and Ms. Grace told her to come to her when she did. She was struggling to hold herself together after Ben's last letter. The tone of the letter was different from any other he'd sent to her. She questioned whether he wrote it or not. It was very different from the previous letters.

Once she finally made it to Thaddeus' house, she opened the gate and paused. Looking up, she stared at the house for a moment, before walking to the door and knocking. It was opened moments later by Thaddeus.

"Kathryn, what are you doing here?" he asked, as he ushered her inside. He didn't see the carriage, and he knew she walked here.

"I need to see your mother, if it's okay," she stated, looking at him.

"Mother is not feeling well, so she is lying down," he informed her. "It's nothing serious just a stomach ailment according to the doctor," he explained, when he saw the look of panic on her face.

"Oh, I'm sorry," she said quickly. "I can just come back," she mumbled, as she moved back to the door.

"Is there anything I can help you with?" He asked placing his hand on her arm. "You look as if you need to talk about something."

Kathryn sighed and wondered why he was the only one to notice. "I do need to talk, but it is about Benjamin," she explained in case he did not want to talk about her fiancée.

"I can help," he said, leading her into the parlor. "I will have some fresh tea bought in for you."

"Thank you," she said, sitting in one of the wingback chairs.

The room hadn't changed since the last time she was here three years ago.

He nodded and spoke quietly to the servant, before looking back at Kathryn. "Now what is wrong with Benjamin?" He asked, sitting across from her.

She gathered her thoughts before speaking. It was hard enough to share this, but it seemed crazy talking about Ben with Thaddeus. "I received a letter from him," she stated. It was the best place to start.

"So he is alive?" He asked, as she nodded. "I don't understand; you seem sad, but if he is alive, it is something to celebrate."

"Oh, it is," she said quickly. She didn't want him to think she wasn't happy Ben was alive. "It's just his last letter is different from the previous ones he sent," she explained.

"I would imagine so, since he lived through Gettysburg," he remarked. "I've heard terrible stories about it, especially the Wheat Field."

She shuddered at the mention of the Wheat Field. It was said to be the bloodiest part of Gettysburg, according to her father. He read about it a few days after the battle. She made him stop after only a few words, because it was just too much to handle.

"Do you think a man can change his entire outlook on life after one battle?" she asked, folding her hands in her lap.

The question plagued her mind since his letter. Since Thaddeus was a man, he would be able to answer her question better than the women in her life.

He leaned back and thought about how to answer her question. He knew his answer was a big deal to her. She was sort of happy to see he took his time to answer her question. It meant he was seriously thinking about his answer.

"Honestly, yes one battle can change a man's outlook," he stated slowly. "Kathryn, the man has faced three years of brutal war. I am surprised it took him this long to change. I can only imagine what he has seen on each battlefield."

"Benjamin is a stable man. I don't think one battle would change him," she voiced, remembering the man Benjamin was. "He has faced three years of war, but didn't change until this one battle," she pointed out.

"It was the one battle," he commented. "Have you read any of the battle reports about Gettysburg?" he asked slowly.

"No, because I wasn't sure if Ben was alive or not," she didn't want to admit she was afraid to read the accounts of the battle.

Her dreams tortured her enough without adding the details.

"You might want to read them to get a sense of what he has gone through," he said, as the servant came in with the teacart.

The servant handed Kathryn a cup, then one to Thaddeus before taking her leave.

"I'm not sure I can manage to read it," she admitted. "I don't want to know what he faced there."

"It was a bloodbath lasting three days, Kathryn. Thousands of men lost their lives while others were wounded and left for dead," he explained watching her closely. "The men who lived probably see the battle over and over in their dreams."

"He said he can't see a future with me clearly anymore," she blurted out.

He sighed before taking a drink and setting his cup to the side. "I'm sure he doesn't," he stated. "You have to remember he just witnessed death all around him. I'm sure he believes he is next or is already dead. If I had to guess, I would assume he is wondering why he is still alive, while those around him died."

"Why would he tell me, though?"

"I don't know, but I know he truly loves you," he stated. "Give him time. The battle is still fresh in his mind. He probably still sees the faces of all the men he served with, whom died."

"I hope time will help," she muttered, before sipping her tea. "I'm just not sure. Ben has never sounded unsure of me or our future before."

"It's not you he is unsure of, it is him."

"I guess, but it still hurts. I feel he is pulling away from me," she revealed.

Looking at her, he tried to think of some way to make her understand. The only thing that would reassure her was Ben. The problem was Ben was the one who caused her doubt. "It is only because he is so far away. When the war is over, he will come back to you."

"I hope you're right," she whispered, as she set her teacup aside and stood up. "Thank you for allowing me to unburden on you. I will think about what you said and pray for Benjamin," she said, as he nodded. "I want this war over, so he can come home to me."

Thaddeus quickly stood up. "I want the war over too, if only for you to have Ben back," he stated. "If you need to talk more, let me know," he said, as they walked to the front door. He opened it for her and waited to see what she would say.

"I will," she promised before walking through the door and out to the street.

She was here longer than she thought. The sun was now sinking low in the sky and it cast a blood orange hue on everything. It looked as if everything around her was bleeding. Was this how Gettysburg looked after three days of battle?

~ ~ ~ ~

A few days after her talk with Thaddeus, she had a surprise visitor. She was shocked when her mother announced Henrietta was here. She quickly made her way out of her room to see Henrietta and the baby.

"Have you heard from Benjamin yet?" Henrietta asked, her as soon as they were alone in the parlor.

Henrietta finally left her house with the baby. It was a joy to see them out and about.

"I did get a letter from him, so he lived through Gettysburg," Kathryn mentioned, as she took the baby from Henrietta.

"You don't look happy to have his letter," Henrietta noted, as Kathryn sighed.

It was hard to explain to anyone, she was happy to have his letter. It gave her the peace of mind that he didn't die, but it also caused her worry.

"I am, but what he wrote disturbed me," she admitted. "He said his vision of our future is unclear. He has changed so much from the man who left here."

"Of course he has," Henrietta said. "He's been fighting in a war," she reminded Kathryn gently.

"I know, but his letters were always hopeful and begging me to marry him, when he came home on furlough," she explained. "This one was so far from those letters. It makes me wonder if he even wrote it."

Henrietta sighed before she spoke. "I will let you know a secret," she started, as Kathryn really looked at her. "When Robert came home on furlough, he was a changed man. He blew up at me for something not even worth fighting about. After several minutes, he blinked and starting apologizing. He was different, but after talking about his life in camp, I understood. War changes everyone including the ones not fighting."

"I never noticed he changed," Kathryn commented, thinking back to her last conversation with Robert. He seemed the same man he was before leaving.

"You wouldn't but he was struggling to keep up appearances," Henrietta remarked. "They march to their next camp and gear up for battle. Sometimes those battles last hours, but sometimes they last days. The soldiers who are still alive and able to fight march again. It's a hard life on them."

"I guess it is," she muttered, looking down at the baby sleeping in her arms. "I'm glad you came today."

"Yeah me too, since you are hung up on Benjamin's letter," Henrietta stated, as Kathryn looked over at her. "I want you to promise me, you will stay strong for him. He will need your strength when he comes home."

"I promise," she said. "I'll need help."

"Of course you will, and I will be here for you," she promised. "You were with me through Robert's death and Robert Jr.'s birth. I can never thank you enough."

Kathryn smiled, as she cuddled the baby closer. "How was it getting out of the house?" Henrietta hadn't left her house since before Robert Jr.'s birth. Kathryn didn't know the last time Henrietta visited her.

"Difficult, but I knew I needed to step outside again. I've been in the house for too long," she replied, as Kathryn nodded.

"What do you parents think of you venturing out?" she asked.

"They pushed me out the door," Henrietta said with a smile. "I think they were praying I would finally leave."

"I'm sure they were, but only to help you."

Henrietta nodded, as the baby cried out. "You know this is the first time he has been off of my parents' property."

"Wow, is it?" Kathryn asked, looking down at the baby. "It's hard to believe, but I guess it's because I go see you."

"Which is why I decided it was high time I came to see you," Henrietta stated as Kathryn nodded.

She was happy Henrietta was out of the house. She needed a friend to talk about Ben's letter. Thaddeus gave her a male's view, but she really needed a female's view. She knew she could have talked about the letter with Hannah, but she was his sister. It would be awkward for her to be in the middle of her brother and her brother's fiancée mess.

Henrietta stayed over an hour until the baby got fussy, and she decided it was time to get him home. They hugged before Henrietta left her alone with her thoughts. If Robert changed in a short amount of time, Ben had plenty of time to change, too. He fought more battles than Robert, so who knows what his mind thought. She would do as she promised Henrietta. She would stay strong for Benjamin while he fought.

~ ~ ~ ~

April 1865

Four years of intense fighting in several states only to lose the war. Many people felt the Confederacy should have never fired on Fort Sumter. They felt we could have left the Union peacefully, if those shots were not fired. Kathryn believed differently. Lincoln would have still called for troops to march against the South. This war tested the nation for four years, but it did not appear stronger for it. Many lives were lost in the pursuit of a lost cause.

Kathryn cried as she read the newspaper. Lee surrendered to Grant only yesterday at Appomattox. No one was really shocked over the surrender. They were waiting to see when Lee would decide when enough was enough. The Battle of Gettysburg was the turning point in this war. If Lee would have won, the Confederacy might have won the war. It was the furthest north the Confederacy got in the war. There were several major battles fought after Gettysburg but none seem to make as big an impact as the small town in Pennsylvania.

The Union win there seemed to spur them on. Sherman took Atlanta, before burning his way to the coast taking the Port of Savannah. He presented it to Lincoln as a Christmas gift last year. His 300-mile march left twisted train tracks, scorched fields, and burned down houses. His goal was to destroy supplies meant for the Confederate troops, and he accomplished his goal in a little over a month. The South was crippled in his wake, along with its troops still fighting.

Sadness hung over the Confederacy, as the news spread of Lee's surrender to Grant. The only good thing was Benjamin would be home. He survived the war. She wondered what he would think when he got home. It was different from when he left four years ago. The land of plenty was barely the land of enough.

Slaves were no longer tending the cotton fields, or at work in the homes. Lincoln freed them with his Emancipation Proclamation. Some of the freed men stayed with their former owners, because they knew it was easier to stay where they were. They were also guaranteed to find work.

Kathryn shook her head as she sat beside her mother. They were on their way home from the Good Friday service at church. All day she thought about the day Ben asked her to marry him. Tomorrow would be the anniversary of when he asked her, which was probably the reason why she thought about it today. Once they made it home, she went to her room. It was her wish that Ben would be home tomorrow to celebrate their anniversary. It was a hopeless wish, but she didn't care. As she got ready for bed, she wondered what tomorrow would bring. There was a sense of dread settling in her heart, but she didn't know why.

~ ~ ~ ~

The next morning Kathryn woke up and made her way into the morning room. No one was up yet, which is why she loved this time in the morning. She noticed the paper was already sitting on the table. One of the former house slaves, who now worked for her family, must have went early this morning to get it. Sitting down, she reached for the paper and read the top headline. As she read the words, her blood turned cold and her body numb. The dread she felt before bed turned to heartache. This couldn't be right, could it? It said President Lincoln was dead.

April 1865
Bluff City Chronicle
President Lincoln assassinated!

Only days after Lee surrendered to Grant, President Lincoln was shot and later died. His death is a blow to the already weak nation. As more Confederate Armies surrender, the people are questioning why Lincoln was shot now that the war is over. His loss is felt by the nation as Vice President Andrew Johnson steps into the President's shoes.

As sadness floods the nation, remember the war is over and our brave men are on their way home. If you see a soldier slowly making his way south, it is encouraged that you help them on their way. They may have a long road home, and you could be the one that helps them get home to their loved ones.

She was still sitting at the table when her parents walked into the room. She wasn't sure how long she sat there, while she tried to shuffle through thoughts.

"Kathryn, you are looking pale, my dear," her mother noted, as she blinked and glanced at her parents. "Did you not sleep well last night?"

"What's wrong?" Her father asked when he noticed the haunted expression on her face.

"Lincoln was shot last night," she stated hollowly.

"What?" Maybelle asked. "Kathryn, now is not the time for jokes."

"I'm not joking. He was shot last night at Ford's Theater and died early this morning," she said picking up the paper.

"Oh my," her mother gasped, as they rushed over to read the paper.

Kathryn watched as her parents read the article over and over again. She needed some fresh air so she stood and made her way outside. Normally it was calm, but this morning there was chaos. People were running down the streets. As the news spread of Lincoln's death, she wondered how the nation, which was weakened by war, would heal now.

~ ~ ~ ~

A few weeks later Kathryn and her mother were on their way to Twin Willows to start planning for the wedding. She looked over at her mother and smiled. Benjamin would be home sometime soon, and she wanted plans in place when he showed up. The carriage stopped in front of the house as they got out. They were greeted by Hannah and Lydia within moments of them knocking.

"I'm so excited," Lydia stated, as she pulled Kathryn into her hug. "I've been waiting for your wedding day for too long."

"We all have," Maybelle stated, as she hugged Hannah. "I'm glad the war is over, so she can start planning."

Kathryn smiled, as Lydia released her. She hugged Hannah before stepping back. It was then she realized she hadn't showed her mother her wedding dress. This would not be a good visit, but it was time to show her mother the dress she planned to walk down the aisle in.

"Mother, I have something to show you," she said grabbing her mother's hand and leading her through the open door. Lydia and Hannah glanced at each other, before following Kathryn and Maybelle upstairs and into Ben's room.

"What's going on?" Maybelle asked, looking at her daughter.

Kathryn took a breath before walking over to her dress. "I didn't tell you when it came in, but this is my wedding dress," she stated, brushing her fingertips over the sleeve.

"Your wedding dress?" she asked, as Kathryn nodded.

"I ordered the material, and the dressmaker made it for me," she explained. "I wanted a white dress."

Maybelle walked over to her daughter's dress and sighed. It wasn't blue, but looking at it now, it was better. She couldn't be mad at her daughter's choice because it was a beautiful dress.

"What do you think?" she asked, trying to gauge her mother's reaction. It was hard because her mother liked to control everyone.

"Honestly, I love it," Maybelle answered, as Kathryn smiled and hugged her mother. "You were right, the white is better for you," she said, as everyone smiled.

They left the room to get started on some of the plans.

~ ~ ~ ~

A month after Lincoln's death the nation started to settle down. Reconstruction of the South began as the soldiers made their way home from the various battlefields. Since most of the rail system was destroyed, the soldiers were on foot for most of their journey; sometimes they were lucky and found rides with people. The rides may only last for a few minutes, but at least they were not walking for those few minutes. Many people helped them on their journey by feeding them what little they had and offering them a place to stay for a night or two. Those little things helped get the soldiers closer to their homes and families, who were waiting patiently on them.

Kathryn wondered when Benjamin would be home. Lee had surrendered a month ago, but there was still no word from Ben. It would have helped if she knew where he was when the war ended. She assumed he was with Lee, but she didn't know for sure. The death and wounded lists were still printed from some of the last battles, as more and more men were found.

"Kathryn, you have a letter," her father said knocking on her bedroom door. She quickly opened the door and took the letter.

"I didn't see it when I came in," she remarked, as she opened it without checking who it was from. "Thank you."

"It was just dropped off," he said, as she looked up at him.

"Why? The mail normally comes in the morning," she said.

"It's one of the new changes," he replied. "I hope it contains good news," he said.

"I do too," she muttered, as he smiled and walked away. She shut the door and walked to her desk. The stack of Ben's letters was in the hidden compartment of her desk. They were held together by a pink ribbon. This one would join the others, once she was finished reading it.

Dear Kathryn,   *April 1865*

Well the war is over at least for Lee. He surrendered to Grant today at Appomattox. It was the hardest sight to see. Lee is a very proud and humble man, but he knew there was no way to continue on. We were all but surrounded and cut off from the rest of the South. Grant's men started cheering as soon as Lee and Grant stepped out of the house, but Grant immediately hushed them. We were once again their countrymen, and he knew there was still an up-hill battle to face.

We will start our journey home tomorrow, and I pray this letter reaches you before then so you know I am on my way. I am not looking forward to seeing all the devastation those 5 years of war has bought to the land. I also do not know how long it will take me to get home. I pray it will be sooner rather than later.

I love you, and if I do not make it home, I want you to move on with someone else. I do not want you to wait the rest of your life for me to come home.

Love,
Your Soldier

He wanted her to move on if he didn't come home? Why would he put it in a letter? He was coming home. She folded the letter and put it with the others. She would talk to Henrietta about this letter. Losing Robert changed her life, but she was starting to live again. Ben wasn't dead, though, so she would not think about moving on. He would come home to her one day, and she intended to wait for him no matter how long it took.

~ ~ ~ ~

Weeks passed as she waited for any word on Ben. Men from the different families in town started appearing. Celebrations were held for each new soldier home from the war, even the families who lost someone celebrated. The men who fought were weary, dirty, and in tattered clothes. It amazed her they could even smile, but they did. Each one gave her hope of seeing Benjamin soon.

"I see you are enjoying this fine day," Grace said breaking through her thoughts.

Kathryn smiled as she looked at Grace. "I am," she said. "How is Thaddeus?" she asked.

The bank was currently closed, as Thaddeus poured over the books. The government wanted him to call in all of the loans. It was something he could not do, because he knew people could not pay those loans. War took its toll on the former Confederate States as they struggled to recover. There was little money, and those who had some were holding it tightly, in case things didn't get better.

"He is worried about the bank not opening," she replied, looping her arm though Kathryn's.

"I do hope he finds a way to keep it open," Kathryn whispered, as they walked across the street.

"I do too, since the bank has been a family business for generations," she stated. "Would you care for a stroll through the park?"

"I would love too," Kathryn answered.

Grace nodded, as they walked through the entrance.

"I'm so glad our town wasn't touched by the Yankees. I couldn't stand to see it destroyed."

"I couldn't either," Kathryn said thinking about Atlanta and other Southern cities.

Some of the cities had Yankee soldiers patrolling the streets. They were supposed to keep the peace, but she knew they caused more trouble for the struggling city.

"The people who lost everything must be devastated."

"I know they are," Grace remarked, as they took one of the paths which would circle the pond. Many people didn't take this route, because it was the longer one through the park.

They walked in silence for a few moments, lost in their thoughts, when Kathryn looked to her left. She saw a man standing there in a gray Confederate uniform. His uniform wasn't in tatters as all the other soldiers, but it was dirty. He traveled miles and miles and his clothes reflected those miles. Something was familiar about him. As they walked the path, the soldier stepped toward them, and she knew who it was.

"Benjamin," she whispered under her breath, as she stopped completely.

Grace paused to see why Kathryn stopped.

"What's wrong?" she asked, as tears formed in Kathryn's eyes.

"I'm sorry Ms. Grace, but I must leave you," she said, looking at the older lady.

Understanding formed in Grace's eyes, as she nodded. Releasing Kathryn, she stood back and watched Kathryn pick up her skirts and run to the soldier. She assumed it was Benjamin, but she couldn't really tell this far away. Kathryn knew though.

"Ben!" Kathryn stated, as she jumped into his arms. "I can't believe you're finally home," she whispered, as she wrapped her arms around his neck and hugged him tight. He felt different from the last time she held him, but it was over four years ago.

"Kathryn," he stated, as he hugged her, before stepping back. "You are even more beautiful than I remember," he remarked, as he brought her hands away from his neck to hold them in front of him.

"Please tell me this isn't a dream," she begged squeezing his hands.

"It's not a dream. I'm really here," he replied, glancing at their hands.

"Do your parents know you're back?" she asked, as he shook his head no. "They will be overjoyed when they find out."

They left the park to go to her house to get the carriage. Her parents hugged Ben before sending them on to Twin Willows. Ben was quiet on the ride to his house, but Kathryn didn't mind. He was back, and they could finally start their life together.

~ ~ ~ ~

The next day Benjamin picked Kathryn up in his father's carriage before driving them to the park. She couldn't stop smiling.

It was like the morning he proposed to her. Four years might have separated them, but it would only be a bump in their life. They were together again.

He stopped the carriage and helped her down. They entered the park and walked the same path she and Grace walked yesterday. It was early, so no one was out yet. They stopped by the water's edge, as he turned to face her.

"Kathryn, I need to tell you something," he began as she smiled brightly. He held her hands between their bodies as he always did. It was such a comfort to have him home.

"Oh Ben, I've missed you. I just can't believe you're standing here in front of me. I've dreamed of this day for years," she admitted, swallowing back her tears.

Now was not the time to cry, even if they were tears of joy.

"I'm sorry," he whispered, as she lost a little of her smile.

Ben was acting different. She would have thought, he would be hugging her close and wanting to plan their wedding. Last night, he only nodded when anyone would talk about anything to do with the wedding. It was as if he didn't want a wedding. He was the one who wanted to get married before he left for war.

"Sorry?" she asked with a chuckle. "Why are you sorry? You're home," she said squeezing his hands. It was unreal he was here, in front of her.

She watched him take a deep breath before looking directly at her. There was no joy in his eyes. Was he not happy to see her?

"I'm sorry because I can't marry you," he whispered releasing her hands.

Her arms fell to her sides, as she tried to process what he said.

"What?" she asked in shock. "I don't understand why you can't marry me," she muttered, trying to wrap her mind around his statement.

The war was over, so they could get married. This was their plan before he left four years ago.

"Kathryn, I love you, but the war has changed me," he stated coolly. It was not the loving tone she loved so much. In fact, he never spoke to her in such a cold voice. "I'm not the man who left here that April morning. I don't know that man any longer."

"What? Yes you are. You haven't changed," she protested.

This wasn't right. She waited for him to come home and complete her life, not tell her he changed.

"I've changed, more than you will ever know," he whispered brokenly.

"I don't understand," she cried. "I've waited over four years for you to come home," she voiced angrily.

"I know Kathryn," he whispered, closing his eyes. "I can't stay with you. I can't marry you. I will not burden you with marriage to me. It's not fair to you."

"No, this is not fair to me!" she shouted, as she held back her tears. "I love you. I want to marry you and start our life together."

"Kathryn, this is hard, and I don't want to hurt you anymore than I am. If I were to marry you, your entire life would change. I can't ask you to give up your life for me."

"Benjamin, I know you've seen more than I want to know, but it's not a reason to call off our engagement," she stated, trying to reason with him.

He backed up and sighed. "I can't explain, but I will never get married," he stated with finality.

Kathryn stood there for a moment, as her heart broke into a million pieces. "Are you sure? We don't have to get married anytime soon. We do have to plan the wedding," she muttered still trying to make this work.

"I am sure," he stated. "I wish I could share what's changed in me, but I can't. Please believe me, and let me go."

"I prayed for you to come home from the war," she whispered. "I prayed for you to come back to me."

The tears threatened to spill, as she bit her lip to control her emotions. She refused to cry in front of him.

"I am sorry."

"This has something to do with the Battle of Gettysburg," she muttered, as she really looked at him.

He was a changed man. The sparkle in his eyes was gone, causing them to be a dull, dark color. It was as if he was cloaked in shadows and hidden away from her, even though the sun was shining on him. It was Benjamin, but then again it wasn't.

"Kathryn," he moaned. "I can't stay here and marry you. Please live your life without me."

"I'm not sure I can," she cried, as she felt him slip away from her. "You've broken me," she whispered, as her lip trembled.

The look in his eyes was one of pure anguish. This was torture for him, as well as her.

"I'm sorry," he said before turning away from her.

She watched him leave through her tears. She let him leave, because there was no way she could keep him. He made sure she couldn't.

Kathryn slowly made her way out of the park. She saw the carriage was gone. It didn't matter because she needed time to think. The future she planned for was gone. It was shattered and unrecognizable. It barely existed beyond one April morning, but it had been real.

She heard footsteps behind her and wondered if it was Ben coming back for her, even though, she knew he wasn't.

"I heard Benjamin was back," Thaddeus stated, as she closed her eyes.

She didn't want him to see her like this.

"Yes he is," she stated, as she quickly wiped her cheeks.

She prayed her eyes were not red rimmed, but she knew they had to be. Turning slowly, she kept her eyes downcast, and hoped he didn't see the tear stains on her cheeks.

"I'm happy he is back. You will be able to get married now," he commented, as she nodded. "I'm not sure if you want a job, but there will always be one open for you," he said, as she bit the inside of her cheek to keep from shedding more tears.

"Did you find a way to keep it open?" she asked, still looking down.

"I did, thankfully. We will open back up tomorrow morning. I know with Benjamin home you will want to spend time with him, so take a few days off."

The mention of Ben's name had fresh tears streaming down her cheeks.

"Thaddeus," she cried, finally looking at him.

"Kathryn, what's wrong?" he asked, looking down at her. His look of concern only made the tears come faster. "Are you hurt?" he asked, cupping her shoulders as she shook her head no. "What's wrong then? Why are you crying?"

She gulped back her sobs, as she took a few deep breaths. "It's Benjamin," she whispered.

"What's Benjamin? Is he hurt?" he asked, looking around her.

"No, he's not hurt, or at least not physically," she replied as he handed her his handkerchief. "He broke off our engagement," she shared, wiping her cheeks and eyes. She refused to blow her nose in front of him, especially on his handkerchief.

"Let's go somewhere so we can talk," he suggested, as she nodded. He pulled her in close and walked her down to the street to the bank. "No one will be here for a while," he said, unlocking the door and ushering her inside.

She looked around, as the sunlight filtered through the glass. "I'm sorry for disturbing your morning."

"I'm not," he stated, as he pulled out a seat for her. "Now, why did Benjamin break off your engagement?" he asked, as she slowly sat down.

"He said he has changed beyond the man he was, and he couldn't ask me to give up my life to marry him," she explained. "I don't understand, and he didn't tell me anything more."

"When was this?" he asked, sitting down on the top of one of the desks.

"This morning, we were in the park," she replied holding back more tears. She could not continue to cry in his presence. "I thought he was taking me out there to talk about our wedding," she admitted. "I never suspected he would call it off."

"I'm sorry, Kathryn."

"You know after he told me, I saw the changes," she voiced, remembering the differences in the man he was and the man he is. "I guess I overlooked them yesterday, in my joy of him being back."

Thaddeus nodded, as Kathryn took another deep breath. He was being caring by talking to her, but she didn't need to break down in front of him.

"I know you don't want to hear this, but maybe he saved you a lifetime of heartache."

"What?" she asked. "I have a lifetime of heartache, by not being with him."

"No, you have a broken heart at the moment," he stated rationally. "Time will lessen the pain, and maybe, even heal it if you let it. You have your whole life in front of you, even if it's without Benjamin," he explained. "Trust me, if he has changed as much as he thinks he has, he did you a favor."

"I don't see it," she muttered. "He broke my heart."

"Kathryn, war is hard on the men fighting, as much as it is on the women waiting for them," he commented. "Did you not see the change in his letters?" he asked.

"Yeah, his letter after Gettysburg was different," she remarked, remembering their conversation about the changes.

"I remember you talking about his letter," he said with a sigh. "Now think about those letters after it, was the tone the same?" he asked.

She took a breath. "Yes, but I thought he was weary and ready for the war to be over."

"I'm sure he was, but he was also a changed man," he said standing up. "He tried to warn you."

"I guess."

"I know it's going to take some time, but you will move past him," he commented, as he pulled her to her feet. "Trust me, this pain you feel will get better."

She nodded, as she wrapped her arms around her body. "Do you need me today?" she asked quietly remembering the bank was back open.

"No, go home and grieve," he replied, as she nodded and left.

She wasn't sure if this pain would get better, but she trusted Thaddeus.

His fiancée died, and he moved past her death, so he would know about getting over the pain of losing someone you love.

The worst part was telling her parents about her broken engagement. They were excited last night when she got home. Her mother started talking wedding plans, until time for bed. This would be hard, but she would have to tell them.

~ ~ ~ ~

Kathryn wiped her cheeks once again as she shut her bedroom door. She told her parents the wedding was off. They thought she was joking, until she explained this morning. Her father wanted to rush over to Twin Willows and talk to Benjamin, but she stayed him. She would not have Benjamin forced into a marriage. She was not compromised, so there was no need for a forced wedding. Besides, she didn't want a husband who did not want to marry her.

Walking to her desk, she pulled out her diary. Yesterday's entry was full of happiness and joy, while today would be full of sadness and pain. She sat and started writing. She hoped this would release her, and help her to heal.

Dear Diary,

I cannot believe how much my heart is breaking. The man I love has changed more than I ever thought he could. He is surrounded by darkness now, which is something I am not used to from him. The war has changed him, like he said, and now he said he cannot marry me. I wish I would have just married him before the war started, like he asked. It was just fear that held me back, and now I realize letting fear rule my life is wrong.

I cannot believe it was only one day ago I was celebrating his return home, and now I have to say goodbye once again. Letting go is the best for him; I cannot ask him to stay. I saw how much being back home hurt him. My momma told me, if you loved someone, sometimes you just had to let them go. Well, I am letting him go even though I wish he would stay.

I cannot picture what my life has in store for me now that he is gone. Thankfully, I still have my job at the bank because of Thaddeus. He checked on me this morning just to make sure I was still working for him now that my Soldier was back. Unfortunately, he was also the one I broke down to. No one else knows I am single again.

I am not sure how to break the news either. It is going to break both of our mothers' hearts when I tell them. They have been planning for five years for a wedding that would never happen now.

Thankfully most of the wedding had not made it past the planning stage though in fear that my love would die before he made it back home to me. I guess in a way he never did, though. I know that a part of him was left on those battlefields up North. There is no way that he can gather those parts up and be whole again.

I wonder what God has in store for me now because the road that I used to believe was my path to my true love is gone. All I could see is a start to a path I would have to forge by myself. It is not even clear if this was the way I should go, but I will trust in God, and see where he will lead me. At this moment, he is the only one that I can rely on. He is my only hope for some kind of happiness in my future. I pray there is happiness in my future.

Once she finished her entry, she closed her diary. It would be the last entry in this one. Tomorrow was the start to a new life for her. Ben chose his path to follow, and now it was time for her to do the same. She didn't have a clue what she would do, but the war was over, and like the South, she would rebuild her life.

Chapter Seven

"Shouldn't you be wearing black?" Maybelle asked her daughter as soon as she saw the green dress she was wearing.

It happened to be one of her favorite dresses, and she needed something to boost her mood today. She wanted people to know her broken engagement did not mean she was broken.

"I am not in mourning, Mother," Kathryn pointed out. "I was not married, and Benjamin did not die. He just decided not to marry me," she would not dye her dresses black because Benjamin broke off their engagement.

After a long night of pacing and worrying, she thought about her situation. As the sun peeked over the horizon this morning, she composed herself and gathered her thoughts. She knew it would be a long road to healing, but she was ready. Mourning was not in her plan; it would only delay her from moving forward with her life and getting over Benjamin.

"You would gain sympathy if you were to wear black," her mother stated, as she refrained from rolling her eyes.

She couldn't be mad at her mother for her statement. It was shocking and unwelcome news

"I do not want nor deserve sympathy," she said, looking over at her mother. Sympathy wasn't what she wanted from the people around her. She didn't deserve it for one, and for another she wanted to move on with her life. "I want to move past this," she stated, looking over at her mother.

Her parents needed to understand what she was telling them.

"You should have let your father go talk to Benjamin last night," her mother voiced. "I think he got cold feet about marrying you. The war is over so he couldn't hide behind it anymore."

Kathryn shook her head. She knew Ben, and she knew he would have married her, if he was able to. He didn't get cold feet about marrying her.

"He wasn't hiding behind the war. You were right last night. If you love someone sometimes you have to let them go. He is not the man he was before the war. He needs to find himself, and maybe when he's ready, he will come back," she murmured, thinking about Benjamin leaving home one day after he came home.

It was a terrible time for him.

"Kathryn, please tell me you are not going to wait for him," her mother said in shock. "If he doesn't want to marry you now, then why would you wait until he does?"

"I'm not waiting for him. I meant if he does find himself, then maybe he could come back and be with his family," she replied. "I will not sit back and wait for him. I am going to find my way without him."

It was a bold statement, but she would put all her energy into doing it. There was so much more to life than one man. It was time she discovered what was out there. Eating quickly, she left the house for work. It was at least the one thing steady in her life.

~ ~ ~ ~

As she walked into the bank, she smiled. The feeling was akin to coming home. She missed this place more than she would have ever guessed. One part of her life may by in shambles, but this wasn't. Sitting down at her desk, she quickly got to work to make up for the work she missed, while the bank was closed. She didn't hear Thaddeus walking towards her until he spoke.

"Kathryn, I didn't expect to see you this week," Thaddeus commented, as soon as he saw Kathryn sitting at her desk working.

She was here early today, which meant she beat Thaddeus to work. She noticed other people were making their way inside.

"I decided I needed to move on and not pine over a lost love," she stated, flashing him a smile.

She wanted everyone to understand she wasn't mad at Benjamin. Fate decreed they were never supposed to be married, and she wanted everyone to accept it. Ben didn't need anyone mad at him.

"Did you get any sleep last night?" he asked quietly, as she sighed.

The lack of sleep was written on her face. She couldn't hide it no matter how brightly she smiled.

She glanced around and saw everyone else was working. They didn't appear to be interested in their conversation, thankfully. "I got some," she admitted. "I feel fine."

"I think you should go home and come back tomorrow. You need rest," he stated, his voice laced with concern.

"No," she said shuffling some papers around. "I told you I feel fine. I don't need you fussing over me. Ben called off our engagement; he didn't die," she pointed out. "I don't need sympathy."

"I'm sorry," he murmured, and she felt bad for getting angry with him. "If you need anything, please talk to me or mother," he said, as she nodded.

She watched as he shook his head and walked away. She knew he meant well, but she had to make people see she was bigger than this.

The rest of the day passed quickly. No one asked her about Ben, which made her grateful. She wasn't sure if Thaddeus warned them not to, but she didn't care. They didn't ask.

Once work was over, she quickly made her way home to get the carriage. She wanted to visit Twin Willows and talk to Ben's parents. She wanted to reassure them she was fine and they couldn't be mad at Ben. It was his decision, and she wanted them to respect him for it. Those plans changed once she saw Ben's parents and Hannah waiting for her in the parlor. Her parents were there quietly talking, as she stepped into the room.

"Oh, Kathryn, I am so sorry," Lydia stated, as she pulled Kathryn into her arms. "I don't know what's gotten into my son," Kathryn heard the sadness in her voice.

It broke her heart to hear it.

"It's alright," Kathryn whispered, as she pulled back to look at everyone. "Is he gone?" she asked, hoping his journey bought him peace and the answers he sought.

"Yeah, he left this morning," Joshua answered. "I wish I could have made him stay."

"No, he has the right to change his mind," Kathryn stated, shaking her head. "I didn't marry him before the war because I thought something might happen to him, which would leave me a widow."

"It's not the same thing," Hannah protested, as tears pooled in her eyes.

It hurt to see tears in Benjamin's sister's eyes.

"It is, trust me," Kathryn voiced.

"Well, I wanted to ride out and have a talk with him last night," Gregory stated, looking over at his wife. "Kathryn asked me not to leave."

"You should have; maybe the two of us could have made him see reason," Joshua commented, as Kathryn shook her head again.

They didn't understand why Ben chose this path. He hurt her with his decision, but at least she did understand it.

"He is seeing reason," she said quietly, as the room fell silent.

All eyes turned to her, and she knew they were wondering what was wrong with her. They couldn't fathom why she wasn't crying over Benjamin.

"Kathryn, you don't mean it," Lydia voiced. "He asked you to marry him."

"I know, and I wanted to marry him, but he has changed," she said. "He is not the same man; even you have to admit your son is different," she said, looking at Ben's mother.

"He was different," Hannah commented. "I thought it was because he was tired from his journey, but it wasn't. When he left this morning, his eyes were dead. I've never seen his eyes look like that."

"Kathryn, you know this is not your fault," Lydia stated, as she nodded.

She knew it wasn't her fault. It wasn't anyone's fault. It was war.

"It's not Ben's fault either," Kathryn stated making sure that fact was clear. "Four years of war changed him. I'm not sure what he saw, but he lost something of himself. Every battlefield he stepped on holds a piece of him. He needs to find a way to get it back."

"You are too kind to him," Joshua muttered. "I only wish my son could find what you say he lost, and still marry you."

"It doesn't work that way," Kathryn said touching his arm. "I love you, and I don't want you to not come around me because of this situation with Ben."

"No worries there," Lydia promised.

"Since you are here, please join us for supper," Maybelle said, before leading everyone into the dining room.

Everyone appeared to settle down and enjoy each other's company. Once dinner was finished the Sawyer's made their way outside to their waiting carriage. Kathryn hugged each of them, before stepping back. Hannah moved closer as her parents said their goodbyes to Kathryn's parents.

"Benjamin asked me to give you this letter," Hannah whispered slipping the letter into her hand. "I don't know what it says, but please read it."

"I will," Kathryn promised, as Hannah nodded and moved away.

Kathryn waved and watched them get into their carriage, before she walked back inside. She quickly walked to her room and sat at her desk. She needed to read what Ben wrote.

Dear Kathryn,

I know I hurt you yesterday, and I cannot apologize enough for my actions. You were so happy, and I ripped your world apart with only a few words. I do love you, but I cannot subject you to this new side of me I've discovered. I'm scared of this side. I want you to live your life and find someone who can share everything with you. I want you to find a man who has no secrets.

You were right yesterday when you said this was about Gettysburg. I wish I could explain it to you, but I'm not sure you would believe me. Sometimes, I don't believe what happened there. I'm sure you're glad you didn't marry me before the war, especially now.

I want to thank you for being my rock throughout the war. Sometimes your letters were the only thing keeping me sane, while we marched and fought endless battles. Your letters made the war bearable. You sent me a little piece of home with each letter you mailed. Thank you for being a wonderful woman. I keep them with me to remind myself of who I once was.

I want you to keep my ring as a reminder of how life can change in the blink of an eye. Asking you to marry me was the happiest day of my life, and I wish the war would have never happened. We could have been married with kids, if Lincoln wouldn't have declared war.

Remember the man I was, the one who got down on bended knee to ask for your hand in marriage, not the man I've become. I pray you find a man who deserves you and who will treat you the way you deserved to be treated. It is my wish for you. I may not be in your future, but some man is. Once you discover him, marry him. I pray you find him soon, so you can start your life together.

Love You Always,
Benjamin

Kathryn re-read Ben's letter several times, before folding it. The candlelight sparkled off Ben's ring when she moved her hand. She forgot she wore it most days, because it never left her finger. Four years later, it was time to remove it. Gripping the ring, she slowly removed the only piece of Benjamin she had left. She tucked it safely in her jewelry box. She didn't know what she would do it with it, but she wouldn't throw it away.

Looking back at the letter, she held it over the candle. The flame didn't quite reach the letter; she would need to lower it. Moments later she pulled it back. She knew this would be the last letter she ever received from Ben. She couldn't destroy his words, even though reading them broke her heart all over again. His words also reminded her of the man he was before the war.

She opened one of the drawers on her desk and placed the letter in it. Closing the drawer, she took a deep breath. The Ben part of her life was over.

~ ~ ~ ~

Kathryn smiled at the driver, as she climbed out of the carriage. She hoped Henrietta was up for a visit, because she needed to talk to someone. Since it was Saturday morning, she hoped it was okay to call this early, as she knocked on the door.

The door opened moments later. "Oh Kathryn, I didn't expect to see you today," Henrietta's mother said, as she opened the door wider.

"Is Henrietta here?" she asked.

"Yes, she is," she said, motioning for Kathryn to come inside. "I'm afraid the parlor is a mess, but with a toddler running around, it is hard keeping it clean," she said with a laugh.

Kathryn smiled, as she stepped inside. Robert was two years old, which meant he was very mobile now. He would turn three in November.

"I understand."

A little boy ran down the stairs as fast as his little legs would carry him. He spotted them near the door and ran to them.

"Kat!" he yelled, as he wrapped his arms around her leg. He couldn't quite say Kathryn yet, so he called her Kat most of the time. "Did you bring me anything?" he asked in his little-boy voice she loved so much.

He was the spitting image of his father with blonde hair and brown eyes. She wondered how Henrietta dealt with her husband's mirror image every day, without slowly going crazy.

"Robert, you do not ask a guest if they brought you a present," Henrietta stated, as she slowly made her way down the stairs.

She was not wearing black anymore, Kathryn noted.

Henrietta was moving past Robert's death, and it was amazing to see. She remembered those months when she thought Henrietta would slip into despair. Looking at her today, she would never know she almost died when the news of Robert's death was released. Time really did heal; Henrietta was proof.

"I'm sorry," he said, hanging his head.

She held her smile; he was too precious. She also didn't want Henrietta mad at her for laughing when she scolded him.

"No worries, but I did bring you something," Kathryn revealed, as he looked at her with hopeful eyes.

"What?" he asked as he bounced around her.

"A big hug from me," she answered pulling him into her arms and picking him up.

His little arms came around her neck as she held him close. She did not squeeze him, because she remembered he didn't like it.

"I'm surprised he let you pick him up. He barely lets me hold him longer than a few seconds," Henrietta remarked, as she walked over to them.

"I get a little longer, but not as long as you," Henrietta's mother said before smiling and leaving them standing there.

"Would you care to join me in the parlor?" Henrietta asked, as Kathryn nodded. "I'm sure my mother warned you, but I will too. The parlor was converted into Robert's playroom. It was the only way to insure the rest of the house stay toy free," she said, as Kathryn smiled.

"I don't mind the toys," Kathryn stated, as Henrietta nodded and led the way into the parlor.

Kathryn followed with Robert still in her arms. He seemed content to be carried, which was fine with her. She loved carrying him.

"How are you feeling?" Henrietta asked, as she sat down.

"Down," Robert said, as Kathryn smiled and released the little boy.

She watched him run to the corner where his toys were located.

"I'm still surprised he let you hold and carry him," Henrietta said, watching Robert sit down to play.

"I'm sure you've heard about Benjamin," Kathryn remarked, as Henrietta looked from her son to Kathryn.

"I heard, and I'm sorry."

"No need to be sorry," Kathryn said. "I know it sounds weird, but I respect his decision."

"I don't know how you could be so brave. You willingly let him go," Henrietta muttered. "I didn't want to let Robert go, even though he died."

Kathryn nodded slowly. "I saw the changes in him and knew I couldn't hold onto him," she revealed.

"It's not easy letting them go, is it?" she asked, as Kathryn nodded. "Robert didn't ask me to let him go, but if he had, I'm not sure I could have."

"It is hard," Kathryn agreed. "If Robert would have asked you, I know you would have found the strength."

"How do you know?" Henrietta asked, glancing back at her little boy.

He was playing with small blocks of wood. He liked to stack them before pushing them over.

Kathryn looked over at Robert before answering. "Because you've raised your child without his father," she noted. "You have more strength than any woman I know."

"So do you," Henrietta voiced quietly. "You waited through each battle, wrote him letter after letter, and then let him go when he came home."

Kathryn nodded, as she thought back on those years of waiting for him. Even if she would have known the outcome, she knew she would do it all again.

"Thank you," she whispered.

"Honey, we have to stick together. Men come and go, but friends stay with you forever," she stated, as Kathryn smiled and nodded.

She was grateful to have Henrietta in her life.

~ ~ ~ ~

A few months later, Kathryn finally found herself enjoying life again. She even celebrated, as more and more soldiers made their way home. Some of them were held in prisons and were only released after the surrender. The stories they told sent chills down her spine. These men endured the horrors of battle, prison cells, and rampart diseases during the war. They deserved a homecoming from everyone in town, including her.

"You know in Washington, they adopted the 13th Amendment last week," Thaddeus informed her. They were sitting side-by-side at one of the celebration dinners. They were the only two left at their table, because everyone else was either dancing or talking to other people.

"I wondered when they would, since it was passed by the Senate and House almost a year ago," she commented. "I see the need to abolish slavery and involuntary servitude."

"You know the Southern States will not be allowed to re-enter the Union, unless they adopt it as well," he remarked.

"I know," she muttered. "The actual war is over, but there will be battles between Washington and the Southern States. The reason for the war is still there," she sighed. "Unfortunately those reasons didn't go away with the surrender."

"Are you worried?" he asked before taking a drink.

Kathryn looked at him. "Yes, I am," she replied. "We don't have representation in Congress, because they turned the elected men away."

"Well, Andrew Johnson is not making friends in Congress, either," he noted. "We are in for a rough few years. Recovery from the war will take longer than the war, if the nation is still divided."

"I know," she voiced. "Do you think Georgia will be readmitted to the Union anytime soon?" she asked.

"Not sure, there is too much hanging on re-admittance. The Northern elected Congressmen want to hang the South for rebellion, while Andrew Johnson just wants the Nation reunited," he answered, as her mother walked over to their table.

She knew the look in her mother's eyes, and it meant she wasn't happy with her daughter.

"Why are you not dancing?" Maybelle asked looking at Kathryn. "It's a celebration, and you should be dancing."

"I'm sorry, Mrs. Alexander, I kept Kathryn from dancing," Thaddeus stated, as he stood. "I will rectify the situation now. Kathryn, would you do me the honor of dancing with me?" he asked, holding out his hand to her.

Kathryn nodded as she stood and placed her hand in his, much to her mother's delight. She let him lead her out to the dance floor.

"You know, you didn't have to ask me to dance," she pointed out, as he pulled her into his arms.

"I know, but I saw my mother looking at us, and decided to ease their minds," he explained, spinning her around the floor between the other couples. "It was easier to dance than to argue with our mothers."

"Sneaky, Mr. Morgan," she whispered. "I may have to tell Ms. Grace what you got her for Christmas for that stunt."

"If you do, then I will tell your mother what you got her for Christmas," he teased. "And I know you had a hard time thinking of what to get her."

"You wouldn't dare."

"Oh, I would if you tell my mother," he said. "I don't have enough time to find her anything else before Christmas."

"I don't either," she mumbled. "I won't tell your mother what you got her for Christmas."

"Good and I won't tell your mother," he said, smiling at her. "Now, how was little Robert's birthday party?"

"Good, I was happy to see his Mr. and Mrs. Jackson there."

Thaddeus nodded. "Is this the first time they've seen him?" he asked because he knew from his conversations with Kathryn, they hadn't been around since Robert Senior's death.

"No, they came by a few weeks ago," she replied. "Henrietta was wary throughout their visit. I don't blame her, but they were very doting on Robert," she explained.

"Were you there for their first visit?" he asked, as the music ended.

He released her, before taking her hand and leading her to their table.

Kathryn sat down in her chair, and Thaddeus did the same. "Well, they showed up while I was there one afternoon; Henrietta asked me to stay."

"I still can't believe they haven't seen him, before now. He is their only grandson."

"I know, but they were grieving for their son," she stated. "They cried when Henrietta let them in to see Robert."

"I bet it was hard for them, since he looks so much like his father," he remarked, as she nodded.

"They plan on visiting Shiloh in April," she informed him. "They want to visit the place where their sons lay to rest."

"Are Henrietta and Robert going with them?" he asked, looking back at the dance floor, as more couples crowded the floor.

"No, they asked her, but she said she didn't want to take Robert that far."

"She probably doesn't want to see the place where her husband died either," he murmured, as his mother made her way over to them.

"You know, you two could enjoy the party," she remarked, sitting beside Thaddeus.

"We did dance, Mother," he commented, looking at his mother.

"One dance. You danced one dance," she pointed out. "You haven't even asked me to dance."

Kathryn smiled at Thaddeus and his mother. Their relationship was special, and she enjoyed their conversations. She knew they grew closer after the death of his father. They were all each other had now.

"Mother, would you join me in a dance?" Thaddeus asked, as he stood and held his hand out to his mother.

"Since you asked so nicely, I will," Grace said standing up and taking her son's hand.

Kathryn watched as Thaddeus led his mother to the dance floor and took her in his arms. She also saw her parents on the dance floor. Everyone was enjoying the night.

"What are you doing sitting by yourself?" Henrietta asked, as she sat down beside her.

"I didn't know you were going to be here tonight?" she said, looking at her best friend.

"It was a last minute decision," Henrietta explained. "The grandparents have Robert tonight, which gave me the excuse to come and dance the night away."

"Which grandparents?" Kathryn asked.

"Robert's."

"Really? I can't believe you let them watch him," Kathryn mused, wondering what Henrietta's parents thought.

They were hurt by the Jackson's lack of attention to the baby, but she also knew they were happy Robert got to see his other grandparents.

Henrietta sighed, as she looked back at the dance floor. "It wasn't easy," she revealed. "They are his grandparents too, and they deserve a chance to get to know him," Henrietta stated.

"They could've known him, since the day he was born," she muttered, remembering the baby Robert was.

"I know they could have," Henrietta said. "I can't hold their grief against them. They lost both of their sons in one battle."

"You lost your husband, it's the same thing," she said, remembering Thaddeus' comments from earlier about the Jackson's. She was letting his thoughts color hers.

"No it's not. I loved Robert, but he was not my child. I did not carry him for almost a year, then care for him until he came of age, only to lose him in a battle far away from home," she explained, as Kathryn nodded, she knew the Jackson's grief was different.

"I'm sorry Henrietta," she said placing her hand on Henrietta's. She shouldn't have spoken against Jackson's. It only made it harder for Henrietta.

"It's not your fault, but please don't judge them too harshly. They are dealing with it the only way they can," Henrietta explained. "They love Robert Jr., and I can't ask for anything more."

Kathryn nodded as she removed her hand and watched as Thaddeus and his mother made their way to the table. She didn't notice the music changing until now.

"You should be dancing," Grace said looking at Kathryn.

What was wrong with her, that everyone thought she should be dancing?

"I'm sorry Mrs. Morgan, I was talking to Kathryn," Henrietta stated as she stood up. "I'm sure all the men thought it was a girl conversation, and decided not to ask either of us for a dance."

"Oh I'm sure you're correct, dear," Grace said patting Henrietta's hand. "How is your little boy?"

"Rowdy," Henrietta replied as Grace laughed. "Every day, I wonder how I will survive with my little terror. He is into everything and all over the house now."

"I remember that age well," Grace commented looking at her son. "I promise you, he will get better. Remember to treasure these days; he won't stay little for long."

"I treasure each and every second I have with him," Henrietta stated. "If little Robert turns out anything like your son, I will be one proud momma."

Kathryn smiled when she noticed Thaddeus' cheeks turn a little pinker than they were. He was embarrassed, but there was nothing for him to be embarrassed about. It was evident Grace was proud of her son.

"I think little Robert will turn out just fine," Grace stated. "Now you girls need to be dancing," she said.

"Henrietta, would you like to dance?" Thaddeus asked, as she smiled.

"I would love to," she said, placing her hand in his.

Kathryn smiled, as the music started up. It was a reel, and she was thankful Thaddeus hadn't asked her to dance this time.

"I don't think my son likes reels too much," Grace said as Kathryn nodded. "How are you, dear?"

"I'm good," she replied. "I'm looking forward to Christmas for the first time in four years," she informed her.

"Have you heard from Benjamin?" she asked.

"No, his family hasn't either," Kathryn answered. "They got a telegraph two months ago. He was in Missouri or Arkansas."

Grace nodded before looking at her son. "Henrietta is not wearing black," she noted.

"No, she told me she was done mourning Robert's death," Kathryn said with a smile. "She said she will always love and remember him, but she needed to move on with her life."

"I think she is moving on."

"Yes she is," Kathryn agreed, as the music stopped and Thaddeus and Henrietta made their way back to them.

The celebration continued on as Kathryn joined her father on the dance floor and a few of the other men in town. The last dance of the night, she found herself back in Thaddeus' arms. Thankfully, it wasn't a reel but a waltz. He held her close, but not as close as Ben held her during a waltz. It was then she remembered the last time she danced a waltz.

"You're thinking about him," Thaddeus muttered, as she looked up.

"How do you know?" she asked, as he spun them from the other couples.

"You get this lost look in your eyes," he replied. "Are you okay?"

Kathryn smiled. "I'm fine. I was remembering the last time I danced the waltz."

"When was that?" he asked keeping them in time with the music.

"With you," she answered looking up at him. "We danced three dances that night, and one of them was a waltz."

Thaddeus nodded. "I remember, I also remember your mother was not happy with the fact we danced three dances."

"No, she wasn't, but since the war was going on, she couldn't fault me. Most of the men were fighting, so it was okay to dance so many times with you," she explained.

"What about tonight?" Thaddeus asked. "This is our second dance," he pointed out.

"I think she's okay with it," she replied. "I mean, she is the one who wanted me to dance."

"True," he murmured. "I forgot to tell you earlier, but you look lovely tonight."

Kathryn smiled and lowered her eyes. This was the first compliment Thaddeus gave her, and she liked it.

"Thank you," she whispered.

"So you're shy?" he asked, bending his head lowered to whisper in her ear.

"Not normally," she answered, looking back at him.

He smiled, as the music faded into nothing. "Thank you for the dance, Ms. Alexander," he said as he released her before bowing.

"It was my pleasure, Mr. Morgan," she said dipping low.

He led her off the dance floor to her parents, before taking his leave. She watched as he joined his mother before disappearing outside.

"Are you ready to leave?" Maybelle asked, looking at her daughter.

"Yes mother, I am," she replied, as her mother nodded.

They said their goodbyes as they made their way outside to the waiting carriages. The driver opened the door, as Thaddeus appeared at her side.

"Allow me, Kathryn," he whispered, as he held out his hand.

She nodded, as she placed her hand in his, and let him help her into the carriage. Releasing his hand, she sat down and arranged her skirt around her.

"Thank you," she stated, as he nodded before helping her mother inside.

"Thank you, Thaddeus. You are such a dear man," Maybelle exclaimed, as she settled across from Kathryn.

"You are most welcome," he stated, before turning away.

Kathryn sighed, as her father entered the carriage. Once he was settled, he tapped on the side to signal the driver to go.

~ ~ ~ ~

The week before Christmas, Kathryn finally found the nerve to give Thaddeus his gift. She wondered if it was wrong to give her boss a gift, but after four years of working for him, she didn't care. He did a lot for her this past year, and she wanted to thank him. It wasn't a big gift, but one she knew he would like. Standing up, she walked into his office. She knew he didn't have anyone in there, since his door was open, and he just walked in.

"Kathryn, is something wrong?" he asked, standing up.

"Oh, no, nothing's wrong," she rushed to say. "I bought you a gift," she said, handing him the wrapped package.

"Kathryn, you didn't have to get me anything," he said, as he took the gift from her. "I didn't get you anything."

"You don't have to; this is my thank you gift to you," she stated. "You have done a lot for me this year."

"I didn't expect a gift for helping you," he remarked.

She smiled. "I know you didn't," she said. "Open it."

"Okay," he said, as he slowly peeled back the plain brown paper to reveal a jewelry case. "Kathryn, what did you buy me?" he asked, looking over at her.

"You have to open it to see," she voiced.

"This is entirely too much."

"How do you know? You haven't opened it yet," she pointed out, as he sighed and opened the case.

Nestled inside was a pair of cuff links. She ordered them from New York and was happy to see them come in a few weeks ago.

"Kathryn…," he said, pausing to look at her. "Thank you," he whispered, as she smiled.

"I knew you would love them," she said, turning to leave.

"Wait," he said, as she stopped.

He came around the desk and stood in front of her.

"Did you get these just as a thank you?" he asked, staring intently at her.

"Uh, yes," she replied, not really sure what he meant. She told him it was a thank you gift.

"Are you sure?" he asked, titling his head to the side. He was looking at her differently than he had been.

"Yes, as a thank you, but also for being there for me through this year," she answered. "This year wasn't easy for me, but you helped by always being there for me," she explained.

He slowly nodded. "Thank you, I do love them," he stated, as she smiled before leaving his office.

She had a funny feeling something shifted in their friendship, but she didn't know what it was. She was happy to have him in her life.

Chapter Eight

Kathryn walked down the hall to the parlor. Her mother told her she had a visitor, but didn't tell her who it was. It was odd for her mother not to tell her who was waiting for her, but she brushed it off. She knew it wasn't Hannah, since the Sawyer's were gone for the holidays to visit their family in Savannah. It wasn't Henrietta, because she was celebrating Christmas with Robert's family today.

No one else came to visit her, so she really didn't have a clue who it could be. Stepping into the room, she paused when she saw Thaddeus, standing near the windows.

"Is something wrong with Ms. Grace?" she asked, walking toward him.

It was the only thing that came to mind, when she saw him waiting for her. Images flashed through her mind of his mother sick.

"Oh, no, mother is fine. She is in perfect health," he said, as she sighed.

She was happy Ms. Grace wasn't ill, because she knew it would not be welcome news for Thaddeus.

"I came to bring you your gift," he stated, as she stared at him.

Did he buy her a gift, and if so why?

"You said you didn't get me anything," she stated, as she sat and motioned for him to sit.

"Well, I was raised if you got a gift, you gave one," he explained, as he sat across her. "It's not much, and I admit mother helped me pick it out," he said, handing her the wrapped package.

"You didn't have to get me anything," she voiced, looking at the package.

She wasn't sure why she was hesitant to open it, but she was.

Thaddeus smiled at her. "I know I didn't, but I wanted too," he stated. "I really hope you like it."

She smiled, as she finally un-wrapped the brown paper to reveal a cameo brooch. "This is too much," she whispered, as she ran her fingertips over the image of the woman. She always wanted one, but they were expensive. They did last, because her mother wore one. It was a family heirloom, and was passed down mother to daughter. "Thaddeus, I can't possibly accept this," she said, looking over at him. "This is meant for someone else," she uttered.

"Kathryn, I bought it for you," he stated, unwaveringly. His eyes never left her face.

"This is the one from the General Store," she mentioned, as he nodded in agreement. "Thaddeus, it really is too much," she said, thinking about the price tag she saw on the brooch the last time she was in the General Store.

It was more than double the price she spent on the cuff links. How could she possibly accept his gift? They were friends, and this was a gift a man gave his mother or his wife.

He shook his head before speaking. "I want you to have it," he said standing. "Please," he whispered, as he moved next to her, and sat. "Mother has one, and she once told me it was her most prized possession, besides her wedding ring."

"My mother says the same thing," she commented, looking down at the brooch again. Could she accept it?

"Please accept it," he urged, placing his hand on hers. "This is my gift to you for the past four years. You have been a wonderful friend and a great help to me and my mother. You love my mother, more than I think I do," he said with a smile. "Please, all you have to say is thank you."

She saw the pleading look in his eyes and knew she couldn't turn down his gift. He didn't turn hers down, and she knew he wanted to.

"Thank you, Thaddeus," she stated, as she looked at the brooch again. "I do love it."

"You don't know how relieved I am," he commented, as she glanced at him. "I was at a loss on what to get you."

"Why?"

"Because the cuff links were special, and I needed to get you a gift as perfect as them," he replied. "I finally asked my mother for help yesterday. She remembered how much you fancied the brooch."

"I can't believe she remembered. She was with me one day back this summer when I saw it in the case. I told her how much I wanted one, since my mother had one," she explained. "She told me about hers and how it was passed down from generation to generation, just like my mother's."

"Yes, hers is from my great-great grandmother," he commented. "I don't think I've ever seen her leave the house without it," he remarked, standing once again.

"I don't think I have either," she voiced, thinking back to all the times she saw Ms. Grace. She always wore her brooch, no matter where she was going.

"I hope you have a Merry Christmas with your family," he said, as she stood.

"Thank you, and Merry Christmas," she said, as they left the parlor and walked to the front door. "Thank you again."

"It was my pleasure." He said reaching for her hand, and bringing it to his lips. "Have a good day," he said, before opening the door, and walking to his carriage.

She watched him leave, before closing the door. Looking at her brooch, she smiled, and went in search of her mother. She was a little shocked her mother didn't join her and Thaddeus. He was a male caller, so it was almost a requirement for her mother to sit with them. She wanted to know what was going on and if something was wrong.

~ ~ ~ ~

"Did you have a good chat with Thaddeus?" Maybelle asked, when she saw her daughter walk into the morning room.

"You didn't join us," Kathryn stated, as she sat beside her mother. She was sewing, so nothing was wrong.

"No, I thought Thaddeus wanted to talk to you about work. I thought it best to leave you two alone," Maybelle explained. "Does he want you to come into work?"

"No, and we didn't discuss work," Kathryn said.

"Then why was he here?" Maybelle asked. "He has never called on you before."

Kathryn smiled, as she handed her mother the brooch to show her. "He came to bring me my Christmas present," she announced.

"Thaddeus bought you a present?" Maybelle asked, as she set her sewing to the side. "Oh my, Kathryn, you can't possibly accept this from a man who is not your intended or husband."

"Why?"

"It is not right," Maybelle stated. "He is a single man. You are not courting or engaged; you must give the brooch back," she instructed.

"Mother, he asked me to take it," Kathryn explained. "I got him a pair of cuff links as thanks for the past four years. He has provided me a job, asked about Benjamin, and offered me a shoulder to cry on."

"You got him a gift?" Maybelle asked, as Kathryn nodded. "Does Thaddeus mean something to you?" she asked.

"He is a friend, Mother. I just got out of a long engagement; do you think I need to enter into another one?"

"No, which is why you cannot accept this brooch," Maybelle stated, as she handed it back to Kathryn. "You shouldn't have given him a pair of cuff links, either. You obligated him to buy you a present, to return the favor."

"Mother, everything is fine. He kept the cuff links, so I'm keeping the brooch," she said, as she pinned the brooch on her collar.

Maybelle stared at her daughter before sighing. "Fine, but do not buy any man any gift, unless he is your father or your intended."

"I promise."

"How did he know you fancied that brooch?" Maybelle asked, as she picked her sewing up. "It is the one from the General Store, correct?"

"Yes, it is. One day I was in there with Ms. Grace, I told her how much I liked it," she explained. "Thaddeus wasn't sure what to get me, so he asked his mother. She remembered how much I liked the brooch, and told him."

"Well, he did a good job, but please do not accept any more gifts from him."

"Okay, Momma," Kathryn agreed as she stood up. "I think I'll take a stroll."

"Take your wrap, and don't stay out too long. You do not need to catch your death, because you wanted to take a stroll."

"Yes, Momma," she said as she left the morning room.

On her way to the front door, she grabbed her wool wrap and opened the door. It was cold, but she still intended to take her stroll.

~ ~ ~ ~

A few days after Christmas, Kathryn made her way out to Henrietta's house. She didn't want to intrude on any family gatherings, so she waited until after Christmas to visit.

"You spoil my son more than my mother does," Henrietta pointed out, as Kathryn knelt down next to Robert.

He'd already opened his present, and was playing with it.

"I couldn't help it. I saw the ball and knew he would love it," she said, as Robert smiled and rolled the ball to her.

"I thought about getting him one but went with a stuffed animal instead," Henrietta said.

"Does he sleep with it?" Kathryn asked, as she got up and walked over to sit next to Henrietta.

"He does," she confirmed. "My mother tried to put it away before bedtime last night, and he threw a fit. I just let him have it, since it's his, and he doesn't sleep with anything else," she explained.

"Well, hopefully, he won't want to sleep with the ball," Kathryn mused.

Henrietta smiled. "If he does, I'll get it once he falls asleep," she stated. "I've learned to let him go to bed with whatever he wants, and if I don't want him sleeping with it, I sneak in, and get it out of the bed. He never knows the difference."

"I can't see him throwing too many fits," Kathryn remarked, looking over at the precious little boy.

He was growing too fast, because she remembered when he was only a baby.

Henrietta laughed. "Believe me he does," she declared, as her mother walked into the room.

"Kathryn, I didn't know you were here," she said, as she looked down at her grandson.

"I wanted to give Robert his Christmas present," Kathryn said. "I think I wanted to give him his Christmas present more than I wanted to open mine."

Henrietta and her mother laughed as Robert picked the ball up and threw it. "I'm thankful this is his playroom now," Henrietta said. "He will not hit anything breakable."

"When the weather gets warmer, he will be able to play with it outside," Kathryn said, as Robert threw the ball again.

"He will enjoy it too," Henrietta said. "He loves going outside."

"Yes he does, I always find several sticks in the house, once he comes back inside," her mother agreed. "I think I will go check on your father and let you two ladies talk," she said, standing up.

"Where is your father?" Kathryn asked, as soon as Henrietta's mother left the room.

"Chopping wood," she replied. "He's not great at the task, and mother tends to worry about him injuring himself."

"My father isn't great at it either," Kathryn said, as she adjusted her wrap.

"Oh, I love the brooch," Henrietta gasped, as she looked closer at it. "Did your mother give you hers?"

"Uh, no," she answered. "Thaddeus gave it to me."

"Thaddeus gave you a Christmas gift?" she asked in shock.

Kathryn nodded and knew she needed to explain. "He has been so great this year after everything with Ben. I decided to give him a Christmas present."

"What did you get him?" Henrietta asked calmly; Kathryn knew she was processing every word.

"A pair of cuff links," she replied. "He apparently thought he should get me something in return."

"I think it was more than that," Henrietta murmured, looking at the brooch. "What do you think about Thaddeus?"

"How do you mean?" Kathryn asked. "He has been a great friend throughout the war, and even better after Ben left. Some days, I wasn't sure if I would be able to get out of the house," she revealed.

"I know how those days feel," Henrietta remarked with a far-off look in her eyes, before focusing back on Kathryn. "I meant, what do you think of him, as a man?" she asked.

Kathryn sat for a moment, while she tried to process what she thought about him, as a man. "I'm not sure I ever thought of him as a man."

"Well, you might want to start," she suggested. "No man gives a woman a brooch because she got him a gift."

"I think he was being nice," Kathryn commented.

"Are you sure?" Henrietta asked, as Robert ran over to them.

"Ball," he said holding his ball.

"Yes, ball," Henrietta said, as she smiled at her son.

Kathryn watched as the little boy smiled and tossed the ball again. He didn't catch it but did chase after it, as it rolled across the floor.

"No, I'm not sure," Kathryn mumbled. "I've only seen him as a friend," she admitted.

Henrietta looked from her son to Kathryn. "Kathryn, I've seen you with him, and he is more than a friend to you. I'm not telling you to run off and marry him, but please think about what he means to you. There could be something you're missing. It could be something great," she whispered.

"I will think about it, and I'm not running off to marry anyone," Kathryn said with a smile, as the ball rolled to her feet.

She picked it up and handed it to Robert, as soon as he got to her side. She was happy he loved her gift, but the best part was talking with Henrietta. She just put everything into perspective.

~ ~ ~ ~

Months slipped by as the nation tried to reunite. Today marked the anniversary of the surrender, and the only big difference was there were no actual battles involving guns and cannons. The battles were fought with words and actions at home. Congress was still split like the nation. The Southern States did not have anyone representing them yet, since they would not ratify the 13th Amendment. It was almost as if they regressed to the point of being colonies again.

The War of Independence was fought for representation and independence from the Crown of England. Why were the former Confederate States forced back in time? It made no sense, and caused many battles between the North and the South. Lee should have never surrendered, since they had fewer rights than they did before the war.

After the New Year, they learned of a new group called the Ku Klux Klan. It was founded in Pulaski, Tennessee by six former Confederate soldiers, one of which was Nathan Bedford Forrest. It was said to be formed in the defense of white supremacy and inviolability of white womanhood. She wasn't sure if it wasn't another way for the former soldiers to battle, without donning on a Confederate uniform.

They called this new group a male social club. What club wore robes and masks while riding around the country? She heard reports of them burning crosses on the properties of supporters of the emancipated slaves, as well as flogging, mutilating, and murdering the newly freed blacks. It was a scary time, and one she wished would stop.

Some of the men in town joined, as soon as they heard about it. Men she would have never thought to join such an organization. They were respectable business men, shop keepers, and elected officials. Thankfully, Thaddeus did not join. He told her he believed it would set back the reconstruction and hinder the south from healing. She agreed with him, whole heartily. Tensions were high enough, without adding fuel to the fire.

Big changes were happening as well. More and more people seemed to move into the area. They were Northerners looking to capitalized on the rebuilding effort. They didn't want to help out the South; they just wanted the money involved. She also saw more and more members of the Republican Party visible in town. The Carpetbaggers were Republicans from the North, and the Scalawags were the Republicans from the South. The two combined tried to force the new laws for the blacks. It caused more fights than it helped.

This new South was being forged by fire, and she wondered if it would survive the process. When a metal is forged, it is weaker than it started, and sometimes it breaks. Would the South break, or would it come out stronger than it was? She just didn't know anymore.

Pushing those thoughts out of her mind, she looked out the carriage window at Twin Willows. Time seemed to stand still here, and she wondered if it would always be this way. The April winds picked up as she clutched her wrap tighter around her shoulders. She was glad she grabbed it now to ward off the chill from the wind. She smiled as she saw Hannah waiting for her to exit the carriage. As soon as she was out, Hannah rushed to her side. Hannah reminded her of little Robert sometimes. They were always so happy to see her; they practically bounced around her.

"I wasn't sure you would be here. I know how much you do not care for the cold," Hannah stated, as Kathryn smiled.

Hannah wrapped an arm around Kathryn's shoulders as they walked up the steps and into the house. It was nice and warm inside.

"It's the wind, because when it's actually calm, it's quite nice outside," Kathryn stated as she followed Hannah to the parlor. "I can't believe I haven't been here in forever."

"I know," Hannah remarked. "My parents were upset they couldn't be here to see you," she informed her as they sat down.

"Where are they?" she asked as the teacart was bought into the room.

Since it was unheard of for a single, unmarried woman to be left alone in the house, Hannah's aunt and uncle on her mother's side were staying at the house with her, while her parents were gone. She saw them yesterday in town. This wasn't their first time in town, so she easily recognized them.

"They traveled to Atlanta for Momma's birthday," she replied. "It was surprise trip or it was supposed to be."

"I thought everyone knew your father was taking her away for her birthday," Kathryn commented, as she poured the tea into two cups. She handed one to Hannah before taking the other.

Hannah sipped her tea before answering. "Everyone knew, which was why it wasn't a secret anymore. No one seemed to know where he was taking her though, so a part was still a secret for her," she replied. "How was your Christmas?" she asked.

"Great, did you enjoy your trip?" Kathryn asked.

They got back into town three weeks ago, after staying four months with her extended family. Since she was busy at the bank, this was the first chance she got to come and visit Hannah.

"I wish we would have come home sooner, but the trip was good. I missed everyone here," Hannah stated. "I knew they wanted to get away this Christmas because of everything with Ben and you."

"How are they?" Kathryn asked, ignoring the pain of hearing Ben's name.

Hannah sipped her tea before answering. "They are dealing with him not contacting them. I think it hurt them more than they want anyone to know."

"I wish it could have been different."

"Me too, at least for their sakes," Hannah said sadly. "What are you going to do about your wedding dress?"

"I honestly don't know. I forgotten it was here," she said, before sipping her tea.

"It's still in Ben's room," Hannah commented. "It can stay here until you do get married," she suggested, as Kathryn shook her head.

"No, it was to be the dress I married your brother in. I can't get married to another man in it."

"Are you going to throw it away?" Hannah asked.

"No, I'm not sure what to do with it," she said glancing down at her hands. "I can move it so it won't be in your way."

"It's not in my way. If Ben ever comes home, it will be in his," Hannah said, placing her hand on Kathryn's. "I doubt he comes back."

"I do too," she whispered.

"Momma closed off his room," Hannah supplied. "His uniform in is there with your dress."

Kathryn nodded, as she thought about the wedding she would never have with him. She wanted him to wear his uniform, until his letter about never wanting to wear it again. The image of the wedding was so clear in her mind. She was standing in a field somewhere, with him standing beside her in his uniform. They were surrounded by people, but she couldn't see their faces. They were blurry.

"Kathryn, are you alright?" Hannah asked, as Kathryn jerked.

"Yeah, I'm fine," she answered, as she set her teacup on the side table and adjusted her wrap. "Let me know if I need to move the dress."

"I will, but I doubt you will have to," Hannah said. "Your brooch is beautiful."

"Thank you," Kathryn said touching it. "It was a Christmas gift from Thaddeus," she stated, remembering Henrietta's suggestion to start thinking about what he means to her.

She was still confused about her feelings for Thaddeus. He was a friend, and she didn't want it to change. She didn't want to lose him as a friend.

"You must be doing a great job at the bank," Hannah commented. "It must have cost a fortune," she said, getting a closer look at it.

"Actually, I gave him a gift, so he got me something in return," she explained, not wanting Hannah to think it was because of the bank. No one else at the bank got a gift.

"What did you get him? Actually, the better question is why did you get him a gift?" Hannah asked quickly.

"I got him a pair of cuff links, and it was a thank you for being a great friend," Kathryn replied. "He's been really great after everything with Ben," she mentioned.

"Do you care for him?" Hannah asked, setting her cup to the side.

She seemed very interested in Kathryn's answer. It was a little unnerving. Why did everyone want her to care for Thaddeus, as more than a friend?

"As a friend, yes."

"I think you care for him as more than a friend," Hannah commented.

Why did everyone think she and Thaddeus were more than friends? Their behavior was above reproach, since for most of their friendship, she was an engaged woman. Thaddeus never stepped out of line of their friendship.

"You know Henrietta thinks Thaddeus likes me more than a friend, and you think I like him as more than a friend," Kathryn muttered, remembering her earlier conversation with Henrietta. "I think you're both wrong."

Thaddeus was a great friend but nothing more. How could they not see it? He was there for her when Ben broke her heart.

"I don't think we are," Hannah said with a smile. "But I can see it makes you uncomfortable, so I'll drop the subject."

"Thank you," Kathryn said, before picking up her teacup. "Where are your aunt and uncle?" she asked, when she realized she didn't see them when she came in earlier.

"They are out riding," she answered. "They wanted to see the property, since they've never seen it entirely."

"Well, it is beautiful," Kathryn voiced, as Hannah nodded.

Twin Willows was a large plantation covering hundreds of acres. Ben promised her after they were married to take her around.

"What do you think about the new social club?" Hannah asked moving past Twin Willows. "What do they call it?"

"The Ku Klux Klan or KKK is the name, and I don't approve of it," Kathryn responded, remembering one of the burning crosses printed in the paper.

"There was a lot of talk about it in Savannah. Most of the men there were rushing to the meeting. My uncle, cousins, and father went to the first one," Hannah informed her.

"What did they say?" she asked, because no one she was close to went to a meeting. She refused to ask the men in town; they probably won't tell her anything, anyway.

"My cousins liked it. They said it was a great way to take care of things, since the Union soldiers patrolled the streets. My uncle and father didn't think it was a good idea," she explained. "Did you father go?"

"No, he didn't, and neither did Thaddeus," Kathryn supplied. "I asked him the next morning hoping he went, so I could ask what it was really about."

"So, all we know is from the news which isn't good," Hannah noted, as Kathryn nodded. "I guess we will have to wait."

"Probably not long, since the reports are bad," Kathryn remarked. "I'm not sure I approve of them burning crosses."

"Neither do I, but what can we do?" Hannah asked. "They say they are doing it to protect the women."

"We have always been protected, so why is it necessary to form this social club?" Kathryn groaned. She just didn't understand why they thought they needed a club to protect the women. None of it made any sense.

Hannah shrugged, "I don't know, Kathryn. They're men, and think differently than we do."

"Yeah, they do," Kathryn sighed. "I wish we could go to one meeting."

"Why?"

"To see what is said to turn rational, God-fearing men into destructive and murdering men," she answered.

"It's a flock mentality; the sheep follow after each other just as the men do. They probably don't see anything wrong with what they are doing," Hannah remarked. "I mean, when has Mr. Smithville ever hit another man?"

"He's in the club?" Kathryn asked, as Hannah nodded. "He is too old to be doing anything dangerous."

"I know, but I overheard Momma saying he was suffering from a broken hand from punching out some man," Hannah explained.

"You know, I wondered what happened to his hand," Kathryn muttered. "I asked him about it, and he just shrugged it off. I can't believe he would punch another man."

"Me either, but he did."

Kathryn thought about Mr. Smithville's kindness, as she waited for the death lists. He told her he prayed each night for the soldiers to come home, especially Benjamin. He said it wasn't good for a man to leave a woman like her, at home. She always smiled, and thanked him for his prayers. She would have never guessed he would need prayers for the course he was on now.

~ ~ ~ ~

Kathryn made her way to the bank, when she noticed many people dressed in black. She wondered what happened, but thought it was probably something to do with the new social club. She didn't want to know if it was anything to do with the KKK. It was better she didn't know.

"Honey, you're not in black," Grace said, as soon as she walked into the bank.

She noticed Ms. Grace was in a black dress and knew it didn't have anything to do with the club.

"What happened?" she asked, as she sat down at her desk.

"It's the anniversary of President Lincoln's death," Grace replied.

"It is?" she asked, as Grace nodded. "I forgot all about it, but why is everyone wearing black? He wasn't really adored here."

"The only people I saw wearing black was the black people," Grace said. "I knew not many people would wear black for him, but I thought you would."

"What? Ms. Grace everyone I saw outside was wearing black," Kathryn said, standing up before walking over to the windows.

Shots rang out down the street, as she grabbed Grace and pushed her to the ground. She hoped she didn't hurt her, but they needed to get down.

"Is everyone alright?" Thaddeus asked, running out of his office. "Mother?" he called out.

Kathryn looked around and saw everyone else was on the ground, too. She couldn't see Thaddeus, which meant he probably couldn't see them either.

"Thaddeus, I'm fine," Grace called out, as she looked at Kathryn. "Do you think it's okay to get up?" she asked, as more shots were fired.

"I would say no," Kathryn replied. "Thaddeus, we're by the front window," she called out, when she realized he was probably looking for them.

"There you are," he stated, as he knelt down next to them. "Are you hurt?"

"I'm not, but I think I hurt your mother, when I slammed her down," Kathryn said looking at Grace.

"Oh, no, dear I'm fine. I'm just thankful you were quick to react," she stated. "Did you see the shooter?"

"No," Kathryn answered. "I did see people in white robes, though."

"What?" Thaddeus asked. "Were they firing this way?" he asked, gripping Kathryn's arms.

"No, not that I know of," she replied. "Why would they fire at the bank?" she asked, as he released his grip on her.

"Because I didn't join them," he muttered. "They said there would be repercussions for not joining them."

"What?" Grace asked, "You did not tell me they said that."

"I'm sorry, Mother. I assumed they were bluffing, since they made the threat months ago," he explained.

"I don't think they were aiming at the bank," Kathryn voiced. "It looked as if they fired into the crowd of mourners," she said peeking above the windowsill to look out. "In fact, I know they did."

"What?" Thaddeus asked, as he eased beside her to see what she was talking about. "I think they hit some people," he noted, as she nodded. "I'm not sure if anyone is dead."

"Do you think we should move away from the windows?" Grace asked, as Thaddeus and Kathryn turned to look at her.

"We haven't heard another shot. I guess we can," he said. "Stay low," he ordered, as Grace nodded and crept away from the window to the back of the bank.

"Are you okay?" he asked looking at Kathryn.

"I'm fine, but you should have warned everyone who works here," she declared. "We have a right to know if anyone has threatened you."

Thaddeus sighed and ran his hands through his hair. "I know, but I thought it was a bluff. They were just mad because I didn't join," he explained.

"I don't believe they were bluffing," she muttered. "You need to keep your mother safe. They know she is everything to you."

He nodded before looking over his shoulder at his mother. She made it to the back of the bank and was talking with the other workers to help calm them down. "I need to keep you safe, too," he admitted, looking back at her.

"What?" she asked.

"Kathryn, they know you mean a great deal to me," he whispered.

She sat back and looked at him while trying to process what he just said. She meant a great deal to him?

"Did you hear me?" he asked, taking her hands in his.

"I think so," she gulped. "You meant, I mean a great deal to you as a friend, right?" she asked, as he shook his head no, "Then, what?"

"You mean more to me than my own life," he answered. "I could never see you hurt because of this mess," he said, releasing one of her hands to brush his fingers against her cheek.

"I don't..." she stuttered, "I don't know what to say," she said, closing her eyes. Henrietta and Hannah were right.

This was more than friendship, at least for him. She didn't know how to respond to his declaration. She still wanted him to be her friend.

"Please, promise me you will be extra cautious," he stated as, she opened her eyes to look at him.

She saw worry and concern written across his face.

"I promise," she whispered.

He sighed and stood, before reaching his hand down to her. She looked up at him and slipped her hand into his. He helped her to her feet but didn't release her hand. She didn't know what he wanted from her, and she was afraid to ask. The fragile bond of their friendship was at the point of snapping.

"I don't think anyone was killed," he said, looking over her shoulder at the chaos, just beyond them.

She turned slightly and saw people running around, while others were helping the injured people. She noticed there were no white people outside. Grace was right; the only ones wearing black were the blacks. It made them easy targets for the men to shoot. She was ashamed of the men who dared to fire into an open crowd. They were cowards hiding behind their new social club to target people because of the color of their skin.

"They should be arrested," she stated. "Someone could have died."

"Who would arrest them? The sheriff is one of the members along with his two deputies," he explained.

She didn't know the sheriff was in it. He was another man who was kind to her after Ben left.

"The sad thing is this will bring soldiers to patrol the streets. They just made the situation worse for everyone else."

"Do you think the soldiers will come?" she asked looking at him.

"Yeah, because they fired into an open crowd and won't be arrested. We will be under martial law, since we are not an official state," he explained, as she closed her eyes.

Soldiers patrolling the streets? How much more would the people have to suffer before everything righted itself? It wasn't fair, and she knew they were nowhere near being healed. In fact, they were probably farther back than they were when the war actually started.

~ ~ ~ ~

"Thank you for seeing me home," Kathryn said, as Thaddeus helped her out of his carriage.

After the shooting this morning, Thaddeus made sure everyone got a ride home. He didn't want anyone to walk today. He took a few people home throughout the day.

"I wish being seen with me would not put you in danger," he stated, as he released her hand.

She sighed; this guilt was messing with his mind. "Thaddeus, everyone around town has seen us together for the better part of five years. They know I work at the bank. They know we are friends, so you taking me home is nothing out of the ordinary," she commented. "Please do not worry. There is nothing you can do to change their minds."

"I could join them," he observed.

It would not have been her first thought of what he would say.

"Yeah, you could, but then you would sacrifice your beliefs to protect your mother and me," she said, taking his hands in hers and squeezing them. "You will get through this, as long as you keep those beliefs and principals."

"I hope you're right," he muttered. "Will your father bring you to work in the morning? I do not want you walking into work for a while."

"I will ask him, if it will ease your mind."

"It will," he confirmed. "I'll find a way to solve the problem."

"Without joining them?" she asked, because she didn't need him joining the enemy to protect her.

"Without joining them," he confirmed. "Now, I need to get mother home," he said, as she nodded.

Grace was still waiting in the carriage. She refused to go home earlier when Thaddeus asked her.

She walked up to her door, before turning to watch him climb in the carriage and signal the driver. Shaking her head, she opened the door and went to her room. She wanted to collect her thoughts before she joined her parents. She hoped they already heard about the shooting, and knew she wasn't in any danger. It would make it easier to tell them about Thaddeus' worry. She also wanted to ask her father if he was threatened. It could be her father's connection to her that would get her killed.

Chapter Nine

After speaking with her parents, she was more than a little worried. Her father was warned, the same as Thaddeus, for not joining the group. Both men were worried about her, because of her connection to them. They didn't think it was a good idea for her to walk to and from the bank, so they each took turns driving her. It made her feel helpless, but she was thankful one afternoon.

She was riding in the carriage beside her father as shots rang out. The carriage stopped suddenly, which threw her into the door. Thankfully, it was latched because, if not, she would have gone flying through it.

"Are you hurt?" her father asked, as he looked over at her.

"No," she answered, as screams pierced the air. She tried to look out the window only to be pulled back.

"Be careful," he warned, before more shots rang out. "We need to get out of here."

"What about those people?" She asked, as she leaned up to look. "I think they hit someone," she remarked.

"They've been taking out the men who attacked one of the farmers last week," he stated. "According to the farmer's family, five black men came onto his property. They beat and killed him before raiding the house."

"Why didn't they attack the family?" she asked, as she watched a woman kneel down next to the man lying in the street.

"The family hid in the cellar until they were sure the men were gone," he answered, as he tapped on the side of the carriage to signal the driver to continue. "Kathryn, this situation is serious."

"I know."

"Your mother and I have talked; we think it may be for the best to move," he voiced.

"What?" she asked. "You want to move? This is our home, and I don't want to run away."

"Honey, I know, but it's my fault you are in danger. I can't lose you or your mother," he mentioned. "We could move to a place where the Klan is not there."

"Where would that be?" she asked. "According to the paper, it's all over the south," she stated.

He looked away for a moment before looking back at her. "We were thinking out west. The frontier is growing every day, and there are plenty of opportunities for a fresh start."

Kathryn took a deep breath and looked away from him. She loved her home, and couldn't image moving away from everything she knew and loved. "I don't want to move."

"Kathryn, this situation is deadly. You saw what those men are capable of doing."

"I know, but no one has actually targeted you. They could have been bluffing," she said, though she knew they were not.

"We haven't made any decisions yet," her father said quietly.

She nodded as the carriage stopped in front of their house. She was quiet, as they exited the carriage and walked into the house. Thoughts bounced around, as she tried to figure out a way to make her parents change their minds. She knew moving away would not keep them safe. They couldn't run away from their lives because someone threatened them.

~ ~ ~ ~

She was still working through her thoughts, when she walked into the bank the next morning. Nothing out of the ordinary happened on the way to work, which eased her father's mind. She barely made it inside when Thaddeus came up beside her and ushered her back to his office.

"Are you alright?" he asked, closing the door behind them. "I heard about the shooting on your way home yesterday."

"Thaddeus, I'm fine," she replied, as she sat down.

This would not be a short conversation, so she might as well get comfortable. Thaddeus' worry was pouring off of him in his words and actions.

"Tell me what happened," he demanded, as he rounded his desk and sat down behind it.

He looked ready to kill someone, but it didn't frighten her. She knew he would never hurt her.

"We were on our way home, before the carriage suddenly stopped. I was tossed against the door, as shots rang out. I looked out the window, and saw a man lying in the street with a woman kneeling down beside him," she explained quickly. "Father thought it was something to do with the farmer who was attacked."

"Yeah it was, according to a friend of mine," he muttered. He was tense even after she told him she was okay. "How many rounds of shots did you hear?" he asked.

"Two, but why does it matter?" she asked. What did it matter how many rounds of fire? They were not aiming at the carriage as far as she knew. Her father checked the carriage over for any bullet holes later. She knew he didn't find any because her mother told her this morning.

"Just wondering, how are you feeling?" he asked softly, as he finally relaxed behind his desk.

She looked at him and knew it was best to answer honestly. "I'm okay physically, but I'm angry at the situation. My parents are talking about moving out west. They want to leave behind our lives because of this social club," she stated in a huff.

It still made her mad at the thought of her parents packing everything up and moving.

"You're moving?" he asked. He looked hurt by the news.

"Well they're not sure," she replied. "I don't want to move because my life is here," she remarked, as he nodded. The sad thing is, it wasn't her decision. She knew her parents would decide without asking her. They thought it would remove the threat, but she knew it wouldn't.

"When will they decide?" he asked.

"I don't know," she answered sadly. "If I ask you a question will you answer me truthfully?" she asked, leaning forward in the chair. It was a question she wanted to ask her father but knew she couldn't. He would lie to her, if only to ease her mind.

"Yes," he replied. "Ask me anything, Kathryn."

"Did the Klan threaten me personally?"

"What do you mean?" he asked, not understanding her question.

"My father is worried about me wandering outside alone. You are worried about me traveling between the bank and home. Did they threaten just me?" she asked.

"No, or at least they didn't with me. They just know how important you are to me," he explained. "They know not to come after my mother, but you are the only other person close to me."

"What about my father? I mean, as far as I can tell, he's not worried about momma as much as me."

"It's the same thing for me with my mother. You would be an example to us," he commented. "It might be a good idea for your family to leave."

"No," she stated standing up. "It would not be a good idea. Have you not read the papers recently?" she asked. "The Indians are causing problems for the people moving out there. Troops were sent out west to protect the settlers. We would trade one problem for another," she remarked angrily. "Moving will not solve anything."

"I didn't realize troops were sent out. I knew the settlers were having problems, but not as much so the Army was called," he voiced. "I can't place all the blame on the Indians, though."

"I can't either. The settlers are taking more and more of their land along with the government. The West is not big enough for the Indians, settlers, and the government," she said, as he nodded. "It didn't help when Colonel Chivington massacred all those Indians at Sand Creek."

"He believed it was honorable to kill the Indians," he muttered.

"It was not honorable to kill women and children camped out," she growled. "Custer was sent out west to help deal with the Indian problem. Why they sent him, I don't know. The situation will get worse before it gets better," she informed him. "It would not be a good idea to move right now."

He nodded. "Talk to your parents. They may listen to reason, especially if you explain about the Indians."

"I plan to," she said.

"Sorry for burdening you this morning. I needed to know if you were okay after yesterday," he said, standing up. "If you need to talk just come find me."

"I will," she promised, before turning to leave his office. She prayed the day would be uneventful for everyone. There was enough excitement in her life, so she didn't need any more.

~ ~ ~ ~

Once the workday was over, Thaddeus walked over to her desk. It was his day to take her home, and she wondered if anything would happen this afternoon. According to the paper, all the men involved in the crime were dead. The last one was killed late last night near the back edge of town.

"Are you ready?" Thaddeus asked, as she looked up at him.

"Yes," she replied, standing up. Moving around her chair, she pushed it under the desk, as Thaddeus placed her wrap around her   shoulders.   "Oh,   thank   you."
"I paid a visit to your parents at lunch," he informed her. "They have rethought their plan about moving. I explained your worry about the Indians and soldiers. They agree the situation is too unstable to move into."

"You went to see my parents?" she asked, spinning around to face him.

He left the bank earlier, but she didn't know it was to see her parents.

"I did," he acknowledged but didn't explain.

"Why?"

"I knew you were worried about moving out west, so I talked to them. I knew you would not be calm when you discussed everything with them, so I did," he answered. "I also asked them if it was okay for you to join me for supper."

"You want me to eat with you?" she asked, as he nodded. What was going on here? "Where?" she tried, searching his face for answers, but it was blank. None of this made any sense.

"My house and mother will be there," he added. "If it's okay with you?"

Eating with him and his mother wouldn't be a problem. It wouldn't be the first time she'd eaten with them. The question in her mind was why he asked her parents.

"Of course, its fine," she said, as he led her outside to his waiting carriage.

She didn't know when he gave his driver instructions to be out front, but she wasn't complaining. Tonight should be interesting. It was a few years since his mother's quarantine, which was the last time she shared supper with them.

He helped her up into the carriage and signaled the driver to go. "Kathryn, are you okay eating with me?" he asked quietly.

She turned to look at him and wondered why he asked. "Thaddeus, why wouldn't I be?" she asked instead of answering. What was going on with him?

"You seem uncomfortable," he remarked.

"No, I'm not uncomfortable," she stated. "I guess a little nervous, because the last time I ate with you and your mother, was during her quarantine."

"I can promise you, you will not be quarantined this time around," he said, as she smiled.

"I'm not worried about being quarantined. It wasn't bad last time," she remarked. "Thank you for talking to my parents."

"I needed to talk to them after speaking with one of the members of the Klan," he commented.

"What? You talked to one of the members of the Klan?" she asked, as he nodded. "Are you crazy? They could've killed you."

"I am fine, as you can tell. I spoke with them about threatening you through your father and me," he explained. "I warned them if you were harmed, I would tell the soldiers who exactly is in the social club."

"Thaddeus, you placed the threat squarely on your shoulders by threatening them," she exclaimed.

"Everything is alright now."

"How can it be alright?" she asked, grabbing one of his hands. "They will kill you for threatening them."

"No, they won't," he stated. "I made it very clear to them. If anything happened to me, the list of members would be released on my death. They would not be able to stop it."

"Why would you draw their fire?" she asked, when she felt him rubbing the back of her hand.

"I cannot allow you to be harmed," he said, squeezing her hand. "I reminded them you were an unmarried woman and deserved their protection more than their contempt. Their motto expressly stated they were to protect women."

"What did they say?"

He smiled, as the carriage slowed down. She knew they were close to his house. "The man agreed and told the men to leave you alone. They said you have been through enough in your short life."

"What did they mean?"

"Ben," he replied softly. "They all know Ben left you after the war was over."

"So they feel sorry for me?" she asked, as the carriage came to a stop. She heard the driver jump down to open the door for them.

"No, they do not feel sorry for you. They admire your strength," he replied, as he climbed out of the carriage and reached for her. "You've earned their respect, and for a woman, it is a high honor."

She thought about what he said, as she let him help her out of the carriage. "Thank you for going to talk to them," she said, as her feet touched the ground. "It will ease my parents' minds."

"It eases my mind as well," he noted, as he lead her up the steps and into the house. "I could not let anything happen to you because of something I didn't do," he muttered, as his mother met them at the front door.

"Kathryn, I'm so glad you could join us tonight," Grace said, as she pulled Kathryn into her arms. "I hope my son didn't just drag you here, but asked you politely."

"Ms. Grace, your son would never drag a woman here against her will," she said with a smile. "He helps her into the carriage and has the driver bring them here."

Grace laughed as Thaddeus shook his head.

"Can I take your wrap?" Thaddeus asked, stepping behind Kathryn.

"Thank you," she said as he eased it off her shoulders, placing it on the entry table.

"Dinner is ready, if you are," Grace stated, looking at her son. He nodded as she smiled, and looked back at Kathryn. "Follow me."

Kathryn walked into the dining room beside Grace with Thaddeus right behind them. Once they entered the room, he walked past them to pull out one of the chairs. She knew it wasn't his mother's chair, so it was for her. She walked over to the chair and sat. "Thank you," she said, as he pushed her closer to the table.

He then walked, to his mother's side, and did the same to her.

"Thank you," Grace said, looking up at her son. He nodded, as he walked over to his chair at the head of the table and sat down. As soon as he was seated, two maids walked into the room with their food.

"This looks amazing," Kathryn said, as the food was set before them. "Thank you again for inviting me."

"Trust me; it is our pleasure to have you here," Grace voiced. "Thaddeus told me about the shooting yesterday. I cannot imagine being close to the action."

"You were at the bank for the first one," Kathryn pointed out. "The men fired into the crowd behind the carriage."

"We were behind the brick walls of the bank during the first shooting. You were only in a carriage yesterday afternoon," Grace remarked. "Big difference, my dear."

"I agree with mother," Thaddeus said. "The carriage would not stop a bullet, but you're fine."

"Yes, perfectly fine," she agreed. "I am still a little shocked the men of town would even succumb to this level of violence."

"It's fear," Thaddeus declared. "They fear the unknown."

"What's unknown to them?" Kathryn asked, as she began eating.

"The blacks have always been slaves with no rights," he stated, as she nodded. "They have rights now, or at least they will when Georgia adopts the 13th Amendment. If every former slave stayed in town, they would outnumber the white population. They can run for office and own land."

"Only the males," Grace piped in.

"Yes, only the males," Thaddeus agreed. "It is their fear their world will come crashing down with a shift in power."

"It doesn't make sense; they would need to get voted in," Kathryn said. "The white men in town would not vote for a black man."

"They have the numbers to vote someone into office," he informed her.

"They would, if every black male stayed in the area but most have moved up North," she stated. "Actually, they moved up North when they were freed during the war."

"She's right; they don't have the numbers they once did," Grace said between bites. She was enjoying the conversation. Kathryn could hold her own against her son.

"They still have enough to make a change. The South is not what it once was; the economy is almost non-existent since cotton production is down. Tennessee is the only Southern state readmitted to the Union," he explained. "One voice is all it would take to change the delicate balance."

Kathryn nodded as she looked away from him to her plate. "Is something not to your liking?" Grace asked, as Kathryn glanced over at her.

"Oh, no ma'am, everything is perfect. I was processing what Thaddeus was saying," she commented, as Grace nodded. "One voice can make a difference, but it can also be lost in a sea of voices."

"True, but the Klan is worried just the same. They may have lost the war, but they will not lose their homes," he expressed.

"No, they will just fire into an open crowd," she muttered as she pushed her empty plate away.

"Would you join me for tea in the parlor?" Grace asked, as she pushed her plate away and stood.

Kathryn smiled when Thaddeus stood. He was a true gentleman who stood when a lady was standing.

"I would," Kathryn said, as Thaddeus walked over to her chair and helped her up. "Thank you."

"I will leave you ladies to your tea," he said, before turning to look at Kathryn. "I will be in the library when you are ready to leave."

"Okay," she said, as she watched him leave the room before shifting to look at Grace.

"You ready?" she asked, as Kathryn nodded, and followed her out of the dining room and into the parlor.

Once their tea was delivered, Grace settled in one of the wingback chairs. "Are you really okay after the shooting?" she asked, as Kathryn added a sugar cube to her tea.

"I am," she answered. "Your son worries too much," she commented, as she sipped her tea. "I wasn't hit and neither was the carriage. My father was with me, in case anything happened to me. I explained everything to Thaddeus this morning."

"My son wears his heart on his sleeve," Grace remarked, before sipping her tea.

"What?" Kathryn asked in surprise. They were talking about the shooting, not Thaddeus' heart. "What does his heart have to do with the shooting?"

"He waited in marrying Sarah," Grace stated, as Kathryn stared at her in confusion. "He didn't realize life was short, but he does now."

"Ms. Grace I'm not sure what this has to do with the shooting," Kathryn voiced. "In regards to your statement, I think Thaddeus knows how short life is. I know I do; the war drilled it into my head." She remarked, thinking about Robert and his brother William both dying at Shiloh.

"He does know life is short now," she agreed. "This trouble in town has made him realize a few things."

"What?" Kathryn asked, finishing her tea. She wanted to know why Grace was talking cryptic about Thaddeus.

"I think you will understand in time, my dear," Grace stated. "Are you finished with your tea?" she asked, as Kathryn set her cup to the side.

"I am, and I believe it is time for me to go home. I do not want to worry my parents or keep Thaddeus out late," she said standing up.

"I do not want your parents to worry, either," Grace said standing. "I'll inform Thaddeus you are ready to leave," she said, before leaving the room.

Kathryn picked up her teacup and placed it on the teacart, as Thaddeus and Grace walked into the room.

"Mother says you are ready," he said, as she nodded. "I will take you back then."

"Thank you again for the meal and tea," she said, walking over to Grace. "It was a pleasure to share your meal."

"You are welcome, my dear," Grace said, hugging Kathryn close before releasing her. "I will see you tomorrow."

"Yes, I will see you tomorrow," Kathryn said, as she followed Thaddeus out of the parlor. He grabbed her wrap, and held it out for her. "Thank you."

They walked out of the house, and down to the waiting carriage. She looked at him and wondered when he told the driver to be ready.

"I spoke to the driver while you were having tea with mother," he explained, when he saw the question in her eyes. "I knew tea wouldn't take too long so I informed him to be ready."

"You think of everything," she mused, as he helped her into the carriage, before coming in behind her.

"Not everything," he muttered, as he settled down beside her. "If I did, then your life would have never been threatened."

"Thaddeus, I am fine," she stressed, grabbing his hands. "Look at me, there is no scratch or bump. I am not hurt."

"You could have been," he stated, looking at her. "It would have been my fault."

"No, did you forget they threatened me through my father too?" she asked. "You have a right to turn down membership to a club. They should have never threatened you for not joining."

"I agree."

"You are a good man," she said softly. "Thank you for removing the threat off my life."

"I needed to," he whispered, squeezing her hands. "I didn't just visit your parents to tell them not to move," he stated.

"What else?" she asked smiling. "I mean besides supper."

He took a deep breath before answering her. "Kathryn, I spoke with your parents about you," he said. "I asked them if it would be acceptable if I could ask you for your hand in marriage."

"What?" she asked in shocked.

Did he just say marriage? He asked her parents' for her hand in marriage. This didn't make sense.

"I asked them if I could ask you to marry me," he replied, releasing her hands to cup her cheek. "I wanted their permission before I asked you."

"Are you asking me now?" she asked. This didn't sound like a proposal, but Ben's proposal was the only one she had to compare.

"No," he answered. "I would never ask you to marry me in a carriage," he stated with a smile. "You deserve more than the inside of a carriage."

"So, you only wanted me to know you are going to ask me to marry you?" she asked, still in shock about his statement. She didn't know what to think about him wanting to marry her.

"Yes," he answered. "I told you, because I want you to think about marriage to me. I want you to think about it longer than a few seconds or even a few minutes," he said. "This is an important decision in your life, and you need to be sure. I do not want you to feel pressured to give me an answer, either. I want you to answer without thinking about the answer, because you will already know it."

"Okay, I will think about it," she commented. "Do you want me to give you my answer?" she asked, wondering how this would work.

"No, not until I ask you."

"When are you going to ask me?"

It was odd, but she wanted him to ask her, and she wanted to know when he would ask her. It would give her a timeframe on when to have her answer.

Thaddeus laughed. "You will have to wait, but trust me; it will be soon," he said, as the carriage stopped.

The driver opened the door seconds later as Thaddeus climbed out. Kathryn scooted across the seat and placed her hand in his. He helped her out, before leading her up the steps.

"Thank you for joining us for supper. I know my mother enjoyed your company."

"I enjoyed it," she stated. "It was rather enlightening," she mused, thinking about what he told her.

"I'm sure it was," he said, releasing her hand. "Please think about what I said."

"I will," she promised, as she opened the door and stepped inside. "Goodnight."

"Goodnight, Kathryn," he whispered.

She smiled, as she watched him walk away and climb back into the carriage. Closing the door, she headed to her room. Thaddeus gave her a lot to think about. She wasn't sure what she would have said, if he would have proposed tonight.

When Benjamin asked her to marry him, she said yes without thinking. She didn't have to think about her answer. It was always going to be yes. She loved Benjamin, so it made the answer easy.

She didn't know what her feelings were concerning Thaddeus. He was a kind man who loved his mother. He eased her worry about Benjamin after every major battle and was the first one she broke down too after Ben left her. Over the past five years, he became a big part of her life, by sharing his. He even met with the Klan to remove the threat on her life.

She thought about the last few years, and in the darkest periods of her life, he was there. He was a light in her darkness. The shocking part was most of those dark periods were surrounding her then fiancé, Benjamin. The man she promised to pledge her life to, caused her pain, but the man who was only her friend, eased the pain.

Thaddeus asked her to think about his proposal. She would do as she promised, and think about it. Hopefully, she would have her answer before he asked her. She thought, he wouldn't ask her until he knew, she knew, her answer.

~ ~ ~ ~

"I'm so glad you let me visit today," Kathryn said, as she rushed into the parlor, with Robert in her arms.

Two weeks after Thaddeus asked her to think about her answer, she needed to see someone. She thought about his suggestion every day, and she was farther away from knowing what her answer would be. She knew she needed help in her decision, and Henrietta was the only person she could think of who would be able to help to her. Henrietta also wouldn't push her into a decision. She would help Kathryn see both sides of the decision.

"Your note sounded urgent, which is unlike you," Henrietta stated, as she shut the door. "Is everything okay?" she asked, as Kathryn sat Robert down next to his pile of toys, before sitting down on the chaise.

Kathryn wondered if her confusion was written on her face because everyone asked her if she was okay over the past two weeks.

"Do you think Thaddeus likes me?" she asked, as Henrietta sat beside her. It was one of the questions floating around in her mind. She wondered if he was proposing because he didn't want her to be alone. She also wondered if it was a way for him to protect her. A marriage between them would not work, if he didn't at least like her. She needed to know if he liked her as more than a friend or not. "I mean, as more than a friend."

"Yes, I do," Henrietta answered. "I've seen the way he is around you. I know you don't see the looks he throws your way, but he does care for you. Why do you ask?"

Kathryn sighed before answering. This was the hard part, because she didn't know for sure. It was another problem floating around in her head. "He asked me to think about marrying him," she explained.

"What? Has he asked you to marry him?" Henrietta asked smiling.

"Uh, no, not really," Kathryn replied remembering his comments in the carriage. He told her, she deserved better than a proposal in a carriage. "He asked my parents for my hand in marriage, a few weeks ago."

"Did your parents spill his surprise?" Henrietta asked, tilting her head to the side. Kathryn knew she wasn't sure what she was trying to tell her. "Your parents shouldn't have said anything about Thaddeus wanting to marry you. They have ruined his surprise."

"They didn't spill his surprise; he asked me to think about marriage to him," she explained. "He told me he asked my parents, before asking me to think about what my answer would be."

"I still don't understand," Henrietta admitted. "He didn't ask you to marry him, but to think about what your answer would be?" she asked, as Kathryn nodded. "Isn't it a little odd?"

"Probably," Kathryn replied with a shrug. "I don't think he wanted to spring a proposal on me, so he asked me to think about my answer," she knew it was hard to explain, but hopefully, Henrietta understood now.

"When do you have to let him know?" Henrietta asked.

"When he actually proposes," she answered. "He did tell me it would be soon. I don't know when soon will be, since it's already been two weeks."

Henrietta looked over at Robert to see what he was doing, before looking back at Kathryn. "What are you going to tell him?" she asked.

"I don't know," Kathryn said truthfully. "I've thought about it for the past two weeks, and I can't decide. He has been there for me in the darkest times of my life."

"I agree; he has been there for you, but you can't marry someone just because of it. You need to actually feel something for them, just as they need to feel something for you," Henrietta commented. "What do his actions say to you?"

"He cares for me," Kathryn replied remembering every time he let her cry on his shoulder. He knew when she needed to talk or when she just needed a friend to sit beside her. He never pushed her into anything; he let her come to him when she was ready.

"He does care for you," Henrietta said. "He also doesn't want to push you into a decision, which is why he asked you to think about your answer."

"What makes you say that?"

"Kathryn, he basically asked you to marry him. Instead of asking though, he wants you to think about your answer, before he really asks you," Henrietta supplied. "Do you at least like him?"

"Yeah, I do, but I don't know if it's love," she whispered. "I don't feel for him, what I felt for Benjamin. I knew I loved Benjamin, when he asked me to marry him. I never thought about my answer. It was easy."

"You're older," Henrietta pointed out. "You loved Ben in a dreamy way. Nothing could harm you or could come between you two. You're older now. You know life is short and full of pain and heartache. You loved Ben with a girl's heart, but now you have a woman's heart."

"Several years of war will harden a heart." Kathryn noted.

"Possibly, but when you think about love, you picture what you had with Benjamin. It was quick and all consuming. It basically caught fire," she remarked. "Love does not always come fast. It creeps up and embeds itself in your heart until it can take root. The process is slow and takes more time than you would ever think. It is there before you realize it," she stated. "Love comes fast, and love comes slow, but it is love in either case. It is up to you to recognize the signs."

"How did you get to be so wise?" Kathryn asked, smiling.

"I don't know, maybe motherhood makes me see things I would have otherwise missed. I do know how it feels to lose someone. I also know I loved Robert with a girl's heart," Henrietta voiced. "I'm not saying I wouldn't have loved him with a woman's heart, if he would have lived. I just know the difference. I love my son with a mother's heart, which is something entirely different. When Robert died, I didn't want to live because of the pain. If my baby were to die, I'm not sure I would survive."

Kathryn sat there and listened to Henrietta describe her love for her son. She didn't know there were so many types of love. Was it possible her feelings for Thaddeus were love? "Henrietta, what do I say when he asks me to marry him?"

"I want to tell you to say yes, but it is up to you," she answered. "I think your answer will come to you when he does ask you."

"You think?" Kathryn asked, as Henrietta nodded. "Okay, I will wait until he asks me. I hope I know the answer when he does ask me."

"You will; trust me. When he asks you, the answer will be there for you, even if it is no," Henrietta commented. "Don't worry about you answer now. It will only cause you to doubt what you feel for him."

Kathryn took a deep breath before letting it out. This was harder than she thought it would be. "Okay, I hope you're right."

"Oh honey, I do too," Henrietta laughed.

Kathryn stayed a little longer before leaving. She felt better after talking things over with Henrietta. She would trust her answer to Thaddeus would come, when he asked her to marry him. It was the only way she would be sure she was following her heart.

Hopefully, her answer wouldn't break his heart, if it wasn't what he wanted to hear.

~ ~ ~ ~

A month later, her nerves were on edge. Thaddeus still hadn't asked her to marry him, and she began to wonder if he would. He said he didn't want her answer until he asked, but maybe she should tell him. The waiting was torturing her.

Every time he asked her to join him for the noon meal or supper, she thought he would ask her over their food, or at least on the way to and from the bank. He didn't even mention marriage.

It was confusing her and making her think, he didn't want to marry her anymore. She hoped it wasn't the case, but she needed to face facts.

Later that afternoon, Kathryn strolled beside the church. Since the threat on her life was removed, she didn't have to be driven around anymore. It was a good thing, because she needed time to think, away from everyone around her. It was a beautiful day to walk and think.

"These streets are not safe," a voice she knew better than her own, said behind her.

"They are safe enough, since the threat against my life is gone," she stated, spinning around to face Thaddeus. "Shouldn't you be at home with your mother?" she asked, looking up at him.

"My mother is at the General Store right now," he informed her. "I saw you walking and decided to come over here and keep you company. My mother will be a while," he explained.

"What will take her so long?" she asked with a smile.

"One of the ladies from church is also shopping," he replied.

"So, she is talking instead of shopping?" she asked, as he nodded. "I'm better company than two ladies talking in the General Store?"

"Yes, you're better company," he said, reaching for her hands. "Do you know where we are?" he asked, as she looked around.

"Uh, yeah beside the church," she answered.

Had he lost his mind? The church was only a few feet away from them. Was he sick? If he didn't recognize the church, maybe she should get the doctor.

"This was the place you found my mother, short of breath," he declared. "I didn't know then a pair of blue eyes would change my life. The owner of the blue eyes also happened to save my mother," he mused.

"It was nothing," she muttered, thinking about how scared she was for Grace.

"Kathryn, it was everything to me. I lost my father and couldn't lose my mother so soon. You reacted quickly and were rewarded by being quarantined with us," he voiced. "I didn't realize until later how much those blue eyes would mean to me," he said, as he knelt in front of her.

"Thaddeus?" she asked, as she stood there in shock.

"Kathryn, I love you, and I am asking you to marry me," he said squeezing her hands.

She took a deep breath and stared into his eyes. In a blinding flash, she knew her answer. Henrietta was right; the answer was flashing in his eyes.

"I will," she whispered, as he smiled and stood. "I will marry you," she stated, as she released his hands and looped her arms around his neck.

"Are you sure?" he whispered, as his arms came around her to hold her tight.

Kathryn pulled back to look him in the eye. "I am; I want to marry you," she said with a bright smile.

"When do you want to tell your parents?" he asked, dropping his arms back to his side.

They still needed to be respectful.

"Tonight, you and Ms. Grace can join us for supper," she answered. "We can tell them together."

"My mother would be thrilled with this news," he said, smiling down at her.

"My parents will be too," she stated, still smiling. "When do you want to discuss wedding plans?" she asked.

He laughed before answering. "Slow down, we have time. I want you to enjoy being engaged today. We will discuss wedding plans tomorrow," he stated, as she nodded. "Do you want me to see you home?"

"No, I'm okay. You need to go back to your mother," she said, looking over her shoulder at the General Store. "I'm sure your mother is finished with her shopping."

"She's probably not, but I will get back to her," he said, looking at the General Store. "I will see you tonight."

"Yes, you will," she said, leaning up to kiss his cheek.

Stepping back, she turned, and starting walking toward her house. This meal should be interesting.

~ ~ ~ ~

Kathryn paced her room, as she waited for Thaddeus and his mother to arrive. Since she was on edge, she stayed in her room, to keep from alarming her parents. They would question why she couldn't stand or sit still. It was better to stay out of their sight until Thaddeus got here with his mother. She wouldn't have to answer questions without him at her side.

She walked over to her desk and sat. Opening the drawer, she pulled out the stack of letters lying there. It was almost a year since she read them. She looked at four years of her life. The crazy thing was it was her life with Benjamin, but what she saw was her life with Thaddeus. Each letter either held happiness or sadness, but each was linked to him. She remembered smiling with him over the happy letters and crying on his shoulder over the sad ones.

Henrietta was right; love didn't always come fast. She wouldn't have known she loved Thaddeus, without talking to Henrietta about the different types of love. Rubbing the ribbon around the letters, she was finally okay with Ben breaking off their engagement. There was a small part of her that hated the fact he'd broken up with her, but she was finally okay with it.

Ben was the love of her girl's heart, but Thaddeus was the love of her woman's heart.

There was a soft knock on her door. She knew it was her mother, so she put the letters back in the drawer. Standing up, she walked over to the door and opened it.

"Thaddeus and Grace are in the parlor," her mother stated, as Kathryn nodded. "Are you ready?"

"Yes," she said, as she stepped out of her room and walked beside her mother to the parlor.

Moments later, they were seated at the table, as their food was being served. Thaddeus was beside her, while his mother sat across from them. Her parents were at the ends of the table. She was nervous about telling her parents she was engaged. She felt the calm strength of Thaddeus, and her nerves eased. He was with her, and she could tell everyone with him at her side.

After the first course, Thaddeus stood. All eyes looked to him, including her own. "I want to thank Gregory and Maybelle for having my mother and myself over for supper," he said, as they nodded. "I do enjoy the meal, but there is a reason we are all here tonight," he stated, as he reached for Kathryn's hand.

"Oh," Grace gasped, when she realized her son was helping Kathryn to stand. "Is this what I think it is?" she asked.

"I hope so," Maybelle whispered.

Thaddeus smiled, as he brought Kathryn's hand to his lips. "I have asked Kathryn to marry me, and she has said yes," he stated, as Maybelle and Grace jumped to their feet.

"I knew it," Grace said, as she rushed around the table to her son's side. Maybelle was at Kathryn's side the same moment.

"You said yes?" Maybelle asked, as Kathryn nodded. "I wondered when he would ask you," she whispered, as she pulled her daughter into her arms for a hug.

"I'm so happy you finally asked her," Grace said, as she hugged her son, before pulling back. She moved around her son to see Kathryn.

Gregory stood up and slowly made his way over to the group. "Congratulations," he said, shaking Thaddeus' hand.

"Thank you, sir," Thaddeus said.

"Welcome to the family," Grace said, hugging Kathryn. "I couldn't ask for a better daughter-in-law. You are perfect for my son."

"Thank you," Kathryn whispered, as Grace released her.

"When is the wedding?" Maybelle asked.

"We haven't decided, but you will be the first to know," Thaddeus answered, as Kathryn nodded.

"I think this calls for some wine," Gregory said, as one of the servants walked out of the room to find the wine. He reentered the room with the wine and began filling the empty glasses one of the maids handed them.

Kathryn reached for Thaddeus' free hand, as they raised their glasses. They toasted their engagement and upcoming marriage. This wasn't the grand toast when she and Ben announced their engagement, but it was okay. She was surrounded by family with Thaddeus at her side. This was a perfect toast.

~ ~ ~ ~

A month after they told their parents, everyone in town knew. Their parents told everyone they saw within the first few days. If there was any question to whether they were happy or not, it was laid to rest.

Most people told her they wondered when Thaddeus would ask her. Apparently, they knew he was in love with her, even when she didn't. It was still shocking to her for someone to come up to her and congratulate her.

Everyone wanted to know when the wedding would be. She wondered why everyone wanted to know, but her mother explained everyone wanted to attend the wedding, since they watched the relationship grow for so many years.

She was happy to finally tell people a wedding date. It would be in a month. The crazy thing was it was almost a year since Ben broke off their engagement. It was funny how things worked out. Last year around this time, she was worried about Ben coming home from the war. This year, she was ready for her wedding to a different man.

Turning the corner, Kathryn was stopped by a woman in a black cloak. It was odd since it was summer and too hot for it. She noticed a boy at the woman's side. He looked to be about thirteen. They were not people from the town, and she wondered where they were from.

"Can I help you?" Kathryn asked. They looked weary, and she wondered when they last ate.

"I am looking for a man by the name of Benjamin Sawyer," the woman stated. "I was told he lived in Bluff City."

"Yeah, he does, or well he did," Kathryn said, as thoughts swirled around in her mind. Was this woman the reason Ben broke up with her? He said it was a battle, but could it be a woman?

"What do you mean, he did?" The woman asked, brushing back her hair. "Did he die?"

"No, at least I don't think he did," Kathryn answered. "He moved away after coming home from the war."

"Oh, do you know where he went?" The woman asked.

Kathryn didn't know why this woman needed to find Benjamin, but she wished she could help. This was obviously important to the woman.

"No, I'm sorry, I don't. How do you know Benjamin?" Kathryn asked, because she had to know. This was the first person who asked about Ben.

"I was a nurse during the Battle of Gettysburg," she stated, as Kathryn's mind whirled at the word Gettysburg.

"You were at Gettysburg?" Kathryn asked. Could this woman possibly know what changed Ben? Was it possible she would finally have her answer on why he changed so drastically?

"Yes I was," the woman confirmed. "I wanted to find him and apologize for what I said to him on the battlefield. I'm afraid I said something in anger."

"I wish I could tell you where he is, but he hasn't contacted his family in several months," Kathryn said. "I'm sure he's not mad at you for your words. He knows it was during a battle."

"My words will still be with him," the woman muttered as Kathryn just stared at her. She didn't know what to say to her statement. "You're Kathryn," The woman said, as Kathryn's eyes widened.

"How did you know?" she asked, not even thinking about denying it. How did this woman know Ben well enough to know her name?

"I was with the Army for a while. Benjamin talked about his fiancée, Kathryn, back home. He said she wrote the best letters, and he couldn't wait to get back home to her," she explained. "I assume you are not married if he is gone."

"No, we're not married," Kathryn confirmed. "He said he was a different man, and he couldn't marry me."

"I am sorry." The woman said sadly. "I know he loved you very much. You were the only woman he discussed. The other guys teased him and asked if you were real, because only angels were as perfect as he described you."

Kathryn smiled at her statement. It was nice to know Ben talked about her with the other soldiers. "Oh, I'm sorry. I didn't even ask your name," Kathryn said.

"I'm Mildred, and this is my son Cole." The woman said as the little boy looked up at her.

There was something strange in the boy's eyes, but she couldn't place it. If he was older, she would say his look said he'd seen death and lived through it. He wasn't older, though.

"It is nice to meet you, and thank you for telling me about Benjamin," Kathryn said, holding out her hand to the woman. "If I hear or see him, I will let him know you are looking for him," she promised.

"I hope to find him soon," Mildred stated, as she took Kathryn's hand and shook it. "You are going to be married soon," she stated.

"Yes, the wedding is in a month," Kathryn said.

She wondered how the woman could possibly know, but shrugged it off. She probably had the look of a woman about to get married.

"I wish you many blessings in your marriage," she said, still shaking Kathryn's hand. "May your family be blessed with sons for generations to carry on the family name."

"Thank you," Kathryn said, as the woman finally released her hand. "If you are still in town, you can come to the wedding."

"No, I'm afraid I won't be here," Mildred stated, as Kathryn nodded. "I know you will have a wonderful life with your future husband."

Kathryn smiled, as she watched Mildred and Cole turn and walk away from her. They didn't stop anywhere else. She wondered how they found out Benjamin lived here. It was really nice of her to stop and apologize for words uttered in the heat of battle.

Shaking her head, she continued down the street, and pushed thoughts of Mildred out of her mind. The woman was a little odd, but if she was a nurse during any battle, odd could be forgiven.

Chapter Ten

After meeting Mildred in town, Kathryn decided to visit with Hannah and her parents at Twin Willows. She should have visited with them before everyone in town knew about her engagement. As soon as the carriage stopped, she climbed out and made her way up to the front door. Knocking, she waited for someone to answer the door. She wasn't sure if Hannah was home, but she prayed she was. Moments later, the door opened to reveal the exact person she wanted to see.

"Kathryn, I didn't expect to see you this close to your wedding," Hannah said, as she motioned for Kathryn to come inside. "I assumed you would be too busy with wedding plans to pay a visit."

"I'm never too busy for a visit. I haven't been by in a while, and I wanted to speak with you," Kathryn stated, as she stepped inside.

"Did you get my note?" Hannah asked as she led Kathryn into the morning room.

"Yes, and thank you. I loved it," Kathryn stated, as both women sat in the wingback chairs.

A few days after her engagement, she received a letter from Hannah. It was the first congratulations note she got. There were more notes and letters now, but Hannah's was the first.

"I wanted to visit and tell you my congratulations in person, but my parents are worried about the Klan. The attacks between here and town have picked up over the past few months. They are mostly at night, but they didn't want to take a chance of an attack during the day," Hannah explained.

"I haven't heard of any attacks lately," Kathryn commented, wondering if she needed someone with her other than her driver.

The papers were not reporting the attacks, which she found odd.

"I haven't either, but one of the men from town stopped by about a month ago and told us to stay close. The road is the only one leading into town. It makes sense for the attacks to be along it."

"It's unbelievable. These attacks are getting out of hand," Kathryn muttered. "Anyway, I wanted to tell you in person about my engagement, but it's been busy."

"We understand, and I know my parents are happy you are getting married. They were worried about my brother turning you into a spinster," Hannah voiced. "They love you as if you were their daughter."

"I love all of you. Are you truly happy with my decision?" Kathryn asked.

Hannah sighed before answering. "I am; I wanted us to be sisters, but with Ben gone, I know it's impossible."

"I wanted us to be sisters, too," Kathryn revealed, with a sad smile.

"Do you love Thaddeus?"

"Yes, I do," Kathryn answered without hesitation. "I didn't realize it, until he knelt in front of me. He asked me to think about my answer. I stressed about it for weeks until Henrietta told me to relax. She is the one who told me my answer would come when he really did ask me," she voiced. "She was right."

"Wow," Hannah gasped. "I really am happy you are marrying him. Thaddeus is a good man. I'm actually shocked he asked you. He knew how much you loved Benjamin."

"Have you heard from Benjamin, lately?" Kathryn asked, thinking about Mildred and her son again.

Would they be able to find Benjamin and apologize? She wasn't sure they would, because he could be anywhere.

"No, and my mother thinks he could be dead," Hannah remarked. "The last telegram came from Colorado. He was mining or fighting Indians. I'm not sure."

"How long ago was it?" Kathryn asked.

She wondered why the Sawyers didn't tell her about the telegram. They thought they were protecting her by not telling her, but she was worried about him. They may not be together anymore, but she wanted him to be safe.

"A few months ago," Hannah answered. "Mother read about the Indian raids, the cave-ins, and the harsh life in the west, which is the reason she thinks he's dead. I don't think he's dead, though. He survived the war, so I know he can survive the west."

"Neither do I. He might be in trouble, but he can take care of himself," Kathryn stated. "I just want him to be happy. Hopefully, he will find someone who can make him happy out there in the wilds of the west."

"Do you think he will?" Hannah asked, wringing her hands.

"Your brother is a great man; he will find someone who can make him figure out everything he saw in the war. When he meets her, I have no doubt, he will marry her as soon as he can," she said, placing her hand on Hannah's. "Who knows, one day you may see him with a wife and several children," she said smiling.

"I hope so," Hannah mumbled. "Did you come for your wedding dress? Did you change your mind about wearing it to marry another man?"

"No, I actually ordered another one," Kathryn explained. "It is blue."

"You ordered a blue dress?" Hannah asked. "I thought you wanted to get married in a white dress the same as Queen Victoria. I remember several comments concerning your preferred color of your wedding dress."

"I did," Kathryn confirmed. "I decided to follow my mother and grandmother's tradition. They wore blue, and I will too. There is something to be said for tradition."

"I agree, and you will look beautiful in blue. How is the wedding plans coming?" Hannah asked, as the teacart was rolled into the room.

Hannah got up and poured their tea, before handing Kathryn a cup.

"They are going good, my mother and Ms. Grace are driving me crazy, though. They want to make sure everything is perfect, and I just want to get married," Kathryn explained with sigh.

"Why are you rushed?" Hannah asked. "Thaddeus isn't leaving anytime soon, so you have time."

"I thought I had time with Ben," Kathryn whispered. "I didn't marry him before the war; it is the one thing I do regret," she revealed. "I won't make the same mistake with Thaddeus. No one knows the future. I don't want to assume I have time, but then don't. We may have 100 years together, or we may only have one, and I'm taking it."

"I understand," Hannah whispered, as she touched Kathryn's hand. "You've learned to take your happiness when it's in front of you."

"It wasn't an easy lesson, but I did learn it," Kathryn confirmed before taking a sip of her tea. "Where are your parents?" she asked remembering she did not see them when she came in. Normally, they would be sitting in the room with them.

"They are out checking the back 40 acres. Daddy wanted to check the crops," Hannah explained. "I'm not sure why my mother is with him, but she is."

"She wanted to spend time with him," Kathryn said with a smile. "How are the crops?"

Hannah finished her tea, before answering. "I don't know. I guess they're good," she said with a shrug. "Oh I forgot; you do not have the head for business," Kathryn remarked, and Hannah nodded. "When you decide to marry, make sure the man does have head for business and crops."

"Don't worry, I will," Hannah promised, as Kathryn laughed. "It will also give my father someone to talk too," she mused.

"I better go before it gets dark. I don't want to encounter anyone on the road," Kathryn said, while standing. "Thank you for the tea and conversation."

"I just wish I could have seen you before now," Hannah said standing. "I've missed our talks."

"I have too. You are coming to my wedding, right?" Kathryn asked, as they left the room and walked to the door.

"We will be there, don't worry," Hannah replied. "I wouldn't miss your wedding day for anything. Plus, I can't wait to see what your wedding dress will look like," she said, as she hugged Kathryn.

"I'm ready to see it too," Kathryn said as she hugged Hannah back. "Bye," she said, as she left the house, and climbed into the waiting carriage.

It wouldn't take her too long to get back to town, which would be well before nightfall and any attacks. Leaning back, she looked out the window and watched, as Twin Willows faded into the distance. The plantation was still beautiful with the trees lining the driveway and the willows covering the graves of two stillborn babies. She never wanted the house to fade or crumble into despair. It could not be allowed to follow in the footsteps of other great houses in the county.

~ ~ ~ ~

"How was your visit with Hannah?" Thaddeus asked, as he helped her out of the carriage the following morning.

"It was wonderful. I have missed seeing her," she answered, as she wrapped her arm around his.

They walked through the park entrance together.

"I'm glad you enjoyed your visit. Is it okay to walk through the park?" he asked, as they started on the longer path.

It was the path she always took with Benjamin.

"Yes, it is perfectly okay. I can't stop going places because it was somewhere Ben took me," she stated, as he nodded. "If I did, then the only place I would be able to go would be your house and the bank."

"Well, it will cut down on your visiting," he remarked, as she laughed. "Have you thought about a best man and maid of honor?"

"I think we shouldn't have any," she stated.

"Why? I thought you wanted Henrietta or Hannah standing next to you," he stated, as they pass a man and woman feeding the ducks.

"I did, but then I realized, I only wanted you standing beside me," she explained. "Besides, who would be your best man? You are not close to anyone but your mother."

"And you."

"Yes, and me," she agreed.

"I'm sure I could talk one of my relatives into being my best man," he commented. "They are coming for the wedding anyway."

"It's fine; we will be each other's best man and maid of honor," she stated, as she paused.

He stopped and turned to face her. "What's wrong?"

"I want a happy memory here," she whispered.

"What?" he asked.

"All the places I've been with Benjamin are cloudy. I can barely walk by some of them, including the park," she admitted. "I want to replace those memories with you."

"Okay," he said, running his hand across her cheek. "How many places are we talking? I don't know if we can visit all of them today, but we can try."

She smiled and sighed. "We don't have to visit all of them today. I just wanted to explain why walking in the park with you is fine."

"Are you sure? I mean we can drive really fast," he stated, as she shook her head. "Okay, so a walk in the park it is."

"Yeah, and it is a beautiful day for it," she remarked, as they continued to walk around the park. It was peaceful here.

~ ~ ~ ~

"Kathryn, you never told me what color your dress would be," Grace said, as she wrapped a ribbon around the stems of flowers. The flowers were the last on the list of items to get done before the wedding, thankfully. The past month passed in a whirlwind of activity. The wedding was tomorrow, and she was happy everything came together with little problems.

"She hasn't even told me," Maybelle stated, as she tied a ribbon around the flowers in her hand. "I'm sure it's white, since Queen Victoria wore a white one when she married Prince Albert several years ago," her mother commented.

She didn't say anything about Kathryn's first dress. Grace knew about the dress, since Kathryn told her about it when she ordered it. She wasn't sure if Grace knew the dress was at Twin Willows or not.

"A white dress? It's different, but it could work. I can see you wearing white," Grace remarked, without looking up from her flowers.

She had a talent of tying bows on the flowers, which Kathryn envied. She couldn't make her fingers work as fast as Grace could.

"I saw the dressmaker this morning, she has my dress finished," Kathryn stated. "It's not white," she informed them, as she waited for her mother's reaction. She wanted it to be a surprise.

"What color is it?" her mother asked looking over at her. "Please tell me it's not red or some other strong color," her mother begged.

She knew her mother wanted everyone to know she was pure, and a red dress would not accomplish her goal.

"It is not red or some other strong color. My wedding dress is blue," she replied looking at her mother. She hoped it eased her mind. She noticed the tears forming in her mother's eyes and knew she was happy. "I thought about it and decided to keep with the traditions of the family. You and Grandmother wore blue on your wedding day; I will too."

"You will look beautiful in blue," her mother whispered, as she wiped the tears away.

"I agree, blue will look so pretty against your skin," Grace stated, as she wiped away her tears. "Your eyes will shine even brighter."

"Thank you," Kathryn said, as she tied the last ribbon.

The flowers were done. They would sit in jars of water over night. She didn't want some dried-out flowers, as she married Thaddeus.

"I can't believe my baby is getting married tomorrow," Maybelle said, as she glanced back at Kathryn.

"I know; I wasn't sure I would see Thaddeus married," Grace commented, as Kathryn thought about Thaddeus' first fiancée, Sarah. "You know, I think this is the first wedding in town since Lee's surrender to Grant."

"You're right," Maybelle stated. "It's no wonder everyone in town is planning on coming. I thought it was odd for so many people to want to attend a wedding."

"Will the church hold everyone?" Kathryn asked, as she placed the flowers in the jars. There was water already in the glass jars.

"Probably not, but if they don't get to see you in the church, they will wait for you outside," Maybelle replied. "You are not to worry about who is coming."

"Your mother is right; you need to only worry about getting married," Grace said, looking at Kathryn.

Kathryn nodded, as she looked around the room. This would be the last night in her house. After the honeymoon, she would move into Thaddeus' house. It was a good thing she admired his house.

Later that night, she looked around her room. She was a little sad to leave the house, but her desk, trunk, and clothes would be moved into Thaddeus' house. She wouldn't need her bed. With some of her things at his house, it would make it easier. Sitting on her bed, she blew out the candle and lay down. Tomorrow was her wedding day, and she couldn't wait to get married.

~ ~ ~ ~

Kathryn closed her eyes as she waited to walk down the aisle. This was the first moment she had to herself. As soon as she woke, the rushing began. The dressmaker dropped off her dress and helped her into it. Her mother weaved flowers into her hair before giving her a lace handkerchief to carry down the aisle.

"This was your grandmother's," she said, as Kathryn smiled. Maybelle then pinned the veil into her hair. "This is from my wedding."

"Your veil?" Kathryn asked, looking up at her mother. "Are you sure?"

"It has been my dream for you to wear my veil," she stated, as she eased the front piece over Kathryn's head to cover her face.

Kathryn stood up, before flipping the veil back. "I can't see with it in front of my eyes," she explained. She was happy her father would be leading her down the aisle, since the veil made it hard to see. "I'll make sure to put it back in place," she promised.

"You look beautiful," Maybelle said, as she hugged her daughter. "You make a beautiful bride."

"Thank you," Kathryn said, as she took a deep breath. "Are the flowers okay?"

"Yes, and they are in place in the church," Maybelle replied. "Your bouquet is with your father."

"Is it time?"

"Are you ready?" Maybelle asked, as Kathryn nodded. "Then let's go," she said, as she walked her daughter out of the house and into the waiting carriage.

Her father was beside the carriage and helped her inside.

"You look beautiful, Kathryn," Gregory stated, looking at his daughter.

Kathryn smiled but didn't say anything. She was nervous, but she knew she could do this. Everyone got married, there shouldn't be any nerves. She was marrying the man she loved.

The carriage stopped in front of the church. People were crowded around the door, which meant the church was crowded. Her parents exited the carriage and helped her out. Maybelle kissed Kathryn's cheek before leaving them to take her seat inside.

"Many blessings on your marriage," several people called out, as Kathryn smiled at them.

She walked up to the door with her father beside her. As she neared the door, she flipped her veil back over her face and took her father's arm.

"I'm ready," she whispered.

"Close your eyes, and take a moment," Gregory whispered, as Kathryn nodded and closed her eyes.

She could see Thaddeus standing at the altar waiting for her. He was beckoning her forward. Opening her eyes, she softly laughed.

"I am ready," she said, stronger this time.

The church doors opened, as her father led her down the aisle. Her eyes immediately found Thaddeus and didn't move. She didn't know who was in the church besides the preacher and Thaddeus. If anyone was speaking, she didn't hear it. Everything in her was focused on the man waiting for her at the end of the aisle.

They reached the front of the church, and her father handed her over to the Thaddeus. He gripped her right hand, as they faced each other. The preacher began to speak, as Kathryn took a deep breath.

Thaddeus was smiling which eased her nerves completely. Everything was a blur, as she repeated her vows and listened as Thaddeus repeated his. It was over before she knew it. Thaddeus raised her veil and kissed her softly on the lips, before easing her arm around his. Everyone was clapping, as they walked back down the aisle and out of the church. She was still unclear on who was there but it didn't matter. She was married to Thaddeus now.

~ ~ ~ ~

"The blue looks great," Hannah stated, as she walked over to Kathryn. "I'm surprised you went with the smaller hoop for your wedding."

Kathryn smiled. "I discussed it with the dressmaker, and she said the large hoops are out of style. She recommended a bustle, but I couldn't do without a hoop," she explained.

"Oh no, I know I would have worn a hoop," Hannah stated. "I don't think I like the idea of going without one."

Kathryn laughed, as she hugged Hannah. "Don't worry; I don't think the style will last long."

"I hope not."

"You hope not, what?" Henrietta asked, walking over toward them.

"She hopes the new style of dress will not last," Kathryn replied. "It's something called a bustle."

"Really?" She asked as Kathryn nodded. "I'm with Hannah, I need my hoop," she said patting her skirt.

"Your son likes it too," Hannah said, as Robert peeked around her skirt at Kathryn.

"Kat!" he said, as he came around Henrietta to get to Kathryn.

"He loves you more than me now," Henrietta muttered, as Kathryn smiled and bent down to the little boy. "I think I need to stop letting you bring him toys."

"You think the toys are bribing him?" Hannah asked.

"Oh yes, she brings the good toys, according to him," Henrietta stated, glancing down at her son and Kathryn.

"Of course I bring the good toys. It's my job to spoil him," Kathryn stated, as she picked him up. "How are you, Robert?"

"Good," he said throwing his little arms around her neck. "You look pwetty."

"Thank you," she said hugging him. "You look so handsome, in your little suit."

"I'm just glad it fit," Henrietta muttered. "He will need a new one for Christmas."

"Oh, he will look so precious," Hannah gushed as Kathryn nodded.

"He does for a few minutes, and then he tries to take it off," Henrietta informed them. "Is Thaddeus taking you on a honeymoon?"

"Yeah, but he will not tell me where," Kathryn replied. "All I know is we will be visiting some of his family."

"It should be fun, then," Hannah said, as Henrietta nodded.

"I hope so," Kathryn said as she set Robert down and hugged Henrietta and Hannah.

She needed to make the rounds, and thank everyone for sharing her special day. Once she thanked everyone, she and Thaddeus slipped away. They would leave in the morning for their honeymoon.

~ ~ ~ ~

Three Months Later

"Kathryn, are okay?" Thaddeus asked, as she leaned against the wall.

Her eyes were closed, while trying to take deep breaths. Apparently, she stood too fast, because her head felt odd.

"Fine, I was just a little dizzy," she replied, as she opened her eyes to look at her husband.

They only got back to Bluff City the week before from their honeymoon. He took her to see his family in Atlanta. The trip was great, but also sad. Atlanta still showed the effects of war, and the people were weary.

The city was gaining its feet, though, as the rest of the South. People were rebuilding the businesses and homes. Union soldiers still roamed the streets, but it didn't worry the people. They went about their business as if the soldiers were not there.

"Kathryn, are you sure?" Thaddeus asked, gripping her shoulders. "You haven't felt right since we got back home," he pointed out.

She knew he was worried about her, but she wasn't sick, or at least she didn't think so.

"I'm sure, actually I feel better now," she stated with smile. "Don't worry; I think I'm still adjusting to living in your house and being back from our honeymoon."

"Our house," he corrected, as she smiled.

"Our house," she said, as he nodded and backed up to give her some space. "I am paying Henrietta and Robert a visit, do you want to come?" she asked.

"No, I need to get to the bank and make sure everything is in order," he said, as she nodded. "Tell Henrietta and Robert, I said hi."

"I will, and have a great day at work," she said.

"See you tonight," he whispered, as he kissed her before leaving their room.

She sighed, as she left the room. She couldn't wait to see Henrietta and Robert today. There was a lot to tell, and she wanted to give Robert his birthday present.

~ ~ ~ ~

"I've missed you," Henrietta exclaimed, as soon as Kathryn exited the carriage.

Kathryn laughed, as she hugged Henrietta. "I've missed you too," she said

"Kat!" Robert yelled, as he ran down the steps and launched into her arms.

"I've missed you too, little man," Kathryn said, as she hugged him close. "You've gotten so big while I was gone."

"I'm four," he said, as she set him on his feet, and handed him his toy. It was a stuffed animal she found in Atlanta. "Thank you," he said, looking up at her.

"Yes, you are four, and you're welcome," she agreed, as they made their way into the house. "I can't believe I've been gone for three months."

"Did you enjoy your honeymoon?" Henrietta asked, as they walked into the parlor and sat down. "How was Atlanta?"

"The honeymoon was great, and Atlanta was burned," Kathryn answered. "It will be years before the city is back on its feet. I'm not sure if it will ever be what it once was, but it is recovering."

"You know, even though I married Robert before he left for war, I still wanted a honeymoon," Henrietta revealed. "We discussed going on one when the war was over."

"Where did he want to take you?" Kathryn asked.

"He didn't know; he told me to be thinking about where I wanted to go," she replied. "I thought about somewhere along the coast."

"Our lives are not what we thought they would be," Kathryn remarked.

"No, they are not; they're better," Henrietta commented.

"I agree," Kathryn stated. "It's just weird because we both had different plans."

"Yes, we did. I never thought I would be raising my son without his father."

Kathryn nodded, looking over at Robert playing on the floor. "You've done a wonderful job. Robert is a well-rounded little boy."

"Thank you. I have his Aunt Kathryn to thank for some of the well-roundedness," Henrietta stated, as Kathryn looked back at her.

"Thank you," Kathryn said. "When did you know you were pregnant with him?" she asked. "I remembered you were pregnant when Robert died, but when did you know?"

"If I remember correctly, I found out a few days before the Battle of Shiloh," Henrietta replied. "Do you think you might be with child?" she asked, looking excited.

"I don't know. I haven't felt myself since coming back home."

"It could be all the traveling or the disruption in your life," Henrietta voiced. "You did just get married, a big change for you."

"True, but my health is worrying Thaddeus."

"Of course it is; he lost his father to an illness along with the girl he was engaged to."

"Sarah," Kathryn supplied, as Henrietta nodded.

"Sarah, right. Anyway, he doesn't have a good track record with diseases."

"I guess not," Kathryn muttered. "Do you think I should go to the doctor?"

"If it worries you, then yeah, go to the doctor. He will be able to tell you if you're pregnant or not. He will also tell you if you caught anything while on your honeymoon," she pointed out.

"Guess I'll see him tomorrow. I really hope I didn't catch anything," Kathryn stated. "Thaddeus will have me in bed all day until I'm better."

"How do you know?"

"When his mother was sick, you know when I was in quarantine with them, he was always telling her to go to bed. The doctor told Thaddeus, Grace needed to get up and move around, so it didn't settle in her lungs," Kathryn explained. "I think she begged the doctor to tell Thaddeus."

"I bet she did, too. Ms. Grace is not one to take orders."

"No, she's not," Kathryn agreed.

They talked for a while, before Kathryn got up. She needed to get back home to Thaddeus. On the ride home, she placed her hand on her lower abdomen. Was she with child? She knew she would see the doctor first thing in the morning because she needed to know. It would also ease her mind.

~ ~ ~ ~

"What exactly is ailing you, Kathryn?" The doctor asked as Kathryn sat on his exam table.

She was nervous, but she needed to know if she was pregnant or not.

"Since coming home, I've been dizzy, short of breath, and sleeping longer," she explained. "I thought I might be with child," she whispered.

"With those symptoms, you might be, but I will do an exam to check. You could just be adjusting to married life," he said, as she nodded. "Lie back."

She did as he asked, and closed her eyes. Thankfully, the exam was over quickly, as he helped her up.

"I will be the first to offer you my congratulations," he said with a smile. "You are expecting your first child."

"I am?" she whispered, as he nodded.

"Is this good news?" he asked, as she nodded. "You are in the early stages, but I can safely say you are pregnant. You will need to take it easy, get plenty of rest, and eat. The baby will take a lot out of you."

"Am I okay though?" she asked a little worried.

"You are perfectly fine and very healthy," he stated. "I will not tell anyone. I will leave it up to you to tell everyone your news. You might want to tell Thaddeus first."

"It's close to Christmas; do you think I can wait until then?" she asked.

"I don't think it will be a problem. You will not actually start showing until later," he explained, as she nodded.

"Thank you," she said simply, as he nodded. "This will be a great Christmas in the Morgan household."

"I'm sure it will be," he said. "Now I want you to come back and see me if you have any questions or concerns. Once you get closer to confinement, I will check on you."

"Okay," she said, as she gathered her wrap and left the exam room. She paid for her visit before leaving the office.

It didn't take her long to get home, but it could have been because she was excited. She couldn't wait to share her news with Thaddeus. All she needed to do was keep her secret until Christmas morning. It was only a few weeks away, and she knew she could keep the secret, as long as she didn't get sick between now and then. If she got sick, especially in front of Thaddeus, she would have to tell him. He would demand to know what's wrong with her, or rush her to the doctor.

~ ~ ~ ~

Over the next few weeks, Kathryn didn't get sick, at least not in front of Thaddeus. She also managed to hide her news from Grace. It was hard, but she was determined to reveal her news to

Thaddeus on Christmas morning. Everything was planned out, and the only thing left was for it to be Christmas morning.

"Do you want to exchange gifts early?" Thaddeus asked, as he led her upstairs to their room.

"If you would have asked me last week, I would have said yes." She remarked. "Since Christmas is tomorrow morning, I think I can wait a few more hours."

"Are you sure?" he asked. "We can exchange gifts tonight, and sleep in tomorrow morning."

Kathryn smiled, as he closed their bedroom door. "Your mother warned me about you always wanting your gifts early," she stated. "You can wait. I promise you are going to love your gift."

"Well, I really want to give you yours," he said, walking over to her. "I don't care what you got me."

"I can wait too," she said, as she turned around to let him unfasten her bodice. "Trust me; tomorrow morning will be special for both of us."

"Do you know what I got you? Is it the reason why you can wait?" He asked, as she glanced over her shoulder at him.

"No, and I didn't ask your mother what you got me, unlike somebody else," she commented. "She told me you have asked her every day this week."

"Well, I couldn't find it in here," he revealed.

"Thaddeus! You were looking for your present?" She asked, as he nodded. "You are worse than Robert. Henrietta said he tries to find out what she got him, but he doesn't hunt for them."

"I make no excuses; I just wanted to know," he commented, as she shook her head at him.

"You know I could make you suffer and not give you your gift until tomorrow night," she warned.

"Mrs. Morgan, you are a cruel woman," he said, as she laughed.

She quickly changed into her gown, before getting into bed. She hoped he was still happy in the morning when she revealed her secret.

~ ~ ~ ~

Kathryn woke up slowly, as the sunlight filter through the window. Slipping out of bed, she grabbed her house coat, and made her way downstairs. She grabbed the bow she stashed under the tree and tied it around her waist. Once she was finished, she sat in front of the tree. Moments later, she heard someone coming downstairs. She knew it was Thaddeus because Grace didn't walk heavy.

"Merry Christmas," she said, as soon as he appeared in the room.

"You're up early," he noted, as he walked over to her. "Why are you sitting in front of the tree?" he asked.

"Well, it has to do with your present." she answered. "Do you want to open yours?"

"No, I want you to open yours first," he said, as he reached behind the tree for her present. Once he pulled it out, he knelt down in front of her. "Open it," he requested, as he opened his hand to reveal a small wrapped present.

She took it from him and slowly un-wrapped the brown paper to reveal a small box. She opened the box and gasped. "Thaddeus?" she asked looking up at him.

"Try it on," he whispered, as he lifted her left hand, and removed the ring from the box. "I didn't have a chance to order an engagement ring before I asked you," he said, slipping the ring on her finger next to her wedding band. "I still wanted to get you one to accompany your wedding band," he explained, as she smiled.

"I love it," she whispered, as she looked down at the ring.

It was so pretty. She was a little worried now because she didn't get him anything this grand. She just had the news of their child as his Christmas gift.

"I was worried you wouldn't like it," he admitted.

"No worries there," she said, kissing him. "Now your present isn't something you can wear," she said.

"It's fine," he voiced. She bit her lip, as she took his hand and placed it on the ribbon around her waist. "Dear, I love you, but are you giving me your body?" he asked.

She laughed. "No," she replied. "Your present will not arrive until next summer."

"What did you order?" he asked, still not understanding. "Nothing takes that long to come in."

"Well, I didn't order it," she voiced.

"Okay, I don't understand," he admitted.

"Our family is growing," she said. "Next summer, we will have a little Morgan keeping us up late at night."

"You're pregnant?" he asked, as she nodded. "We are going to have a baby?"

"Yes, we are going to have a baby."

"When did you find out?" he asked as he rubbed her belly under the bow.

"A few weeks ago, I was nervous about getting dizzy," she explained. "I saw the doctor, and he told me."

"Have you told our parents?" he asked.

"No, I wanted you to be the first one to know," she answered. "I knew it would be the perfect Christmas gift. I know we just got married, and this may be soon, but are you happy with my news?" she asked.

"Kathryn, I love you, and starting a family with you is all I want," he declared. "It is not too soon for me."

"I love you too," she whispered, as he paused. "What's wrong?" she asked, noticing how still he was.

"Say it again," he whispered.

"What?" she asked.

"Tell me you love me."

"I love you," she stated, as he cupped her cheeks.

"You know this is the first time you've told me," he said. "I never thought I would hear you say those words to me. I know you loved Benjamin, but he hurt you by leaving."

"Thaddeus, I love you," she said again. "I talked to Henrietta and discovered there are different types of love. I should have told before now. I love you."

"You know this baby will be spoiled," he stated, as she laughed.

"Oh yeah, since we are only children," she muttered. "We will have to have more children quickly."

"We haven't even delivered this one yet, and you already want more," he remarked, as she nodded. "You know this baby may kill us both."

"Don't talk about my baby," she said smiling. "We will survive this child and every other child after."

"Yes we will," he agreed, as his mother came downstairs.

"Have you two already opened your presents?" she asked, as Thaddeus helped Kathryn stand.

"We have," Kathryn replied.

"Please tell me he didn't persuade you to open gifts last night," Grace said, as she sat.

"No, he did not," Kathryn said. "He tried, but I made him wait."

"I knew I loved you," Grace stated with a smile. "So what did you get each other?" she asked.

"He got me an engagement ring," Kathryn answered, as she held out her hand for Grace to see the ring.

"My son bought the ring? He does have good taste."

"Of course I do, Mother," Thaddeus remarked. "Anyway, Kathryn topped my gift."

"What did she get you?" Grace asked.

"He doesn't get it until next summer," Kathryn voiced.

"What?" Grace asked, as she noticed the bow still around Kathryn's waist. "Are you with child?"

"Yes, she is. We are going to have a baby," Thaddeus stated, as Grace jumped up and rushed over to them.

"This is the best Christmas present. You know you will never top her gift," Grace said, looking up at her son.

"I know, but I'm going to try," he stated, as he hugged his mother. He released her moments later.

"Congratulations, my dear," Grace said, as she hugged Kathryn. "If you need anything, let me know."

"I will," she promised.

At lunch, she shared the news with her parents who were over the moon. Her mother and Grace immediately went into grandmother mode. This next year should be pretty fun with everyone watching over her.

Epilogue

June 1867

"You know your confinement is almost over," Thaddeus remarked, as he handed her their son.

He was walking their son around the room to settle the baby. Their son loved to be walked around.

"Oh yeah, I know. I can't wait to step out of this house," she stated, as she cuddled their son close.

He was such a good baby. She couldn't believe how much she loved her son. Henrietta was right; a mother's love was something different. It was stronger and all consuming. She loved Thaddeus for bringing this love into her life.

Pregnancy was easy for her, and she had a relatively easy delivery. The hardest part for her was the confinement. She hated to be confined to the house, but she experienced some problems near the end of her pregnancy. The doctor ordered her on confinement and as much bed rest as she could get.

She was not happy when he ordered the confinement, but she knew it was best for the baby.

Thankfully, her friends visited her several times, to keep her from going crazy. Henrietta and Robert were at her house almost every week, and sometimes more than once in the same week. Henrietta told Kathryn she could never repay her for all her kindness, so a visit was the least she could do.

Hannah and Lydia also popped in to see her several times. Of course, her mother was at the house almost every day to check on her and to visit with Grace. Thaddeus joked once; their house had more visitors than the bank some days. She smiled and nodded.

"Are you okay?" he asked, sitting beside her.

She knew she worried him those last weeks before giving birth. If she could have spared him from seeing her weak, she would have. Thaddeus barely slept because of his worry for her.

"I'm fine, just ready to go visit someone at their house," she explained, leaning into his side. "You know I never knew I could love someone as much as I love our son."

"What about me?" he teased, wrapping an arm around her shoulders.

"Oh I love you, too," she said. "Are you sure about the name?" she asked, looking at their son.

They decided on a name a few days after he was born, but they would reveal his name tomorrow at the christening. She wanted to make sure he was still okay with it, before it was revealed.

"I am. Are you?" he asked in a whispered voice, when he noticed their son was asleep.

"Yeah, I think it fits him perfectly," she whispered. "I can't believe he's going to be a month old tomorrow. It doesn't seem real sometimes."

"I know; it doesn't seem real to me either," he admitted. "You realize, we haven't been married a year, yet?" he asked.

"We work fast, apparently," she laughed softly. The baby didn't stir at the noise. "So are you ready for another one, yet?"

Thaddeus laughed and shook his head. "Let's give him some time. I've heard they are really good when they are this small, but when they get older, is when we have to worry."

"Well, as long as he is like Robert, we will be fine," she commented, picturing Henrietta's little boy.

"How is Henrietta?" he asked.

"She is good," she replied. "I never thought she would move into town, but I'm glad she is close. I want our sons to be close to each other."

Henrietta was the new schoolteacher, so she moved into town to be closer to her students. She confided to Kathryn that it was weird she was once married and never left her parents' house.

He nodded, as he looked down at their son. "His name does fit him," he commented. "Are you ready for bed?"

"Yes, since he is asleep, we better go to bed. He will be up in a few hours for a feeding," she said, as he stood and helped her to stand with the baby in her arms.

Once they were in their room, she placed the baby in the crib before getting into bed. She needed to get her rest for tomorrow.

~ ~ ~ ~

Kathryn held her son, as she stepped into the church with Thaddeus at her side. Today their son would be christened in a christening gown, worn by all the men in the Morgan family. She handed her son over to the preacher and watched as he sprinkled water over her baby's head and blessed him.

"Your son's name?" The preacher asked looking at Kathryn and Thaddeus.

They were standing side-by-side holding hands.

"Aaron Daniel," Kathryn stated proudly.

"I present Aaron Daniel." The preacher said, as he handed the boy back to Kathryn. "May you answer God's charge on you to take care of your son."

Kathryn smiled, as she nodded. Thaddeus placed his hand on her shoulder as they left the church. Their family and friends were waiting for them outside the church.

"Aaron Daniel, I love it," Maybelle said, as she reached for her grandson. "It's a good strong name," she said looking down at the baby in her arms.

"It is a name he can grow into," Grace remarked with a smile.

"Yes it is," Kathryn agreed.

They made their way to the house to celebrate Aaron's christening and name reveal. Their parents along with friends joined them for the noon meal.

After everyone left, she sat down at her writing desk. Aaron was in his crib beside her as Thaddeus slept peacefully.

Reaching for her pen, she remembered she hadn't written a letter in a while. This letter would not be a normal one for her, because it would not be mailed. It wouldn't leave her possession for a long time. She got the idea from her grandmother. Before her mother left earlier, she handed her a letter addressed to her. It was from her grandmother. Her mother was instructed to give it to her once she christened her first child.

The letter was full of advice for raising children and making your husband happy. It was something special from a woman she never met. She decided to do the same thing. She would write a letter to her first granddaughter. When she grabbed her pen to mend it, she saw Benjamin's ring and remembered the bag she packed. No one ever knew she packed a small bag in case Benjamin asked her to go away with him.

Since he asked her to keep the ring, she thought about passing it down. It wasn't proper to pass it to a son, since the ring was from another man, but she could pass it to a granddaughter. The ring needed to be out of her drawer, so it was perfect to give it to a granddaughter not even born yet. The letter would explain the ring, Ben's letters from the war, her small packed bag, and her love for Thaddeus, she hoped.

Dear Granddaughter,

I hope that this letter finds you well. Since you have found this note, you probably guessed there is something special about this ring that made me hide it. Well, there is.

This ring came from a very special man, my first fiancé. I have placed it in here so my husband does not find it. He thought I had already given this back, but my first fiancé did not want it back. He told me to keep it to pass down my line.

Since this ring is so special, I knew I wanted it to go to a very special woman. Please take care of this ring and know the man that gave it to me loved me as much as I loved him. I do wish he would have asked me to leave with him after the war. I had this bag packed and ready for his question, but he never asked. Instead he just left.

I pray you find a man like him. He gave everything up just to make me happy. The war changed him in ways I will never know, but if he would have just asked me to run away with him, I would have.

So if a man asks you to run away to be with him, go. You will not regret it, as long as you truly love each other.

Do not think I do not love your grandfather. He is a great man and a great father to our children. I cannot believe how lucky I was to be loved by two great men.

Love,
A woman who wished for something more but got everything she needed

Once she finished the letter, she noticed she wrote children at the end. She didn't go back and change it, because she knew they would have more children. Folding the letter, she grabbed the ring and placed them in the hidden compartment of the bag she packed to go away with Benjamin. She would hand the case to her granddaughter, when the time came.

"Is everything okay?" Thaddeus asked, as she blew out the candle.

"Yes, go back to sleep," She whispered, as she climbed into bed, and fell asleep.

~ ~ ~ ~

Sixty Years Later
June 1927

Men. She was surrounded by men. "You know I believe this family is cursed to only have boys," she muttered, as she looked around the room.

Apparently, when you married a Morgan, you were destined to only have boys. Three generations of children and not one baby girl in the lot.

"You raised three of the men here," Thaddeus pointed out as he kissed her cheek.

"I know we had three boys. Why couldn't we have been blessed with one girl?" she asked. "I'm outnumbered with all these men."

"You have three beautiful daughters-in-law, along with seven beautiful granddaughters-in-law, and twelve great granddaughters-in-law."

"Yes, they are beautiful, but they are not of my blood," she muttered. "Every baby born into this family is male."

"I guess we know male is dominant in this family," Thaddeus remarked. "Don't worry, dear. You will have a beautiful granddaughter one day. No family can have only boys."

"You promise?" she asked, looking at her husband.

"I promise you, this family will have a girl. When she is born, there will be a huge celebration in Bluff City; everyone will know there is finally a Baby Girl Morgan," he said.

She smiled and looked back at her family. There were many changes over the years with more than her family. She thought back to those dark days after the Civil War ended. It took many years for the Southern States to be readmitted to the Union with full voting rights.

Georgia was readmitted to the Union on June 25, 1868, but returned to military control, when they kicked the recently freed blacks out of the legislature. It was finally readmitted to the Union on July 15, 1870, for good.

The Ku Klux Klan ran rampart for a few years until Nathan Bedford Forrest disbanded it in 1869. It outreached its original propose. The members still took justice into their own hands; it was without the backing of the social club.

The Nation also grew in size, when Alaska was purchased from Russia. It wasn't the wisest decision, which was why it was called Seward's Folly to this day. She couldn't believe the amount of money spent on a piece of frozen land.

The West was settled after the Indian Wars were over. The Indians fought bravely for as long as they could. They even killed Custer at the Battle of Little Bighorn. She wasn't happy he died, since death isn't something to be happy about, but she couldn't say she missed him either. Custer wasn't liked, because of his treatment of the Indians. The remaining tribes were finally granted U.S. citizenship in 1924. It was very late in her opinion, but at least they were now considered citizens of their own land.

Four years before the Indians became citizens, women got the right to vote. The 19th Amendment was passed in 1920. It was something the women and some men fought for since the 1840s. Some of the women included Elizabeth Cady Stanton, Susan B. Anthony, Amelia Bloomer, and Elizabeth Blackwell, the first female doctor. They worked hard for many years, before they walked up to the polls and cast their first vote.

The last 60 years were not peaceful for America. Besides the battles with the Indians in the West, soldiers fought in Cuba, the Philippines, Mexico, and Europe during the First World War. World War I scared her more than the Civil War did. It was on a grander scale than the Civil War ever was. Instead of one country fighting another or itself, it was several countries fighting several countries. She was happy when the war ended.

Sighing, she moved outside to the back yard. Everything was different than she thought it would be. She never thought she would live in a house in town. The house she dreamed about when she was younger was Twin Willows, on the outskirts of town. This was her dream now.

She turned to look in the direction of Twin Willows. The house was empty now. Hannah moved away when her mother and father died. She married some man and moved out west. It was sad the big house sat empty. It needed a family. Thinking about Twin Willows always made her think about the man of the house. The house needed him to liven up those empty spaces. She wondered if Benjamin ever married and found what he was missing.

She felt someone looking at her, but she knew it wasn't a stranger. She felt those eyes before on her. Turning slightly, she saw a man standing next to a tree beyond the back yard. "Ben," she whispered.

It couldn't be, though. The man standing there could be no older than 25. Ben was older than she was. He would not be 25, but the man did look like Benjamin. It could be one of his children or grandchildren. If it was, he was the spitting image of Benjamin. Something in her, told her it was Ben. It couldn't be possible, unless her eyes were playing tricks on her and it wasn't really him.

"Grandmother, how can we have your birthday party if you are outside?" Nathan, her oldest grandson, asked.

She smiled and looked at him. "Lead the way," she said as he nodded and offered her his arm.

He led her back inside to Thaddeus' side. She pushed all thoughts of the man outside out of her mind. It was only her mind conjuring up Ben's image with thoughts of Twin Willows.

"Happy Birthday, Kathryn," he whispered. "I love you."

"I love you," she stated. Her life may be different than she planned, but she wouldn't change anything. "Thank you for asking me to marry you all those years ago," she stated.

"I'm happy you said yes," he commented as they sat with their family to celebrate.

Unknown to her, the man was real. He wanted to check on her to make sure she lived her life after he left all those years ago. Seeing her family gathered around her, wishing her a happy birthday eased his mind. He was right in leaving her; she would not have the family she did now. The man looked one last time before turning and walking away from the love of his life. He would not be back; she was happy.

~ ~ ~ ~

1989

"Congratulations Mr. Morgan, you have a beautiful daughter," the nurse said handing the baby to him.

"A girl?" he asked looking at the baby in his arms. Shock registered on his face, as he tried to form a thought.

He had a girl.

"Yes sir, a baby girl," the nurse replied with a smile.

"But the doctor said it would be a boy, according to the ultrasound," he murmured, as he ran a fingertip across his daughter's cheek.

"Ultrasounds are not 100% accurate," the nurse explained.

She understood the man's shock now. This was not an unusual occurrence with ultrasounds.

"This is the first girl in my family in generations," he remarked. "There hasn't been a girl since before the Civil War," he informed her.

"Not one in over 100 years?" She asked in shock.

"No," he answered, looking at her. "She is the first."

"Well, congratulations, you have some bragging rights now," she stated. "What are you going to name your daughter?" She asked since she knew they didn't have a girl's name picked out.

"Alexandria," his wife whispered.

"Why Alexandria?" the nurse asked; she knew this name meant something to the family, since his wife mentioned it quickly.

"It is after my so many greats-grandmother. She chose to marry a man who wasn't her first choice and begin a legacy," Mr. Morgan stated. "Her name was Kathryn Alexander, so my daughter will be Alexandria Kathryn Morgan."

"A strong name for a girl," the nurse commented.

"It is her legacy. I know she is destined for great things," he said smiling at his daughter.

She was destined for great things because she was a Morgan.

ACKNOWLEDGEMENTS

I want to start by thanking my parents and my sister, April. You never demanded anything, but to be myself.

Big thanks to my friends and family for supporting me through this process. Thank you for being my cheerleaders, and for spreading my work around. If it wasn't for you, then only a select few would even know my work. You were there through each chapter, and demanded me to write faster.

I have to give a special thanks to Jodi Springer. She was the first to read Cursed Soldier, and demand Kathryn's story. I know she has been looking forward to this story since I sent her Cursed Soldier. Also many thanks on the helping with the summary.

Many, many thanks to my wonderful beta readers Lisa Mae Egan and Claire Baran. You two seen my raw work, and gave me feedback on what worked and what didn't. I couldn't wait for you to read this book.

Thank you to Catherine DePasquale for taking me on at the last minute for editing. I know my story was riddled with flaws, and thankfully, you shaped it into the story I envisioned. I was worried about what you would say with each edit, but you made the process easy and painless.

Thank you to Christina (French) Malone for your beautiful cover work. I loved the cover you created for Cursed Soldier. You put up with my crazy ideas, and turn them into art. This wasn't I pictured when we sat down to run through ideas; its better. This cover is amazing and better than I could have ever imagined.

Thank you to my Aunt Kitty for letting me use her pictures for the early teasers. Also big thanks to her and Keith for showing me around Gettysburg, giving me a behind the scenes tour of the homes, and for giving me the opportunity to hold an Enfield rifle used during the Civil War.

Thank you to my Aunt Beverly and Jerry for taking me to Gettysburg, and allowing me to see the place that inspired me. It was an awesome birthday gift and one I will never forget.

Thank you to the book bloggers who took a chance on a new author, and shared my page, status updates, and links to my book. A special thanks to First Class Books for being my first reviewer of

Cursed Soldier. You don't know how happy I was when I saw your review on Amazon and Goodreads.

Thank you to my Clean Romances group on Goodreads for providing me an outlet for my books. You reassured me that there are people still willing to read clean romances.

Special thanks to Sara Beth Carsen for helping me with the ending scene. I wasn't sure if it would make sense, but you told me to go with it. I'm glad I did.

The biggest thanks of all goes to my readers! It is because of you that I wrote Kathryn's story. I hoped you enjoyed getting to read her story, and seeing how she overcame losing Benjamin.

Do you want to know what happened to Benjamin? Check out his and Alexandria's story in <u>Cursed Soldier</u>. Turn the page for Chapter 1.

Cursed Soldier

July 3, 1863

Ben peeked over the ridge as he prepared his rifle. The Whitworth rifle was far superior to his Enfield musket, he used back at home. The Yankees were closing in, and he knew that the battle was all but lost. He would continue to fight until there wasn't breath left in his body. He would fight for the cause, no matter the outcome.

Flipping back, he took aim and fired again. The cannons were firing away at the Yankee line, but it didn't seem to make any difference. They would still be there firing back at them. He loaded once again and took aim before firing away.

Out of the corner of his eye, he watched as the little drummer boy marched on. He was playing Dixie, like he had since he had taken up the drum two days ago, at the start of the battle. Benjamin looked over at him, and saw that a solider was making his way towards the boy. He could call out a warning, but that would reveal his position, which would put his General in jeopardy. His only job was to protect his General with his life, if it was necessary, even if he was upset over the fact that he was about to watch that little boy die.

He watched as the solider pulled out his knife and killed the boy, without hesitation. The only good thing was the boy had died instantly, and hadn't suffered like so many soldiers before him. Ben couldn't look away from the massacre, nor could he save the boy. Reloading quickly, he took aim and killed the Yankee before reloading again. It was the only way that he could get revenge for the boy.

In that moment though, he heard a woman's scream pierce the air. Women were only allowed as nurses, so they only saw the worst of the battles, the aftermath. Normally, they did not scream as they encountered the gruesome sites so he knew that something was wrong. Looking behind him, he saw that his General was still there, it wasn't his death that had the woman terrified.

"Benjamin, go see to that woman. We cannot have her running around the battlefield." The General called out as Ben nodded and moved from his perch. He ran to the woman, dodging cannon fire the entire way, praying he could calm this woman before going back to protect the General. He needed to get her off the battlefield, before she was killed as well.

"Woman, cease this screaming." Ben stated as he grabbed the woman's shoulders, and began to shake her trying to get her attention. She had a crazy look in her eyes that was a little frightening, but he couldn't focus on that, he had to get her to listen.

"My son!" She screamed, "My son has been killed," She said as he sighed. He hated when mothers of soldiers joined as nurses, because they knew instantly when and how their sons died. They always caused trouble, as well. Did they not know that this was war, and that there was a good chance that their son would be killed?

"I am sorry but you cannot be here." Ben stated in a firm voice. "It is not safe for you."

"But it was safe enough for my ten year old son!" She screamed as she looked down at the boy lying at her feet.

Ben looked down and recognized that it was the little drummer boy. He hadn't taken noticed that she had been rushing to him. "I am sorry." He said because there was nothing else to say. What could you say to the mother of a dead boy? "I did kill the man that did it." He stated hoping that would help her cope with her son's death a little easier.

"You!" She screamed pulling out of his grip on her shoulders. "You could have saved him, but you chose to keep your position quiet." She yelled as he nodded. It was his job, and he had done it. He couldn't feel regret over that. "You let a little boy die!" She shouted, poking him in the chest with her finger.

"Surely, you understood that your son would die when he took up the drum. This is war." He calmly said in a cold voice. The reason that her son was selected, in the first place, was the other boy had been killed. It was a fact; death was a part of war.

"I think that you think your life is better than my son's." She said pointing at him before reaching into her brown cloak tied around her neck. "If you treasure your life that much, then life you shall have, forever." She yelled as she threw some black dust at his face. He started sneezing, and wondered what the woman had thrown on him. Things became blurry as he fell to his knees. His body felt on fire as he tried to push through the pain. What was in that black dust she had thrown at him? It must be some kind of poison, he thought.

"What have you done to me?" He questioned trying to focus on her through the blurriness. It looked like there was three of her circling in front of him.

"You wanted life, and now you have it, forever." She stated. "Know that you can never die, no matter what you may try, but you will watch all those that you love taste the moment of death." She said, before she vanished from before his eyes.

He struggled to get up, and take his place in front of his General once again. The pain seemed to be lessening, but he still wanted to know what she had thrown at him. Everything seemed out of focus, but then again, it wasn't. The battle raged on, before the generals called for a retreat, to save the men that they had left. The Yankees won that battle, and then the war two years later. It had been a hard day when General Robert E. Lee had surrendered at Appomattox Court House. It wasn't as hard as what Ben had faced, when he learned what the woman had meant that day, about not ever dying.

~ ~ ~ ~

May 2005

"That we here highly resolve that these dead shall not have died in vain, that this nation, under God, shall have a new birth of freedom, and that government of the people, by the people, for the people, shall not perish from the Earth." A small brunette girl stated loudly with a huge grin.

"Thank you, Alexandria. Perfection as always," Mrs. Blanton said as Alex made her way back to her seat. Today everyone had to recite whatever speech that Mrs. Blanton had given them at the start of the semester. Alex had been given the Gettysburg Address, which had made her smile at the time. All of the speeches were part of American History, so everyone had been familiar with them when they got them in January.

Alex sat down to listen as Clara Carter, her best friend, began to recite her speech. She had had to memorize FDR's speech after the

attack on Pearl Harbor. Alex had helped her since she had known
that one well. In fact, she knew the entire class' speeches; she was
known as the history buff at school. Everyone had had her to help
them throughout the year, but she had been okay with it.

She liked history, it had come from living in the South, she
supposed. The history that surrounded her everyday didn't hurt
either; it just seemed to come alive everywhere she went. She was
minutes away from the historic Shiloh Battlefield, one of the
bloodiest battles of the Civil War. Every class trip was a visit there,
and that made her very happy. There was nothing like stepping onto
the battlefield, and feeling the history of that place. Even today,
there's still a sense of soldiers marching around.

Every year, she attended the reenactment of the Battle of
Shiloh, a battle that had raged for two days, before resulting in the
defeat of the Confederate Army. She had studied the movements of
both sides, and had done extensive research for the park. Every
summer, she worked at the park giving tours to visitors. It always
gave her joy to teach others the history she so loved.

The Civil War was by far her favorite part of American
History. It wasn't like the other wars, where there was a common
enemy where the American people had to band together against.
Every country basically had a civil war to test the nation; it was
almost like a rite of passage for them. The American Civil War
tested the nation, and America came out stronger for it, even if it had
taken years to realize. Reconstruction had taken years, but the nation
was once again united.

Since she loved history so much, she knew what job she
wanted once she graduated college. She wanted to work at
Gettysburg National Military Park. Since she had done well at
Shiloh, she had contacted the people at Gettysburg, and learned that
a degree in American History was required to be considered for
employment. She knew that it wouldn't be a problem since that was
her goal anyway. She couldn't wait to actually work there, and walk
that battlefield with the soldiers to learn its secrets.

It would be a new experience for her and she couldn't wait to
get started, even if that was a few years down the road. Gettysburg
was the bloodiest battle in the Civil War, and it lasted three days
before the Confederate generals called for retreat. The Confederacy

never really recovered, even though the war did go for almost two more years.

~ ~ ~ ~

February 2013

"Wait, you want me to have those storage buildings cleared out by the anniversary?" Alex asked as she walked beside her boss, Cole Fort. He was an older gentleman, who had been over Gettysburg for the past 20 years. He was a veteran, but he also loved the environment at Gettysburg. He was the reason the park was one of the most visited parks in America; everything was as historic as he could make it. He was also very relatable, and all his employees loved working for him. The one thing that he didn't like was being called Mr. Fort. He once told her that he felt people were asking for his grandfather instead of him so everyone at the park called him Cole instead.

"Yes." He replied. "You are the one that wanted to see what was in them, and now that we know, I want those items on display." He stated as she nodded.

"I can't do it by myself in that short amount of time." She commented. "I'll need help." He stopped beside his office door, and looked down at her. She was quite a bit shorter than him, but that didn't mean that she was a push over by any means.

"Well, you can pull one of the summer workers to help you." He suggested as she shook her head. "Why not?"

"They are great with keeping the fields cleared, and everything organized, but they do not know enough about what those storage buildings hold. I need someone who knows more about Gettysburg than the summer help." She stated.

"Fine, hire someone." He said as she stared at him.

"You want me to hire someone?" She asked, not sure she had heard him right.

"Well, you are going to be the one working directly with the person. I want you happy in the coming months. I'll be there in the interviews to ask the correct questions, while you quiz them." He said smiling at her.

She quirked an eyebrow at him before saying anything. "You think I'm going to quiz them?" She asked while folding her arms across her chest.

"I know that you're going to quiz them, I just hope that you find someone before time runs out." He said opening his office door. "Now, you better get out front for your tour in 15 minutes." He said, checking his watch.

"Thanks, Cole." She said before walking away from him to get ready for her tour. Today she was leading a tour for the local fifth grade class at the elementary school. She loved giving tours to students because they just seemed to listen to her more than adults.

Cole watched Alex walk away from him. These interviews would be hard, and he wondered if she would find who she was looking for, not many people knew as much about the park as she did. This would be a difficult hiring process, but hopefully, if he cast the net wide enough, they would get lucky. Finding someone to work with Alex on the buildings would be difficult since she was passionate about the contents they held.

~ ~ ~ ~

April 2013

"You shall be cursed to live." Ben jerked awake before opening his eyes. He rubbed the sleep from them while trying to push those images out of his head. It was always the same dream that plagued his sleep night after night. The event may have been almost 150 years ago, but it still seemed like yesterday. Every day he wished that he would have saved that boy. He knew if he would have, then he wouldn't be cursed to live forever. Hindsight really was 20/20.

He felt like he was no closer to the truth than he had been that day. It was a terrible burden to know you could never die no matter how much he risked his life. Some might think that it would be awesome, but they didn't see the other side of the coin. He couldn't stay in one place too long because people would begin to question why it seemed as if he never aged. They also didn't know the pain of watching everyone that you love die, and know that you would never join them in death.

This cursed life also meant that he could never be close to anyone, ever. He had been engaged before the war, but he couldn't go through with it once he realized the curse was real. He had let her go once he returned home from war. His only explanation had been he had seen too much to ever fully recover and be a good husband. She had married a banker exactly one year later by the name of Thaddeus Morgan.

Ben didn't blame her for moving on because at least she lived her life fully before she died. She had had three children with him. He had painfully kept up with her grandchildren and great grandchildren until it became too hurtful to do so. The one thought that ran through his mind when he saw her family was it could have been their family instead of Thaddeus. He could have shared all those special moments with her, but instead, he was forced to watch from the sidelines as she aged gracefully and beautifully.

He had realized the curse was real after the Battle of Gettysburg. He had been on the retreat when he had been shot by musket ball. It should have killed him in seconds, but that wasn't the case. The doctors and nurses said it was a miracle that he hadn't perished; he didn't see it as that. The ball had pierced his chest close enough that it should have hit his heart. He had seen others with wounds close to his that died, before they hit the ground, but not him. The scar that it had left was ugly, due to limited medical treatment, but it didn't bother him. No one ever got close enough to see it.

Standing up, Ben stretched and worked out the kinks from sleeping at his desk. He should have gone to bed last night, but he had been reading through a new book that he found on curses and witchcraft from the Civil War. It hadn't provided him with any new information that he didn't already know. This search was getting him nowhere, and he wondered if he would ever be free of the curse, and able to live a full life.

After the war was over, he had done all that he could to help rebuild the South. He had volunteered at hospitals, orphanages, and jailhouses to see if it could break the curse. He had even moved out West, to fight with the Indians. They fought against Custer and his men that had been ravaging the reservations. He thought that if he had sacrificed his family, money, and home that it would break the curse, but nothing happened.

He became angry and thought, 'Why couldn't he just die?' Over the years, he had witnessed and experienced a lot. The invention of the telephone, light bulb, and automobile were something to see. Modern technology would be his downfall though. He had to move more often now, because he couldn't afford to be on the radar. He had no idea what would happen if someone got to wondering about his past, and put two and two together. It was just better to stay on the run.

Normally, he stayed in rural areas so that he could be there a little longer. People kept to their own business as well. He did tend to stay in the South though. It would always be his home, even if he didn't live in his hometown anymore. He couldn't handle it to go back there to see how much had changed, and how things had remained the same.

"Mr. Sawyer, I found something that may interest you." Mildred said walking into his office. She had been with him for the past ten years, and he knew that it was almost time to let her go. She would begin to ask questions, when she realized that he never grayed or got wrinkles. He still looked like the 25 year old he had been that day on the battlefield. He would miss her though, since she was good at her job, and she kept her mouth shut when people questioned her about him. She made sure that his life stayed private, just like he liked it.

"What is it?" He asked as she moved closer to him. He noticed that she was in one of her pantsuits that she favored. In fact, he wasn't sure he had ever seen her out of that style, in the ten years that she had worked for him.

"A notice in the Gettysburg paper." She replied, as she handed him the paper calmly. He wasn't quite sure why she had been reading a paper from Gettysburg, but once he looked at the notice, he was glad that she had. This could be his golden ticket.

"They need someone to help archive the artifacts found in some old storage buildings." He read as she nodded.

"Apparently they opened up one of the storage buildings that hadn't been opened in several years, and found lots of items that they want displayed during the 149th Anniversary this year." She said with a shrug. He just wondered what was in those buildings that made them post a job opening in the paper.

"150th." Ben corrected without looking at her.

"What?" She asked looking up at him.

"This year is the 150th Anniversary of the Battle of Gettysburg." He replied without hesitation. He would forever know the date of the Battle of Gettysburg since it had changed his life.

"Oh sorry, I forgot that you know everything there is to know about the Civil War." She muttered. "Anyway, I figured that this would interest you, since you always want texts from the Civil War, more specifically Gettysburg. There may be something in them that you haven't seen before." She mentioned as he nodded.

"Thank you, please make arrangements for me. I want to check it out, and see what they have found. It may only be things from the town, and not actually the battle." He stated as she nodded and left the room.

Turning to look at the window, he wondered if this was a sign. Could his answer be in that storage building? There was only one way to find out. He would travel back to the place that had started it all. He would go back to that little town in Pennsylvania called Gettysburg, and face his demons head on, for the first time since the Battle of Gettysburg.

~ ~ ~ ~

"Here we are at Cemetery Ridge. At this stop, you will see what is called the High Water mark of the Confederacy. It is said to represent the closest the South ever came to its goal of achieving independence from the Union, via military victory. This part of the battle is called Pickett's Charge, for Major General George Pickett. Years later, when asked why his charge failed, Pickett replied that he always thought the Yankees had something to do with it." Alex stated, as the tourists laughed, the bus stopped to let them off to check out the precise spot. Alex stepped out, and looked over the land laid out before her.

She looked down the slope, and pictured the Confederate soldiers marching up the hill to the Union troops, lying in wait for them. The Northern line had broken briefly here at the low stone fence. It had been called the Angle. The North had quickly regained from that loss. It was one of the saddest places on the battlefield for her, because it was here that the South had really lost the war. They had never recovered from the defeat on this battlefield, even though it had taken them two more years to realize it for themselves.

"Miss, is there anything special about that fence?" An older woman in her fifties asked, pointing to the low stone wall. It had been maintained over the years since it was a big part of that charge. The fence was the reason that the South couldn't gain the ground. The Union army had hidden behind that fence as they fired away on the Confederates below them.

"Yes ma'am." Alex replied as she began to explain how the Confederate troops had briefly gained that ground, before the North took it back.

Ben listened as the tour guide explained the fence. She knew what she was talking about, that was for sure. He had not been along that ridge, but he had seen it from his lookout point guarding the General. Most of his friends had died here, at the hands of the Yankees.

"If everyone is ready, we will continue on our tour." Alex stated as everyone filed back into the bus for the next stop on the tour, which was the National Cemetery. Ben took a seat near the back of the bus, as the tour guide began to describe the aftermath of the battle. She even explained some of the Southern army had stood on the battlefield, on the fourth morning, waiting for another attack, but never came. General Meade, who had been in charge of the Union Army, had not attacked them because he had felt it would result in even more loss. Meade had always been criticized over not battling that fourth morning, since the South was ready.

Most people didn't even know that there could have been fourth day of battle, but she did. Ben had researched the young tour guide, and knew that she had a Master's degree in American History. It didn't really mean that much, since high school History teachers had a Masters. He did see a fire in her eyes as she described the battle. She knew this battlefield almost as well as he did, and she had only worked here for a year, as far as her records showed.

Alexandria was the youngest tour guide he had ever met. Most were older men and women who gave the tours. In fact she was the youngest working the park system he had found. If there was anyone younger, they only worked part time in the summer. He also learned she had grown up close to Shiloh. It could be the reason she knew so much about the war at her age.

"Okay everyone, we are at our last stop of the day, the National Cemetery. Please remember to be respectful of the men that are buried here. They have more than earned their place here." She stated as the people filed out of the bus.

Ben was the last off the bus, as Alex followed. "You seemed to know a lot about this place." Ben commented, when he realized that she was behind him.

Alex smiled at him as they made their way into the cemetery. "I have loved the Civil War since I was a child." She stated without explanation.

"Why?" He asked wanting to know why this woman before him, cared about a war that was 150 years ago. "Normally, girls are not that interested in war or history."

"Yea that's true, but not for me." She stated. "I grew up close to Shiloh so I guess being that close to a battlefield put that love in me. I can't tell you how many class trips I took there."

"And you loved every one of them, I'm sure." Ben mused watching her eyes light up at the mention of Shiloh. He had been there, and knew that the place was as beautiful as any battlefield had a right to be. He looked out over the cemetery and saw that it was just like the park, a quiet beauty for the men that rested here.

"I did." She said smiling. "I worked there every summer as well giving tours, mending fences, and just walking the battlefield."

"How many times have you walked this battlefield?" He asked looking down at her. She was quite a bit shorter than him, but then again, most girls were since he was close to being 6 foot tall.

"I lost count after the tenth time." She replied as her eyes sparkled like she knew a secret he didn't. "I can't help but walk the field, and picture the battle around me." She said as someone called out to her. "I hope that you enjoy the rest of your day here at Gettysburg." She said before walking away.

He watched her for a moment, before slowly making his way through the graveyard. It was marked off in sections by the regiments. There was one section he knew wouldn't be there though. The Confederate soldiers that died here had been moved between 1871 and 1873 to various locations in North and South Carolina, Georgia, and Virginia. Most had been buried in Richmond, VA, the Capital of the Confederacy during the war.

They should have been buried here along with the Northern men that died with them, but they were not given that honor. Turning, he left the cemetery, and headed to the Visitor's Center, where he would meet with the board and Alexandria about the job. He just hoped that they didn't want to look too far into his past, because they wouldn't find much, since he had been off the radar as much as possible. Mildred had helped create some background information for him, and he hoped that it would good enough. Thankfully she hadn't asked why he didn't have that much background information. She was paid well not to ask questions like that. He hoped to impress them with his knowledge, and not his nonexistent background.

~ ~ ~ ~

Alex finally left the cemetery when she noticed what time it was. She had one interview today for the job that she had posted two months ago. After finally convincing her boss to open the older buildings on the property and finding all that stuff, they had been faced with a huge job. It was one that she could do if she had been given at least 6 months to do. They needed to go through all the stuff, and record everything, which didn't sound like a lot, but for the amount of things they had found, it was more than enough. The biggest problem was her boss wanted to have it all displayed in time for the 150th Anniversary, which was just 3 short months away.

With that limited time frame, she knew that she needed help. She hoped this guy knew his stuff, because the last ten hadn't known basic information about the park. She expected the person working with her to at least know the battle, and when it had occurred. One of the boys that she interviewed hadn't known when the Civil War had taken place. He guessed the 1960s. She didn't even hear the rest of the interview, because she just got up and walked out. Her boss knew she wasn't hiring that one just like she hadn't hired the others.

Stepping into the Visitor's Center, she saw that she was only a minute late. Well that was better than she thought. She made her way to the back room knowing Cole, and the guy interviewing should already be back there waiting on her.

"Alexandria, we were wondering when you would be along." Her boss, Cole said. He was a very good boss, which was a good thing considering he ran one of the most visited places in America. He had, thankfully, been really patient with her throughout this process.

"I'm sorry, I lost track of time with the last tour group." She responded as she walked around the table to face the guy, who was interviewing for the job.

"It's no problem, we were just introducing ourselves." Cole stated as she nodded and turned to the man.

"Oh it's you." Alex said as Ben stood up. She couldn't believe that someone who was interviewing had actually gone on a tour of the park. It unnerved her a little, this guy was about the same age as her, which hadn't been a problem when she had received his resume, but it was now, that she was looking at him. When they were standing in the graveyard, she had felt something between them that she couldn't quite name. It wasn't a spark or maybe it was who knew.

"You two know each other?" Cole asked looking from Alexandria to Benjamin. He had an odd look on his face. She couldn't blame him, because she was probably acting way out of character at the moment. Squaring her shoulders, she composed herself for the interview. This man was here to work if he made the cut.

"No, he was just on my last tour." Alex explained finally getting her thoughts under control. "It's nice to meet you, I am Alexandria Morgan." She said extending her hand to him.

"It's nice to meet you too. My name is Benjamin Sawyer, but I prefer to be called Ben." He said taking her hand to shake it before releasing it. Letting her arm drop back to her side, she studied him for a moment.

"Well Ben, I know that you are at least familiar with the park since you were on the tour, but can you tell me when the battle took place?" Alex asked as she sat down. Cole and Ben did the same.

"July 1-3, 1863, but you know that I could have cheated since you told us that on the tour." He pointed out as she smiled. He was right on that, but she had noticed him on the bus when he thought no one had been looking.

"Yes, you could have, but maybe you were not listening on the bus." She remarked thinking about that faraway look he had had in his eyes at the time.

"I'm not sure that any person could not, not listen to you." He said with a smile, not really correcting her assumption of him not listening.

"Alexandria is our best tour guide at the park." Cole explained hoping to move this interview along. "She knows more about the park than even I do."

"Ask me any question about the battle; I have done my research on Gettysburg." Ben stated looking at Alex. She heard the dare in his voice, and decided that this would really be a test for him. He claimed to know about the Civil War, well she was about to find out if that was true or not.

"Okay, where were the Confederates before Gettysburg?" Alex asked, knowing that she hadn't talked about this on the tour. Normally, she never talked about it unless she was on the extensive tour, or during the reenactment. He should at least know that piece of information; it wasn't really that hard to figure out.

"Lee had just won Chancellorsville, and moved his army north to continue his campaign for the North." He replied, remembering those days of marching north.

"Correct." She said not showing any emotion. "Name the battle that Lincoln used to launch his Emancipation Proclamation?" She asked moving away from Gettysburg. She wanted to know if he knew anything else about the Civil War. Gettysburg wasn't the only one battle in the war. He would need to know the entire thing to help her. She didn't know how much history these storage buildings contained.

"Bloody Antietam." He replied in a confident voice, without hesitation.

"Very good." Alex stated, still trying not to be impressed by him, even though it was getting harder. "What battle was known as Burnside's Slaughter Pen?" She asked, watching him closely.

"The Battle of Fredericksburg." He answered with ease. Apparently, he was going to show out for her, while she tested him. Well two could play at this game.

"Where was the Battle above the Clouds?" She asked crossing her arms waiting for his answer. She had never encountered anyone who knew as much as she did, and it really fascinated her. She wasn't above testing him to see how much he really knew.

"Chattanooga, Tennessee, specifically Missionary Ridge and Lookout Mountain." He replied calmly. He knew the battles and places so he didn't worry about her questions. She could question him all night, and he wouldn't miss one. He was sure about that.

"What was Sherman's Christmas present to Lincoln?" She asked. Cole just sat back and let her fire away. He knew that since she had to work with whoever got the job, that they would have to know the Civil War. It was just best to let her question them, and he was really interested to see if this man could keep up with her, since no one else could.

"Savannah, Georgia." He responded, placing his hands in his lap while trying not to smirk. He was pretty sure that Alex had never met anyone that knew as much as she did. He wondered what she would think if she ever found out that he knew more than she did.

"What year of the war did Grant face Lee on the battlefield?" She asked, remaining calm as she pulled questions from her memory. She knew the war backwards and forwards, she just wanted to know if he did as well. It had just gotten to the point that she was enjoying hearing him answer her questions.

"1864 in the Wilderness campaign." He stated, leaning back in his chair getting comfortable because he didn't know how much longer she would keep this up.

"What did Grant tell his men when they cheered at Lee's surrender?" She asked moving to the next question.

"The war is over; the rebels are our countrymen again." He said, with a quiet voice. He remembered that day vividly. He had actually heard Grant shout that to his men. They had quieted down, but you could still feel their excitement through the silence.

Alex looked at Ben, and wondered why he had been quieter on that answer. His voice had been stronger with all the other answers, except that one. There was something different about him, but she didn't worry about that at the moment. She still had a one more question to ask him. "Okay, last one." She said slowly. "Which regiment did Grant lead in the Battle of Gettysburg?" She asked, as Benjamin smiled.

"That's a trick question, Miss Morgan." He stated leaning forward. "Grant was not in the Battle of Gettysburg, in fact, at the same time as the Battle of Gettysburg he was in Vicksburg, winning it." He stated as she laughed.

"You're correct. I must say I am impressed you knew all the answers." She stated as Cole rolled his eyes. Sometimes, he wondered if Alexandria had actually lived during the Civil War. She could have jumped through time to now, just to show her knowledge of that time period.

"Now that your trial by fire is over, I want to tell you a little about the job." Cole stated as Ben nodded. "First off you will be working with Alexandria so I hope that that is not a problem after the firing squad she just put you through." He said glancing back at Alex who shrugged. She didn't feel bad for asking Ben questions.

"No problem at all, she just wanted to make sure that I knew my stuff." He stated looking at Alexandria who nodded in agreement.

"Okay, well as you know from the ad, we have found some previously unknown items that I want archived, and displayed for the anniversary. You have a short amount of time to get everything done, which is why Alexandria needs help." Cole explained as Ben nodded. "She will be lead in this, but you will do a lot of the work alone, since she will still be giving tours and preparing for the anniversary."

"Okay, that's fine by me." He said keeping the joy out of his voice. He was happy to do all the work, if she would let him. It would give him plenty of time to go through everything, and see if he could find the woman who had done this to him, without someone looking over his shoulder.

"Since it's close to closing time, you can start tomorrow. We will meet outside of the Visitor's Center in the morning at 8 am. I can drive you over to the buildings, and let you get started." Alex informed him as he nodded. "I look forward to working with you." She said standing up before leaving the room. Cole and Ben just watched her leave before they moved.

"Whew, I'm glad that you know your Civil War facts because I didn't know half of the answers, but I knew that she would throw a trick question in there. She did it to one of the other men that interviewed, but he got it wrong. She asked him where Lee had died during the battle. He said that Lee died in the Hornet's Nest which isn't even here, but in Shiloh." Cole said with some disgust. "Don't worry though, she gets a little intense when it comes to the battlefield, but she really knows her stuff, and she respects this place more than anyone else I know." He explained as Ben nodded.

"It's fine, I'm glad that she is very knowledgeable. People can learn from her because of her passion for the job." Ben stated while standing up. He wondered if she knew anything about witches during the war. It would be something that he could ask her, but he would have to be careful if or when he did. She had a quick mind and would want to know why he was asking her. He couldn't answer that question though.

"She does have passion for the job." Cole mused. "Now I probably won't see you again until the anniversary so have fun working with Alexandria." He said before leaving the room.

Ben sighed and followed him out. He had gotten the job. Thankfully, he had worked some kind of background story that hopefully they wouldn't discover was a lie until after he left. Leaving the Visitor's Center, he saw Alexandria get into her car, and pull out of the parking lot. Something about her told him to tread carefully. He didn't know what it was, but she was dangerous to him. He couldn't afford for her to find out his secret, before he found his answer, because if anyone could figure out his secret, it would be her.

~ ~ ~ ~

Alex thought about Ben while she pulled out of the park. There was something very different about him, but she didn't know if it was because he knew the answers to her questions or something else altogether. Shaking her head, she rolled her window down, and turned her music up as she exited the park.

The next three months would be interesting to say the least, but she was ready to see what treasures those buildings held. She also wondered if it would give her a clue about her great grandmother, 9 generations removed, ex fiancée. He had fought here, and had lived, but had broken off the engagement when the war was over, citing that he had seen too much to be married to her. The man had left with a piece of her grandmother's heart. She wanted to know the real reason he had broken the engagement, because she was certain that it hadn't been because he had seen too much.

<u>Cursed Soldier</u>
Available now on Kindle, Nook, Smashwords, and in paperback.

About the Author

Laura Lee McKellips was born and raised in Southern Tennessee. She graduated from the University of Tennessee at Martin with a bachelors degree in agriculture.

Years of reading romance propelled her to write her first book, with the support of her friends and family. When she is not typing away on her next story, she is either reading or playing softball.

If you want to keep up with the latest books or news, like her on facebook (Author Laura Lee Mckellips). You can also find her on twitter (@leeredmarlin).

Letters between Benjamin and Kathryn during the Civil War

Dear Kathryn,   *May 1861*

I pray that this letter finds you well. I know you are reading this with bated breath wondering if this letter finds you too late. We have finally reached the camp, I know you have been worried about me and the other guys as we journey north to join Robert E. Lee's Army. The journey was rough since I knew that it carried me miles and miles away from you and our sleepy little town.

I wish that Lincoln would have just let the South leave the Union peacefully, but after Fort Sumter I knew that he would not. April 15, will forever be etched in my mind as the date that our lives ended. I knew when Lincoln called forth for troops that everything we knew was about to change.

You know I do not support the war, but I do support the reason for the war. I heard more states have joined the Confederate States. The guys say Tennessee finally left the Union so we all wonder when the first official battle will be.

There are rumors that Lincoln wants to attack some of our boys at Manassas Junction, which the Yankees are calling Bull Run for some strange reason. I fear if the Yankees do attack there, that General Jackson will stand his ground. He and his men are ready to die for the cause. The Yankees are not as prepared as those men though. Even though I am in the mist of the camp, I feel like the war is still just a dream. We all wait in anticipation of where the Yankees will strike first, still hoping that the war will be over in 90 days, and we come out the victors.

Please know that I love you, and if I could, I would have married you before I left. If you change your mind when I come home on my furlough, I will have you in front of the preacher that day. I cannot wait until the day that you become my wife.

Please give my love to my mother. I know she worries as much as you do.

Pray for a short war,
Your soldier preparing for battle

My love,   *July 1861*

It was great to receive your letter. We heard about the battle at Manassas Junction, but the papers are calling it Bull Run. I am not sure why there are two different names for the same battle. Apparently, the Yankees name places differently than we do. Were you there in the battle? I did not see your name among the list of dead or wounded so I still have hope that you are alive and well. Please stay that way throughout this war. I could not bear it if you were to die that far away from me.

Your mother wanted to let you know that she loves you and that she was happy to see you had time to write. She also wants you to be careful, and come home to give her grandbabies to spoil. Your father is still not saying much, but I know that he is proud of you for joining the cause even if you do not support the war.

I will not change my mind on marriage until the war is over. I do not want to be a widow because of this war. Many of my best friends are already widows with only this one battle. Please do not pressure me to change my mind because I will not. I love you and will marry you the minute that the war is over, and you come home to me. Not a moment sooner.

I wait for your next letter to know that you are alive and well. Please do not be heroic during battle like I know you want to be. I do want you to come home to me. Remember I love you, and know that I am praying for a short war as well.

All my love,
Kathryn

Dear Kathryn,   *September 1861*

I never realized how slow the mail was until the war. It seems like it was months ago that I sent you that letter. I will try not to pressure you for marriage, but why are you asking me not to be heroic? You know I would not let anyone die if I had the chance to save them. It would be wrong of me to sit back and watch them die because I just stood by. This war is a test to those ideas.

I am sorry about your friends. I know most of the guys from Bluff City are dead. The war has not been easy on us, but with each battle we win we believe victory is within our hands. After our defeat at Cheat Mountain, Lee was sent down to Georgia to secure the port at Savannah. The Yankees are trying to bottle up the harbor and attack from that way. I'm not sure why they had to send Lee since he is needed on the front lines.

We are now under the command of General Johnson. I do not like him as well, but he is a fair man, and we have won a few battles already. We march most of the time until we are near the enemy. It is times like these that I do miss my horses.

I do pray this letter finds you well. Please tell momma I love her, and that I will be home soon. This war can't last too much longer. We are gaining more ground every day and soon we will take Washington.

Love from the battlefield,
Your Soldier

My Love,   *October 1861*

I do wish that the mail was faster. I hate having to wait for your letters. I fear one day I will get one after I have read your death in the paper. I am asking you to not go rushing into the mist of the battle just to save someone. I know you, and I know you will rush into a situation without thinking about it. This war has lost its focus. Those ideals that we held so dear, seem gone with the wind now.

I was sorry to hear about your defeat at Cheat Mountain, but I know that your troop will bounce back and start winning so this war will be over sooner rather than later. I was happy to hear Lee was sent to protect the Port of Savannah. It is one of the ports the block aid runners are able to get through at the moment. The block aid runners are our only hope at the moment for supplies. Hopefully, Lee will take care of those Yankees and get them out of our waters.

Will I even recognize you after all this walking and fighting? I'm sure I will because I would know you anywhere. The only thing I ask is you do not cut your hair. I love your long hair because it reminds me of pirates. It will also keep you warm in those cold winter months up North.

Your letters always find me well. I love hearing from you as does your momma. She wanted me to tell you that she loves you and to be careful. Remember, I love you and want you to come home to me so that we can start our life together.

Oh I do have some good news. Thaddeus Morgan the one that owns the bank, asked me to work for him. He needs help, and since I cannot help in the hospitals because I am an unmarried woman, I told him yes. I start my new job on Monday. Momma's not happy that I am working, but she said that if it would help the cause then it was okay to work there.

All my love,
Kathryn

Dear Kathryn,   *November 1861*

I will try to make sure I don't die so you will not get my letter after reading of my death. We are on the move again trying to secure more ground farther North. Every step I take makes me feel like I'm losing you a little more. The thought keeps me up most nights.

I am happy to see you have a job. I know sitting around waiting for news was never to your delight. Thaddeus is a good man, and I trust he will not overwork you even if you ask for it. The one good thing is you will be working in a bank with set hours.

Talk around camps is of the Yankee soldier named Grant is moving south. I pray our troops will stop his path and keep our land safe. We cannot afford to lose Tennessee at this stage, especially with the access to the Cumberland and Tennessee Rivers. Steamboats, on those rivers, provide our supplies at this stage. I fear if they ever gain control of that area, they will win the war because we will be cut off from our main supply route.

Please continue to be safe and give momma my love. I know she worries about me as much as you do.

Love,
Your Soldier from the front lines

My Love,   *December 1861*

I was so happy to get your letter. I feel like the mail is getting slower and slower. It seems like it has taken months to get this letter instead of weeks. I do at least know that you are safe or was from the last death report from the latest battle. I still pray you make it through this war and back home to me.

Every step you take is not taking you farther from me. I love you more than the day you asked me to be your wife. I fall more in love with you every day because I envision our life together once this war is over.

My job is great. Thaddeus doesn't let me work over at all. He makes me leave in time for dinner, and doesn't want me to come in until after I've had breakfast. He is a good man, and speaks highly of you. I think he wishes he could have joined the fight, but with the bank and his mother's health, there was no way he could have. I think it makes him feel guilty; others are fighting while he is stuck here in Bluff City.

Grant is moving south? This is not good news about Tennessee since it is a Confederate State now. I pray he is defeated shortly and ran back up into Kentucky where he belongs.

Your momma said hi, and she loves you. She also wants you to be safe.

I love you,
Kathryn

Dear Kathryn,   *January 1862*

The mail is getting slower. The postal service has been suspended to the Confederate States since we are not a part of the Union. Thankfully though, there are a brave few that take the letters to the block aid runners so they can sail them into one of the Southern ports and get them to everyone. Don't worry, I am still alive, and I plan to stay that way. Also, please stop reading the death reports. I do not want you to learn about my death that way.

I am in love with you as well. I cannot wait for this war to end so I can make you my wife.

You can tell Thaddeus not to feel guilty over not joining the cause. He is doing his part by watching over you, and keeping you entertained while I'm gone.

The Yankees are closing in on Fort Henry and Fort Donelson, which is not good news at all. Apparently, Grant is preparing to attack the middle of Tennessee first, before spreading down. Hopefully our boys will take care of them before they move lower.

Tell momma I love her, and I'm being safe.

I love you,
Your Soldier

My Love,   *February 1862*

I cannot help but read those death reports. It is just a sick obsession that I have to do. In a small way, if I do not see your name, I can rest easy because I know you are alive for at least another battle.

Our mothers are pressuring me to marry you when you come home on your furlough. I have told them we are not getting married until after the war is over, but they just do not listen to me. They want us married with a baby on the way. Apparently, there is talk about me getting too old to have a child if we wait any longer. It is just utter nonsense. I pray every day for Lincoln to call an end to the war. It just seems never ending even though it has not yet been a year since it started even though Fort Sumter seems so long ago now. I guess it is because our lives have changed from what we had envisioned.

Well, Grant has finally attacked Fort Henry and Donelson, reports confirm. I cannot believe that the Yankees are in Tennessee at all. It is only February, and I can only imagine what the rest of the year will bring for us and Tennessee if they have already lost that much ground.

Thaddeus wants to say thank you for telling him not to be guilty about not being able to join the cause. He said you are the only one that has not made him feel less than worthy of being a man. He also wanted me to tell you he is doing his best to keep me entertained, even though it is a difficult job. Apparently, I worry too much about you, or at least that is what he told me the other day.

Your momma says hi, and she loves you too. Your father is still silent on the issue of you joining. I know he is proud of you; it is just hard for him to think about you fighting. Remember, I love you, too, and expect you to return to me in one piece so we can get married and provide our mothers with grandchildren and great grandchildren.

All my love,
Kathryn

Dear Kathryn,   *April 1862*

It is getting tough here at camp. Winter just seems to drag on which is not good for us. I don't think any of us were really prepared for this cold. Some of the guys do not even have shoes to wear. I am not sure how much longer we will be able to hold out with this cold.

If you must read the death reports, please do not get mad if you do read my death. If they do let you rest better, I cannot tell you not to read them even though I would like to. I will say, please remember I am not fighting in every battle, and I hope that small fact gives you comfort.

You can tell my mother I said to leave you alone. You can also tell your mother that too but I am sure that would not go over very well. I am sorry they are pressuring you, and I am not there to protect you, but I am with you in spirit. I pray this war is over soon as well, so we can get married and start our family.

We heard about Henry and Donelson. Grant is on a mission, but no one seems to know his next target. For the moment, we are in wait and see mode, but hopefully, that will change as soon as possible. General Johnston is ready and waiting for anything to suggest where Grant will be next.

Of course, you are not making Thaddeus' job easy. You were always a difficult woman to entertain, but it is just one of the reasons that I love you. Please be a little nicer to him since he did give you a job.

Wishing I was back home in the warmth,
Your Soldier

My love,   *June 1862*

 I was so happy to receive your letter today. We heard about the battle at Shiloh. Grant has gained access to the lower part of the Tennessee River, which is not good news for your troop. We all thought Spring would bring better news but not anymore. The reports of the battle are horrific, and it is being called the bloodiest battle to date.
 I am thankful you are still in Virginia now instead of closer to me. Tennessee is taking a beating and I fear it will only get worse in the coming months. With the war a year old now, I fear everyone has been wrong. This will not be a quick war. I fear it will take years to resolve, and even after it is over, will there even be peace.
 I did talk to our mothers and finally made them see my side. They are backing off, but I am not sure if it is because I am barely holding it together, or if they have accepted that I am firm in my decision not to marry you until the war is over.
 I love you and I await your furlough so I can hold you in my arms and know you are really alive and well, as your letters made me think you are.

Your wife to be,
Kathryn

Dear Kathryn,   *August 1862*

 We received the news of Shiloh after I had sent your last letter. I cannot believe we lost that battle. I know if General Johnston would have survived we would have won. The fighting is getting more intense, much more than we ever thought it would that far south.

Tennessee is all but fallen into Yankee hands. I fear its loss will spell trouble for us and the entire Confederate Army. I still wish I was closer to you, but I know I am needed here more. I agree this will be a long fought war, and I can only hope there will be peace once the fighting is finished.

I am thankful that our mothers are backing off. I do not like reading you are barely holding it together. The only reason I am strong in battle is because I know you are staying strong at home. Please continue to be my strength.

I am afraid my furlough has been delayed due to General Lee rumored to be taking control once again. I have been promoted to sniper so I should not be on the front lines. I hope this news brightens your spirit and brings a smile to your face. In the last battle, the generals were impressed I could shoot as far as I can. I did explain that I practiced long range shooting at home.
Give momma my love.

Your soldier awaiting the end of the war,
Your Soldier

My love,   *September 1862*

The town is in panic over the Yankees being this close. We know they are at least a month's ride away but with Grant leading them, there is no way to tell where he will attack next. Several families have already left for Europe, or places out west. My parents are concerned, but have made no plans to leave yet. I know I will not go with them if they do decide to leave. This is our home, and I refuse to let the Yankees drive me away.

I will continue to be your strength if it is keeping you stable. I will still keep you in my prayers. I know God will protect you far more than my strength.

It is upsetting to know I will not see you anytime soon but I cannot tell you how happy I am you are not going to be on the front lines. I told your parents and your mother cried, but they were happy tears. She said her prayers have been answered. Your father was quiet, but I know your news pleased him.

Please continue to stay safe so you can come home to me and our life together.

All my love,
Kathryn

Dear Kathryn,   *October 1862*

I know you love Bluff City, but if the Yankees get close to you, I want you to run. I could not stand the thought of Yankees in Georgia marching toward you. Please promise me you will go if your parents do. I will come and find you after the war is over.

I feel like you and God are the only ones on my side and I will take that. I know with both of you I can face the unknown of war.

It is hard to know I will not see you in the next coming months, but I know you are saying extra thanks now for me not being on the front lines. I can almost feel your relief from here.

I will stay safe as long as you do too.

Love,
Your Soldier

My love,   *November 1862*

You asked too much of me! I cannot leave my home. I will fight the Yankees if I have too, but they are not running me out of my home. I will promise to stay safe though and pray that the Yankees never make it to Georgia. My parents have vowed not to leave because this is their land. Do not worry; there are still plenty of people here ready to defend our home.

Do not forget your mother, father, and sister are on your side as well. Your father has finally starting talking about you to everyone. I never thought I would see the day he would be proud of your decision. I think he is just scared to lose you so young. Parents are not supposed to outlive their children.

I know you can feel my relief, and yes extra thanks are resounding this Thanksgiving and Christmas. I look back on this year and wonder how we will ever make it, but I know this is God's plan for us. Please continue to stay safe. I dream of you as I remember past Christmases.

Merry Christmas my love,
Kathryn

Dear Kathryn,   *December 1862*

   Merry Christmas to you, and even though I cannot be there with you, please know that you are in my heart. Just think, when the war ends, we will spend every Christmas together after that. I cannot wait until this war is over, and we are finally married.
   I know you don't want to leave your home, but the Yankees cannot be trusted to leave the women and children alone. There have been reports of them going in and killing everyone, no matter if they are soldiers or not. I am just looking out for your life since I am not there to protect you.
   I know my family is on my side, but they have always been. It is like it is their duty to be on my side. I am happy for my mother and sister's sake that he is finally talking about me, but I need to hear him say I am not a failure before I will accept his change of heart. I still love and respect him since he is my father, but after all that has happened it is not easy for me to forgive him.
   I know this is God's plan for us as well. Please believe me when I say I wish his plan included me with you this Christmas. I will stay safe and dream of you as well. It is the only place I know that I will see you so clearly, and know that you are safe. I love you my darling.

As always,
Your Soldier

My love,   *February 1863*

   I cannot believe Christmas has come and gone again. It seems like it was barely here. The New Year has already done the same thing as well. *There is one thing I am still waiting for, and that is your birthday. Can you believe that you will be 25 in a month? It seems unreal I have not seen you since you were 22. So much has changed between us, but I know I still love you.*

I know the Yankees cannot be trusted, but did you forget you taught me how to shoot? If they are wearing a Union uniform I will not hesitate to shoot and ask questions later. They should not be invading my home, but if they do, I will be ready for them. I sleep with the gun next to my bed every night. It makes me feel safer since you are not here.

I understand what you are saying about them always being on your side. Their support is not something you ever have to question. I know that you do not want to trust what I tell you about your father but please do. He has changed in the past two years. I am not sure if you would know him now. I know it is not easy to accept, but when you get home, you will see for yourself.

My dreams are always of you, and when I get to see you again. Please be safe and come home to me soon. I am more than ready to start our life together. I love you more than I can ever explain to you.

Your fiancée,
Kathryn

Dear Kathryn,   *April 1863*

It really is discouraging how slow the mail has gotten. I already had my birthday by the time I received your letter. You asked me if I could believe am turning 25, and actually, I can't believe I am not older than that. The war is wearing thin on my body, and I feel like an old man at times.

No, I did not forget I taught you how to shoot. I am thankful for those instructions now since I am unable to be there. Be careful and do not shoot a random person. The last I heard, the Yankees were nowhere close to you yet so do not go shooting anyone who walks into your house.

I will just have to trust your word on my father. I cannot believe he has changed in that short amount of time, but then I look at myself and know I have changed in that same amount of time. What happened to us licking the Yankees in a month? Were we ever that young and arrogant?

Hopefully, I will get to come home at the end of July. We are on our way to Chancellorsville at the moment. General Lee seems to have a plan in place. No one us know what to think, but we will follow him where he leads us. He wants this war over just as much as we do, and we do trust him.

I love you.

Love you always,
Your Soldier

My love,   *May 1863*

Oh I'm sorry. I really thought if I rushed to write it you would at least get it on your birthday. I know you are tired, and this war has you thinking you are an old man. I can assure you that you are not. The war will soon be over, and then you can go back to knowing you are a young man.

I do wish you were here to protect me since it would mean you are with me, but I will not shoot a random person. How many random people do you think I see any given day? I think you have forgotten how small Bluff City really is. If there is a stranger to walk into town, he would be questioned by everyone. The person would not stay a mystery for long.

I know it is hard to take in what I am telling you about your father, but you know you have changed, and he has, too. You knew it would take longer than a month though. I remember your smirks at the boys who talked of teaching the Yankees a lesson. Talk is always louder than guns. I do not think you were arrogant at all. In fact, you were the one I remember saying it would take the South longer to defeat the North.

You are coming home in July! I will wait for that day with bated breath. I cannot believe I have not seen you since April two years ago. Of course Lee has a plan, just trust in him. Chancellorsville? I heard the Yankee General Joseph Hooker has been raiding in that area. Please stay safe.

Love,
Kathryn

My love,   *May 1863*

    I just heard the news! Please tell me you are alright. I must know. The death reports are still coming in, and I hope my letter reaches you and finds you safe. How could Lee lead the army in like that? How could he split up his troops who were already outnumbered against two Union armies waiting for you? We heard General Stonewall died as well.
    Oh, please be alright. I cannot lose you this close to getting to seeing you.

Waiting in fear,
Kathryn

Dear Kathryn,   *June 1863*

    I am perfectly fine. I received both of your letters within days of each other. I am sure the reports of the battle are nothing compared to what I have seen. It was torture watching all those men dying. Lee's plan worked though. We won and pushed the Yankees back. Yes, Lee is saddened by the death of General Stonewall. He said it was like losing his right arm. I do not know what Lee will do now with that troop. General Stonewall was already a legend before his last breath. This is a blow to the Confederacy that I fear will spell trouble for us.
    Do not worry; I am just happy I receive your letters at all. We are on the move so much now I fear I will not get them. I will say after that battle, I am more than thankful I feel anything at all. We lost so many good men.
    Well at least Bluff City hasn't changed on that account. They were always protective of their own.

As long as you did not think I was then I am happy. I would hate to have my words come back and haunt me. There are enough ghosts of this war already.

Yes Hooker was raiding the towns which was why Lee had moved that way. He also needed to start gaining more ground. With our win here, we are closer to securing more Union ground. We now make our way North to Pennsylvania. The countryside is beautiful, and someday I would like to bring you here after we are married. I know that you will like it.

Love,
Your Soldier

My Love,   *July 1863*

I just received your last letter before the most devastating news reached me. You said you were on your way to Pennsylvania, and I pray you were wrong or delayed. I pray you were not in that little town of Gettysburg where thousands of men lost their lives. I could not bear it if you were. The death tolls are not expected for another week due to the heavy rains, so every hour I will be praying you were not harmed or even there.

Please write to me as soon as you can because this waiting is killing me. I need to know you are alive and well.

I love you,
Kathryn

Dear Kathryn,   *August 1863*

I received your letter, and I am fine. The battle was intense, and we lost many good men over the course of those three days. I cannot even begin to explain what I saw on that battlefield not I would ever describe it to you. I will tell you that I never want to step foot on that hallowed ground again. I am sure you are wondering why I call it hallowed ground. Well, it is hallowed now because it has been bathed in the blood of Yankee and Confederate alike. I do not know if I can ever get those images out of my head.

I thought when I was chosen as a sniper I would not have to deal with death close up. I was wrong. Death surrounded us for three days, and I am not sure I can even remove it from my skin. It has seeped into my bones and lodged there. Death had always been a part of the war, but nothing like this. This was horror to ever face or even think about.

I experienced something life changing there. I cannot discuss it at this time, and I am not sure I ever could discuss it with you. I do know I am not sure of my future with you any longer. It seems further away than it has ever been. I used to have a clear picture on how our life would be, but now that picture has been covered in blood, my blood. There are some things a man cannot overcome in his life. I do believe Gettysburg will be that one thing for me. I beg that you not worry about me, but pray for those that have died in this war. They are the ones that have been given peace in the time of war.

Please do not ask me about the battle, town, or anything related to those three days. I want to be able to push it to the far reaches of my mind, and never have to worry about it again. The course of my life has been forever changed.

Your Battle Changed Soldier

My love,   *September 1863*

I finally received your letter, and I had to shout for joy. I could not believe you are alive. The death tolls from Gettysburg are still being printed each week when a new body is discovered. I would never ask you to describe the battle even if I wanted to know which I do not. I pray those images leave your mind and give you peace.

I pray you begin to see our future blood-free. I want you to come home to me so we can start out lives together. Please do not turn away from me. I can help heal those demons that haunt you and ease that pain if you will let me.

Loving you through this pain,
Kathryn

Kathryn,   *October 1863*

I guess I am alive if you want to call it that. I feel like I am between life and death. I cannot feel the joy of being alive or the pain of being dead. I am in limbo. I fear your prayers will fall on deaf ears. The images of the battle have not left me these past few months. They are still as fresh as the day they happened.

My future will never be blood-free. It has stained my hands for eternity. No amount of soap or scrubbing will remove that blood. I cannot help but turn away from you. Please do not ask me to come home to you at this time. I need time to banish these thoughts and images. I am sorry. You were my future until that battle.

Your Soldier

My love,   *November 1863*

We read Lincoln has traveled to Gettysburg to dedicate part of the battlefield as the final resting place for those who died there. His address was shorter than anyone thought it would be, but I felt that he said what he needed to for the moment.

I pray this letter finds you in happy spirits, or at least finds you alive now. I hope limbo is finally over for you. I know it may not seem like it, but those images will fade into darkness given time. I can help you.

Let me help you scrub away the blood. Love can heal if you will let it. Please let me love you past the pain. Do not turn from my love or from me. I am your safe place to run. I am still your future as you are mine. I love you, my darling soldier. Please have the faith in me you have had through this war. I am here with my arms wide open, waiting for you.

Love,
Kathryn

Dear Kathryn,   *January 1864*

We heard Lincoln traveled there to give a speech. Short or long doesn't matter because nothing can erase those three days. They shouldn't have gone there and done anything. The ground is already dedicated without the fancy words or ceremonies. I am sorry for being like this, but that ground should have never been walked upon again.

Happy spirits? I am not even sure what happiness feels like anymore. The winter has been rough, and it has only begun. I should be home in a few weeks as long as nothing big happens. I am not even sure if I want to come home now that everything has happened.

I cannot ask you to help me. This is a demon of my making, and I need to handle this on my own. I do not want the blood to stain your hands as well. I am sorry if it feels like I am turning away from your love. It is the only thing that keeps me grounded, and I wish I could explain everything to you. I wish that you were here in this moment so I could hold you and reassure myself that you are real.

I do love you; please remember that in the coming months.

Your Soldier

My Love,   *March 1864*

I understand your reasoning for no one going back to that battlefield, but they wanted to pay their respects to all the soldiers that lost their lives there. Please do not be angry over that fact.

Oh, I wish you did not feel that way. You will be happy again when this blasted war is over, and you are back with me. I pray nothing happens so you can come home and recharge. I know you need to come home after all you have seen. We are all praying for you so you can find your happiness again.

It breaks my heart you will not ask for help. The strongest men in the world ask for help. They know there are some things they cannot do alone. Please just let me be there with you through this difficult time. I am not sure why you think the blood on your hands will stain mine. It will not, and it will come off of yours as long as you allow me to help you. Stains can come out with work. You can explain everything to me when you come home. I need to hear what has changed the man that I love to someone I do not know.

I am real, and I am waiting for you to hold me as well. It has been tough not seeing you in over 3 years. I dream of the day the war is over, and we can finally be married.

I love you,
Kathryn

Dear Kathryn,   *May 1864*

I am not really angry about it, just disappointed in the fact they thought the battlefield needed it.

I hope you are right about me finding my happiness again. At this point, I am not sure. I am also not sure if coming home is a good idea. I feel like a black cloud is hanging over me, and I do not want to bring that home. There is also another problem that may halt my coming home. There are reports we will be engaging in more battles. We have heard rumors Grant has been made General over the Union Army. This is not welcome news.

You know I do not like asking for help. I know I should but this is something I cannot ask for help on. It is a change of heart more than anything else. I am sorry it is breaking your heart. I do not like causing you any pain. I just want you to be happy.

My dreams of being married are fading more and more with each passing second I am away from you. I pray something changes so I can see our future as well. You were right in not marrying before the war started.

Your Soldier

My Love,   *August 1864*

I do not think they thought the place needed it just that it was good for their image. You have to remember the war is not very popular right now. Everyone is calling for a cease-fire. It was in Lincoln's best interest to have the ceremony.

I know it's been over a year now since the Battle of Gettysburg, and I pray the black cloud that darkened your mind has left you. I cannot believe I have not seen you in four years. Some days it feels as if the war just started, but then some days I fear it will never end.

I know you do not like asking for help. It is one of the things I love about you, but this is something you have to ask for help on. I know you do not like causing me pain, and it will get better once you are back at home with me and our families. Remember I love you through your faults. I will be happy once I see your face.

Please do not say that, I wish we were married now. It has just been a long war for both of us. I question my decision every second for not marrying you. I should have just gotten over my fears, and said I do before the war started. Please be safe.

Love,
Kathryn

Dear Kathryn,   *September 1864*

I pray a cease-fire or surrender comes soon. The men are weary and tired. I am weary and tired and ready to not wear this uniform. The day the war ends, I never want to put it on again. All I can see when I look at it is the faces of all the men that have died because of this war. This uniform is cursed.

It does not feel like it has been that long. Everyday feels like I just stepped off that battlefield. The black cloud is still there just not as black. I guess it is more of a gray cloud than anything else. I know what you mean about the war seeming to only have started, but then again, it being forever long. I see your face every day in my dreams and thoughts, but I cannot touch you or even talk to you. I am only allowed these letters.

I know that you love me and want me to ask for help. If I knew how to ask, then I would. This state of mind and body that I am in has me tied on how to ask for help. Hopefully, when I come home I will know how to ask. Please just pray that God will show me the way.

Do not question your beliefs. I understand more now than I did that day I left. We will discuss everything when I see you again. Please do not fret over this; I will be home once this war is over. I love you.

Your Soldier

My Love,   *November 1864*

    We have heard General Sherman is marching through Georgia. They are calling for immediate evacuation of everything past Atlanta to the coast. Can you imagine Yankees in Georgia? Atlanta is deep in the South, and I do not like the Yankees have gotten that far. I still cannot believe he has finally taken Atlanta. I pray you are staying safe.

    The day the war ends, I will help you burn that uniform if you would like. I never want to see you in it past the day you come back home and into my arms. I fear I will always see it as something that took you away from me.

    I am happy to hear your black cloud has lessened. It is the best news I have heard in months. I pray every day that God shows you the path that you should take. I hope that path leads back to me and our life together.

    Thank you for understanding those beliefs, even though I wish I had caved before you saw my side. I will fret because you are still out there fighting, but I will try not to let it bottle up. I love you and remember to stay safe so you can come home to me.

Love,
Kathryn

Dear Kathryn,   *December 1864*

    Please tell me I have a home to come home to. We have heard reports about the destruction Sherman left in his wake. I am afraid of what I will find once this war is over. I do not think I have slept since your last letter about him burning his way to Savannah. Please tell me you are alright. I need to know you are alright.

    Do not worry about burning my uniform. I have thought a lot about your suggestion and have decided to hold on to it. It has become a big part of my life, and I cannot bear to part with it. Years

*down the road, I might change my mind, but as of today I am
keeping it.*

*I am sorry this letter is short, but we are on the move again
trying to stay one step ahead of General Grant. Lee has a plan of
attack, and we are just praying that it pays off. Please stay safe, and
remember I love you.*

Your Soldier

My Love,   *February 1865*

*Everything is fine here in Bluff City. The Yankees did not get
near to us, but Atlanta is burnt. I heard Savannah is no better. Our
closest port is now cut off from us with Savannah in Yankee hands
now.*

*We heard Grant is making waves towards Lee. I pray you
and the men are alright, and Lee will gain the upper hand on Grant.
I cannot bear the thought of Lee on the run from Grant even if it
does mean that you are safe for the moment.*

*I understand about the uniform, I just wished it would not
represent high ideals only to have them crash around the South. I
fear the war is forever lost to the Confederacy which makes me
question why we even fought in the first place.*

*I know if Lee has a plan then it means he is still fighting. I
know you love me, and remember I love you, too.*

*Your Love,
Kathryn*

Dear Kathryn,   *April 1865*

*Well the war is over at least for Lee. He surrendered to
Grant today at Appomattox today. It was the hardest sight to see.
Lee is a very proud and humble man, but he knew there was no way
to continue on. We were all but surrounded and cut off from the rest
of the South. Grant's men started cheering as soon as Lee and Grant
stepped out of the house, but Grant immediately hushed them. We*

were once again their countrymen, and he knew there was still an up-hill battle to face.

We will start our journey home tomorrow, and I pray this letter reaches you before then so you know I am on my way. I am not looking forward to seeing all the devastation those 5 years of war has bought to the land. I also do not know how long it will take me to get home. I pray it will be sooner rather than later.

I love you, and if I do not make it home, I want you to move on with someone else. I do not want you to wait the rest of your life for me to come home.

Love,
Your Soldier

Dear Kathryn,

I know I hurt you yesterday, and I cannot apologize enough for my actions. You were so happy, and I ripped your world apart with only a few words. I do love you, but I cannot subject you to this new side of me I've discovered. I'm scared of this side. I want you to live your life and find someone who can share everything with you. I want you to find a man who has no secrets.

You were right yesterday when you said this was about Gettysburg. I wish I could explain it to you, but I'm not sure you would believe me. Sometimes, I don't believe what happened there. I'm sure you're glad you didn't marry me before the war, especially now.

I want to thank you for being my rock throughout the war. Sometimes your letters were the only thing keeping me sane, while we marched and fought endless battles. Your letters made the war bearable. You sent me a little piece of home with each letter you mailed. Thank you for being a wonderful woman. I keep them with me to remind myself of who I once was.

I want you to keep my ring as a reminder of how life can change in the blink of an eye. Asking you to marry me was the happiest day of my life, and I wish the war would have never happened. We could have been married with kids if Lincoln wouldn't have declared war.

Remember the man I was, the one who got down on bended knee to ask for your hand in marriage, not the man I've become. I pray you find a man who deserves you, and who will treat you the way you deserved to be treated. It is my wish for you. I may not be in your future, but some man is, once you discover him, marry him. I pray you find him soon, so you can start your life together.

Love You Always,
Benjamin